DOCTORAL RESEARCH IN ART

DOCTORAL RESEARCH IN ART

Edited by
David Forrest

Australian Scholarly

© in this edition, David Forrest 2017
© in each contribution, its contributor

First published 2017 by
Australian Scholarly Publishing Pty Ltd
7 Lt Lothian Street North
North Melbourne, Victoria 3051
Tel: 03 9329 6963 / Fax: 03 9329 5452
enquiry@scholarly.info / www.scholarly.info

ISBN 978-1-925588-70-5

ALL RIGHTS RESERVED

The chapters in this volume have been subject to peer review.

Cover: Untitled #6, Robin Kingston, Feb/Mar. 2007.
Graphite, watercolour and gouache on paper. 56 x 76 cm

Cover design: Wayne Saunders

CONTENTS

Doctoral Research in Art: An Introduction
David Forrest 1

The PhD by Creative Practice:
From Student-Protagonist to Artist-Scholar
Colleen Boyle 5

In Pursuit of Female Werewolves Along Tightropes: The Pleasures
and Perils of Balancing Art, Life and Research as a PhD Candidate
Jazmina Cininas 16

Juggling Acts
Rhett D'Costa 32

I Just Had to Do It
Lesley Duxbury 47

'Did We Get Away With It?' Off Stage AND Banter: Musical and
Visual Puns in a PhD Study Involving a Hybrid Art Practice
Phil Edwards 59

It's All About me
Julian Goddard 69

'Crossing No-Man's-Land and Back': A Doctoral Journey Through
Art, War and The Topographies of Emptiness
Paul Gough 78

Walking (With Your Legs, In Particular) While Looking at Your Legs
Walking (But Not With a Mirror): Acts of Balancing in Doctoral
Research in Art
Michael Graeve 89

Please Don't Call Me DR
Ian Haig 100

Coming Out ... Again!
Richard Harding 109

Photographing the Australian Landscape Through Expeditions
Shane Hulbert.. 120

Revisiting Research
Ruth Johnstone 132

Making it Matter
Robin Kingston.. 141

Doctoral Research Around Slapstick Tactics
Laresa Kosloff.. 151

The Heroine of this Story is Me
Keely Macarow 157

Eco Revisited: How to 'Write' an Art Thesis
Maggie McCormick.. 167

The Road Taken
Grace McQuilten... 178

One Day at a Time
Sally Mannall 189

Reading, Writing, Making Foundations
to Image a Contested Space
Nikos Pantazopoulos... 199

On the Consideration of Valuable Times
David Thomas.. 211

What Just Happened?
Darrin Verhagen.. 218

Contributors.. 225

DOCTORAL RESEARCH IN ART: AN INTRODUCTION

David Forrest

This collection started with the simple, yet complex word, 'why'. It's a word that is integral to the research process, including higher degree research. (Parents know the term from a different – but arguably related – perspective with respect to young children!) In the case of this collection the 'why' was in the form of two questions: Why do a doctorate? and in particular, why do a doctorate in art? These have framed a good deal of the thinking and reflection that is evident throughout this collection.

We must keep in mind that doctorates *per se* have a tradition as old as universities themselves, however the doctorate in art, and in particular art practice, is a more recent addition to the academy. Parry (2007) reminds us that 'The research doctorate is a distinctive award. Earning it represents the attainment of a pinnacle of academic achievement. It holds more cache than nearly all other awards' (p. 3). He also suggests that a doctorate 'connotes mastery of a discipline area, confidence and ability in the making and reporting of new knowledge in a particular field, and 'know-how' in the construction of a sustained argument' (p. 3). In the field of art this can be the discovery and reporting of new knowledge through art practice.

In most cases mastery is not achieved quickly – it is a long process (beyond the boundaries of the commencement and completion of candidature) and accentuated with an ongoing desire to understand and make sense of a particular fragment of knowledge. Irvine (1996) described a research degree as 'the academic equivalent of scaling an unclimbed peak' (p. xiv). A doctorate is the highest level of academic degree. Historically, the title doctor was given to a teacher – 'a learned or authoritative teacher' at University (Merrimam-Webster,

2017). Many of the contributors to this volume are teachers and have mastery in their discipline and their licence to teach.

A 'feature' of this volume is that the contributors are all associated with the School of Art at RMIT University in Melbourne, Australia. They range from the earliest PhD in Art awarded by RMIT University from a few decades ago, through to some much more recently awarded doctorates.

This collection marks a point in time and provides a snapshot of thinking about doctoral experiences. Some of these experiences are vividly etched in the memory whilst others have been dimmed and tempered. Undoubtedly thinking and perspectives shift – indeed, evolve.

These individual commentaries offer frank observations and reflections not only on how the PhD in art has emerged, developed and morphed – but also on how the contributors, with a degree of hindsight, view and critically assess the process of their personal PhD journey with its attendant and subsequent revelations. Understandably, some of my colleagues declined the invitation to contribute for a number of reasons. This volume complements my investigations into doctoral research in music education (Forrest, 2003, 2010), art education (Forrest & Grierson, 2010) and drama and dance education (Forrest, 2012). The aim of the series has been to present a range of personal reflective journeys that could be of assistance to future doctoral candidates. (I would like to think that these journeys might also have interest – indeed 'messages' – for supervisors!) In the process I have wanted to know more about the researchers themselves, their quest and the outcome of their research. As with other doctoral pursuits, I was fully aware that the research for the contributors was a 'point-of-time' conclusion.

In 2003 I wrote about one of the great journeymen of history – Odysseus – and some of his encounters. The risks he took and the attendant hazards were manifested as monsters and enchantresses, including Calypso, Circe, Polyphemus, Scylla, and the Sirens. They were there to distract and divert him. In higher degree research the 'sirens' remain and evolve in many different ways for each individual. At the same time there are the 'constants' of supervisors and supervision, the ever-developing administrative systems, regulators, and regulations, examiners, expectations – and, indeed, life itself. But there are also the artistic, philosophical and personal quests that are so much a part of a doctoral experience. It would be a pity, I believe, to lose sight of these.

Research and practice within a discipline are not static: they can expand and evolve. The contributions in this volume add further multi-faceted pieces to the expanding complex mosaic of doctoral research in art. The contributions themselves fall into two sections. The first includes details of the research (title, abstract, and awarding institution) to provide a context for the discussion. In the second section the writers were given the option of reflecting on their experience in undertaking a doctorate or, alternatively, responding to a series of guiding questions. These questions related to such considerations as motivation for embarking on PhD study and the choice of institution, the process of developing the research proposal and how it emerged/changed/developed, the determination of the methodological approach employed, and the development of personal artistic practice over the duration of the doctorate. Added to these were considerations of the organization of work/employment, life (and family), and support throughout candidature. The contributors were asked to identify issues they confronted during candidature and, in retrospect, what they would have done differently. In the light of this they were also asked to consider what advice they would give to prospective doctoral candidates.

In the previous collections reference was made to the opening of Homer's *Odyssey*. It is appropriate to return to it once again. The contributors have written with the knowledge that through these commentaries the journeys of others might be easier – but, hopefully just as adventurous, and in doing so, as Homer said, they 'sing for our time too'.

It is with heartfelt thanks that I acknowledge the support, encouragement and generosity of each contributor.

References

Forrest, D. (ed.). (2003). *The Doctoral Journey in Music Education: Reflections on Doctoral studies by Australian Music Educators*. ASME Monograph No. 6. Melbourne: ASME/Common Ground Publishing.

Forrest, D. (ed.). (2010). *Journeying: Reflections on Doctoral Studies by Australian Music Educators*. Melbourne: Australian Scholarly Publishing.

Forrest, D. (ed.). (2012). *The Doctoral Journey in Dance Education and Drama Education: Reflections on Doctoral Studies by Dance and Drama Educators in Australia and New Zealand*. Melbourne: Australian Scholarly Publishing.

Forrest, D. & Grierson, E. (eds). (2010). *The Doctoral Journey in Art Education: Reflections on Doctoral Studies by Australian and New Zealand Art Educators.* Melbourne: Australian Scholarly Publishing.

Homer. *Odyssey.* Retrieved from http://library.thinkquest.org/19300/data/Odyssey/virtodyssey1.htm.

Irvine, J. (1996). Foreword. In P. Cryer (1996) *The Research Student's Guide to Success.* Buckingham: Open University Press.

Merrimam-Webster OnLine. (2017). Doctor. Retrieved from http://www.m-w.com/.

Parry, S. (2007). *Disciplines and Doctorates.* Dordrecht, The Netherlands: Springer.

THE PHD BY CREATIVE PRACTICE: FROM STUDENT-PROTAGONIST TO ARTIST-SCHOLAR

Colleen Boyle

Title of study: Portion of the surface never seen: The perceptual construction of unseen realities

RMIT University, 2016

Abstract

Imaging technology has vastly extended human perception by enabling access to aspects of reality that may never be seen with the naked eye, such as a distant galaxy or the blinding light of an eclipse. This project proposes that technologically mediated images form a perceptual bridge between what we know and what we can imagine, playing a pivotal role in constructing our perception of the unseen. By drawing on the work of image historians, theorists, and artists dealing with visual perception, this research project explores the specific question of how imagination interacts with photographs in order to perceptually construct an image of what would otherwise remain unseen.

Photographic imagery produced by space exploration is used throughout the project as an example of what may constitute an 'unseen reality' but the notion of the unseen is also explored through the histories of art and of science, philosophy, geometry, the rhetoric of framing, theories of perception and of photography. Imagination is defined primarily through selected philosophical interpretations, and its possible intersection with visual analogy is examined via analysis of historic and contemporary examples from the arts and sciences. A key objective of this project was to produce artworks that form an interface between seeing and imagining in order to explore perception of 'unseen realities'. To do this, a vocabulary of materiality was developed in recognition of the legacy of Modernist artists who explored the visual and conceptual concerns of perceptual experience: light, shadow, reflection, and geometry coming to form the basis of the project's practical work. Creative practice provided a workshop for testing imaginative processes and the tautological idea of visualizing the unseen.

A practice of generic, everyday photography provided a means of exploring photographic perception from the inside, ultimately highlighting the uneasy relationship between objective and subjective modes of seeing that the camera engages in.

It is intended that this research will contribute to understanding the connections between technology, representation and knowledge. In combining creative practice with disparate concepts from science, art, history, and visual discourse, this project attempts to create what Roger Kemp describes as a 'nodal point' where knowledge and imagination meet. This project proposes that imagination has the potential to construct a more holistic reality than the fractured one brought to us by images, albeit one that will never truly be seen.

--

When people within the university system describe completing a PhD, of any sort, they often get a little poetic and refer to it as a 'journey'. The word 'journey' has unfortunately been bandied around so many reality television shows in the last ten years that it has lost its impact. Executing the impossible high notes of ABBA's *Dancing Queen* becomes a journey. Enduring a silent meditation retreat is a journey. Discovering a new single origin coffee in a café that seats only two customers at a time in rural Victoria is a journey worth a Facebook post. People use it in a similar way to doe-eyed new parents who get all nostalgic about the first three months of slaving to a newborn baby, claiming that they would 'do it all again' and that they 'wouldn't change a thing' because its 'all worth it' despite the sleep deprivation, disgusting nappies, and chapped nipples. The rhetoric here hints to a secret society where only those who are in the thick of it actually know the whole truth. Likewise, the word journey when used in reference to a PhD has become clichéd and trite but I nonetheless believe there is something to yet explore under the lid of its opaque rhetoric.

What is a journey, after all, but a set of decisions that lead to actions that lead to more decisions and so on? It implies a linear chain of cause and effect that has a distinct beginning and a conclusive ending. When reading a novel, the reader can ride along with the protagonist, encountering the action as blindly and immediately as they do. Or, the reader can be privy to more information than the clueless protagonist, quite aware of the adventures, betrayals, and successes they are about to encounter. In my PhD experience the former mode of narrative is the student, and the latter is the supervisor.

The student-protagonist

From the perspective of the student-protagonist (as I shall now call them), the outcome of the PhD is unknown and the end of the story remains unwritten. The student-protagonist struts and frets upon the stage, not knowing if the writer has finished the script. Furthermore, in a plot twist worthy of any Christopher Nolan film, it can take some time before the student-protagonist realises that they *are* the main character in a three to four year-long show in which they are also unwittingly writer, producer, and director.

Half way through my candidature I decided to alter my growing antagonism towards my studies by doing a short course on script writing. Not only did it do the job, in that it provided me with a new way of injecting creativity into what sometimes seemed to be an insurmountable task, it also allowed me to see the work of the PhD through two alternative structural frameworks – that of the Shakespearian five-act play and Joseph Campbell's *Hero's Journey*.

Of course, I didn't have those handy frameworks at the very start. At first, I couldn't see the forest for the trees, but as I would later discover this is precisely the place in which all good protagonists should be: lost, and completely unaware that they are the hero-protagonist of their own story and about to embark upon a life-changing experience. For the purposes of this paper, I shall refer to the 'mono-myth' or Joseph Campbell's 'Hero's Journey'.

According to Campbell's (1949/2008) theory this is how any meaningful story must play out:

> A hero ventures forth from the world of common day into a region of supernatural wonder: fabulous forces are there encountered and a decisive victory is won: the hero comes back from this mysterious adventure with the power to bestow boons on his fellow man. (p. 23)

Campbell claims the hero undergoes three rites of passage: separation, initiation, and then return. Although Campbell's theory has come under much scrutiny and received valid criticism (particularly, of late, for its tunnel vision focus on the male journey) I believe it is of use in coming to understand the progress of the PhD candidate.

After finishing my undergraduate studies in printmaking at Monash University, I found I had a hunger for art history, and particularly, theory. In the early 1990s Monash had been primarily concerned with fostering basic studio skills in a rather traditional fashion and the art history program followed suit. When my friends doing architecture at RMIT were talking about 'liminal zones' and 'deconstruction' I found myself struggling to understand. So, I took myself off to The University of Melbourne and ended up theoretically examining the images that I had used so blithely in my practical work: the images of astronomy and space exploration. This Masters by Research prepared the way for me, academically, to later tackle my PhD by Project.

I'd always said that I would do my PhD when I was 60 and bored. Juggling work and study in my late 20s, without a family, had been tricky and I knew I had to knuckle down and find myself a career. For some reason, I neglected my practice and instead focused on solidifying employment in the arts sector and I soon found myself with a good steady job at Museum Victoria.

But I was dissatisfied.

I was stressed.

I was bored.

I'd also had a baby and realised (as so many first-time parents do) that I had been wasting time doing something that didn't make me happy. I'd heard about these 'new fangled' PhDs by creative practice some time ago and, quite frankly, having then just come out of a research MA at 'Melbourne', I was a bit of an academic snob. The fact that the word count attached to these new PhDs was equal to my MA made me laugh. And, how, I thought to myself, can you assess an artistic endeavour as a PhD? How do you mark it? But this was now ten years later and my desire to MAKE was much stronger than my desire to WRITE. RMIT had always produced interesting artists and they would also provide a studio space (which I desperately needed). A work friend of mine, (and now fellow PhD) told me how she had enrolled in the MFA at RMIT and that it had provided her with a fabulous creative challenge when she too, had been bored and stressed, and feeling as if she had nowhere to progress to in her job. I believe she played the role of what Campbell referred to as the 'Herald', a character who plants the seed of adventure in the mind of the protagonist. I told myself that if I got a scholarship, I could quit my job and plunge into the PhD full-time. We would manage financially and my son would spend no more time in day-care than he then did.

I got the scholarship.

I quit my good, solid job.

And then four months later I left my partner.

I was now a very poor single mother doing a full-time PhD.

This hero had well and truly ventured forth from the 'world of common day'. So, where was my 'region of supernatural wonder' and 'fabulous forces'?

The stage/The studio

The supernatural wonder and fabulous forces were, of course, to come from the study itself and the people who surrounded me. I simply cannot imagine how I could have completed this journey without the dynamic 'stage' upon which I and my fellow students strutted, nor without the wise counsel, happenstance conversations, gossip, creative exchange, friendship, and common ground that I shared with my fellow students.

To have not entered into that dynamic space of the RMIT studios would have meant to cut myself off from my peers and remove myself from a centralised point where resources and supervision were readily available. Some well-established artists choose to remain in their private studios and rarely come into the university campus. I think this is a shame. By doing this they not only miss out on a culture of congeniality and community but also miss out on sharing their knowledge and skills with others, which, I believe is part of the process of doing a PhD. You belong to a knowledge community, a community that is contingent upon giving and receiving, not hiding and hoarding. Unfortunately, studio spaces are limited and, when set against the backdrop of a CBD location, are a valuable commodity in the eyes of the university. Whenever I heard a young MFA student complain about the studio spaces I wanted to give them a motherly talking to. Couldn't they see that this was a gift? Studios are a 'room of one's own' (as Virginia Wolf would say) and an extension of one's thoughts – they are to be prized and used.

The studio truly is a stage upon which one sees all sorts of miniature dramas played out upon a near daily basis. The tears, joys, and frustrations of other students all offer knowledge and experience on which the student-protagonist can draw. The studio is a site of informal knowledge exchange and network building that is not listed in any course guide but is there for the taking: *if you will.*

Super-vision: a fabulous force

Choose your supervisors carefully. If you find a good match it will make all the difference to your experience as a candidate. In my time at RMIT I saw many of my fellow students encounter slight issues and difficulties with supervisors that were ironed out quite well. I saw a handful of them encounter some big, big problems that lead to prolonged candidature periods and a great deal of stress.

I chose my first supervisor after viewing her online profile and then asking to have a meeting in order to discuss my proposed project. Her research concerns appeared to be similar to mine in concept. This is important. I don't think it would have mattered if she had been a ceramicist or a painter or whatever, but what did matter was that she understood where I was coming from *conceptually*. Therefore, I could talk to her about *what* the work was doing or not doing. She could *see* where I was coming from and sometimes I literally thought of her as having 'super' 'vision': that she could see straight through me or hover omnipotently above me, seeing exactly what I would do next. Campbell describes a guide or helper who is often supernatural and who offers the hero advice and talismans that will help them on their quest. In my case, my supervisor appeared to miraculously know me inside out, and knew I needed guidance as opposed to advice, and understood that I was cripplingly afraid of making mistakes. Therefore, she understood that for me it was the creative *making* that was the most challenging.

My second supervisor was chosen after I started my candidature and by then it was a case of who was left available. This was a mistake. Both times I met with this supervisor I came away unsure of what I was doing, so I simply stopped seeing them and concentrated on my primary supervisor. Later in my candidature I needed to rapidly 'up-skill' in the area of sculpture and so I changed second supervisors. This was a godsend. The time I spent with this second supervisor, in the workshop, making and learning, was one of the greatest times of my life. Sometimes I regret not having changed earlier, but I simply could not have foreseen *where* my research was going to take me. If I had known that, it would not have been research. As it was, it was my primary supervisor who recognised that I needed a change.

Having had a reasonable amount of life experience and having worked in the 'real world' for over a decade, I developed an understanding of how workplaces operate and how to relate to your manager. Your supervisor is much like a manager in the work place. Some managers are very hands-on and want to stand over your shoulder whilst you work. Some managers are the opposite and you never see them. This last absent kind is the one you will hear complained about most, and absent supervisors in universities are no different. However, what most students (who have not had the experience of working in an office for a decade or two) don't understand is that your supervisor is NOT always thinking about YOU. They have many students and many other jobs to do. They think about the 3 pm appointment they have with you at 2:55 pm and then when you walk out the door you are out of sight and out of mind. If you want to see your supervisor: make an appointment. If you want to get them to read something, email it to them at least a week before your next meeting. Meet them over lunch or a coffee. Invite them to your studio!

Belly of the whale to the road of trials: an initiation to practice

Once the student-protagonist crosses the threshold from normality they enter what Campbell refers to as 'the belly of the whale'. Once again, popular culture comes to my rescue as I can best explain this via Nolan's *Batman* series and the most recent Marvel addition, *Dr Strange*. For both of these characters, a mental revelation occurs when they leave their comfortable day-to-day surroundings and find themselves within the enclave of a mystical temple. Here, they learn that they know nothing, and their so-called knowledge of the world has led them to vanity and misplaced priorities.

The first year of the PhD is just like this: but, without the special effects.

When I first got into my studio at RMIT, I set it up like it was my office. I was accustomed to such an arrangement and it made me feel like I knew what I was doing. I brought in my laptop, put postcards on the wall in front of me, and even organised a little desktop filing system. I started with what I knew. I began to make images on my computer because I was utterly terrified of using the printmaking studio. Although my supervisor had graciously taken me to the printmaking studio and introduced me to everyone I still felt like an alien. 'Imposter Syndrome' set in like a dark fog and I sat paralysed in front of my laptop not knowing what to do or what to make. Talking with other students who were a year ahead of me helped to ease my fears somewhat but it was also my supervisor giving me licence to 'play' that brought me out of my shell and I could finally bring myself to freely experiment with some printmaking.

In the meantime, I had to work on my research proposal in preparation for the first PhD milestone known as 'confirmation'. I had first approached my supervisor with a project about the sublime in images of outer space. She was never entirely convinced that this was 'it' and I am indebted, once again, to her 'super-vision'. After 12 weeks of research methods classes I was still floundering. What was this project? I could talk the theory until it was coming out of my ears, but how these ideas were linking, in an effective manner, to my practice (which I was particularly unsure of) was still eluding me. By the time my confirmation came I had some very elaborate research questions based around old ideas of technologically mediated imagery. My presentation went just fine, but my assessors were not convinced of my questions. I had one month to get them right.

As I sat in the deep dark belly of the whale I wondered what on Earth I was doing. This was not how I imagined it. Why could I not get these questions to align with the concerns of my practice? What were the concerns of my practice? I was utterly confused. I am now the proud owner of many notebooks that are filled with mind maps, spider diagrams, random thoughts, re-written questions, word clouds, lists … you name it, I did it. In the end, perhaps I couldn't see 'it' because 'it' was invisible. My topic turned out to be about seeing itself and what these amazing images of outer space tell us about how we see. It had been staring me in the face but I had to get to it in my own way: in the belly of the whale. The process ended up being a 'drilling down'. I had been too complex in my original approach – using 20,000 fancy words when all I needed was 30 simple ones. I had let my theory head lead too much with what I already knew, when I needed to express what I wanted to discover in the more abstract world of my art.

The 'Road of Trials' then began: one small challenge leading to another and then cascading into larger problems of making and discovering. It was here that my fear of failure came to the fore and held me back considerably. Campbell describes this part of the journey as being about atonement with the father, or, the surrender to what is essentially the shattering of one's ego.

Artists notoriously have quite large egos and I'm not sure that mine was any different. Fear of making mistakes is just another form of perfectionism that is tied to the ego and is often made visible as a form of procrastination or inability to make decisions. However, in order for the journey of the PhD to progress, decisions must be made. Oftentimes, sitting in my studio, pondering whether to do this or that or the other to a piece of work, I would be reminded of a short story by South American writer Jorges Luis Borges: *The Garden of Forking Paths* (English version 1948). This extraordinary story – often cited as inspiration for hypertext fiction, which was so fashionable in the 1990s – emphasises the concept of infinity and that all events in time and space could possibly be occurring at once. This is an idea in opposition to the norm where once a character in a novel makes a decision all other courses of action are locked off and s/he must follow a particular fork in the narrative road until they are faced with yet another point of potential divergence and decision making. Rather than cause me to feel utterly overwhelmed with possibility, remembering this story actually gave my indecisive ego hope. Somewhere, I told myself, in the infinite multi-verse, I made a different decision, which led to a different set of unfolding events, and resulted in an entirely different work. I just happened to be conscious of making this decision, right here, right now. Allowing myself the thought that I had, in fact, made ALL POSSIBLE DECISIONS, gave me solace and I could move on within the forking pathways of my PhD journey.

Of course, making decisions and learning to live with the repercussions is part of the creative process however, the PhD demands a step further. In order to complete the research one must take a leaf out of Dr Strange's book and astral project out of one's bodily form in order to look back and analyse what specific actions might mean in the context of those now faded and yellowed research questions that are stuck to the studio wall. This is where the creative act must be related to the historical and theoretical context of the field of study and it is where many students struggle. It is also, I believe, the least well understood aspect of the PhD by creative practice by those who sit outside it. When I began my PhD I was one of those people. I didn't understand just how difficult this translation of intuitive knowledge into some form of empirical knowledge would be. In fact, I didn't understand that it even occurred and that is why I had viewed the PhD by Project as the 'soft' option. For me, reflexive knowledge that informs creative practice is all well and good, but when it can then be fed into an historical and theoretical context that is when it becomes useful to a much broader field of peers, discourses, and practices.

The return

The vehicle for this iteration of the PhD study is the dissertation. Many students of creative practice have had very little experience with writing large documents and they approach their writing with a certain degree of fear and trepidation. My previous experience with my MA had prepared me well for writing my dissertation and I was already very familiar with a large body of texts. Over the years, I have come to realise that writing is actually very similar to making an artwork, at least when their formal aspects are considered. Each has a form, a structure, a shape that can be manipulated at will. I can move parts of each around and see if they work better in one place rather than another. I can alter their tone; make them colourful or monotone; or, make them snappy and contemporary or more traditional in style. I can group elements together or contrast them against one another … all of these are formal manipulations that apply to both formats: the written or the visual. Once a student can begin to see the creative work involved with writing their dissertation the less arduous the process becomes.

It is also important to keep in mind that writing the dissertation is a type of 'return' in that the student-protagonist is in a state of review and reflection. However, as is the case with all great journeys, home never looks quite the same. If good research has occurred, the student-protagonist will see the world quite differently, be making different work, and be thinking in new ways. My journey took me from being a creator of two-dimensional images to three-dimensional objects; from not understanding the context of my practice to discovering a whole new world of artists, history, and theory upon which I could draw on and feel confidently a part of. I had returned, but I had changed, and this was precisely what I had set out to achieve.

Bestowing the boons

Although the dissertation seems to be the most obvious vehicle by which the student-protagonist is able to 'bestow boons on his fellow man' and disseminate three to four years of research, in reality, very few people will ever read it. Publishing academic papers through your candidature will certainly help distribute your ideas and assist you in getting those first few thousand words on a page. But, again, citations will be few and far between. Even your final exhibition will most likely be seen and experienced by a relatively small audience. The boons of a PhD by creative practice are not fame or fortune and it is unlikely to lead to gainful employment. My reasons for embarking on the PhD journey were entirely personal. I wanted to challenge myself to be a better artist and I feel I have achieved that. The boon I wish to bestow upon you, dear reader, is this: enter into this journey as the student-protagonist with an open mind and an honest heart and like all great heroes you will return from your road of trials victorious.

References

Campbell, J. (1949/2008). *The Hero with a Thousand Faces* (3rd ed.). Novato, California: New World Library.

IN PURSUIT OF FEMALE WEREWOLVES ALONG TIGHTROPES: THE PLEASURES AND PERILS OF BALANCING ART, LIFE AND RESEARCH AS A PHD CANDIDATE

Jazmina Cininas

Title of study: The girlie werewolf hall of fame: Historical and contemporary figurations of the female lycanthrope

RMIT University, 2014

Abstract

This visual project and accompanying exegesis identifies individual women, both real and fictional, from throughout Western history who embody diverse aspects of the werewolf legend, and considers how the female werewolf has served, and continues to serve, as a social barometer of Otherness. This may include other nationalities; other religions; other sexualities; other moralities; other mental states; other body types; other species, and – if female – other gender, the most primary 'Other' of them all. The key outcome is a portrait gallery of original portraits utilising the reduction linocut method that offer novel representations and understandings of female lycanthropy, contextualised within the history of representations of the female werewolf.

The original portraits and exegesis that make up *The Girlie Werewolf Hall of Fame: Historical and Contemporary Figurations of the Female Lycanthrope* have been framed by the following questions:

- Who might fulfil the cultural and/or historical criteria necessary to be

identified as a female werewolf?
- How might one visually represent the 'attributes' that identify an individual as a female werewolf?
- What are some of the ways in which changing representations of female werewolves throughout history serve as barometers for cultural change?

My research uncovered not only many more female werewolves than their relatively low profile might suggest, but also a far more even distribution of lycanthropy across genders in earlier centuries. This suggests that the perception of the werewolf as more 'properly' male than female is a relatively recent phenomenon. For example, during the Early Modern witch hunts in central France and Estonia, women were just as (if not more) likely as men to be tried as werewolves. The suffragette era also witnessed a flourishing of female werewolves in gothic literature in response to chauvinist paranoia in the face of disrupted gender hierarchies.

The correlation between the higher visual profile of the male werewolf in popular culture and contemporary perceptions of the werewolf as predominantly male cannot be overlooked. In creating original portraits of female werewolves my aim was not only to provide a visual counterpoint to dominant representations of (male) lycanthropy but also to shed new light on female narratives that had largely been consigned to the shadows.

--

I commenced my PhD in 2005 soon after I obtained tenure as an academic at RMIT University. Up until that time I had been employed as a teacher in RMIT's vocational sector, where the institutional directive was for staff to obtain teaching qualifications. While it was a requirement of my new position that I undertake doctoral studies, I had always fancied myself as an academic and a PhD was something I had been keen to pursue anyway, so I welcomed the opportunity to do so. I decided on RMIT University as I had had a positive relationship with the institution not only as a member of staff but also in my previous career as an undergraduate and Masters student. I was consequently familiar with the supervisory expertise on offer and confident that I would receive the support and guidance I needed, in both the theoretical and practical aspects of my research. I opted to undertake my study part-time, in order to not only accommodate my teaching obligations, but also the unusually laborious and time-consuming nature of my printmaking medium, the reduction linocut, which might require upwards of 700 hours for a single edition. To make sufficient portraits to justify the 'Hall of Fame' title, I simply needed a lot more time than four years. In the end my PhD took me nine years to complete, including a leave of absence which I essentially used to buy me more time. I also used up the lion's share of my long service leave for the final three months in order to devote myself fully to completing the exegesis. Technically, I submitted early (i.e., before my maximum completion date), although it certainly didn't feel like it at the end of nine years.

The Girlie Werewolf Hall of Fame project came about as the natural evolution of my long-standing investigations into representations of female lycanthropy, and in particular my Girlie Werewolf Project, which first manifested itself in the course of my Masters research project, 'Women and Wolves: Gender in Lycanthropy' (completed in 2002). At that stage my investigations were still largely autobiographical, tied up with my hybrid cultural identity as an Australian Lithuanian.

Much of my Masters research centred on sourcing, compiling and representing existing cultural constructions of the wolf including visual representations of female werewolves in film and popular culture. The findings were displayed as compendia: a book of Lithuanian wolf sightings from a research trip and residency; an album of visual and textual depictions of female lycanthropy; and a projected compilation of film clips depicting female werewolves on screen. I also created a suite of ten 'Survival Hints' – small-scale reduction linocuts illustrating 'laws' of werewolf lore, which were my first serious foray into new possibilities for the medium. The only original, direct representations of female werewolves occurred in a suite of photographs, collectively titled Iron She-Wolves. The photographs featured portraits of women of my acquaintance, all of whom were of Lithuanian extraction, and all of whom were wearing my original, hand printed and hand-sewn Lithuanian Werewolf Suits, consisting of ears, mask, gloves and tail. A number of the women were also dressed in Lithuanian national costume, overtly referencing their – and my – cultural hybridity, which was further referenced in the suite's title (the Iron Wolf is the symbol for Lithuania's capital, Vilnius), and in the graphic fur patterning on the werewolf suits, adapted from traditional Lithuanian knitting patterns. The PhD project signalled an opening up to a broader spectrum of female lycanthropy, and a direct engagement with the novel visual representation of the female werewolf in her myriad guises.

My methodology was largely that of a visual mythographer although the PhD was quite advanced before I was able to identify the correct 'label' for my research strategy. Essentially, the broad sweep of my area of investigation – spanning the centuries from Roman times and the legend of the Capitoline She-Wolf, through the Early Modern werewolf trials, through the eighteenth-century vampire wave, through social Darwinian retrograde hirsutism and Suffragette era gothic fiction, from early cinema through to contemporary popular culture – made it very difficult, if not impossible, to filter the research through a single theoretical framework or methodology. Add to that the broad spectrum of lycanthropic types – from demonic witch-werewolves to aristocratic she-wolves with vampiric proclivities, from folkloric shape-shifters to hairy sufferers of 'werewolf syndrome', from moon-affected lunatics to menstrual werewolves to defenders of the wilderness and all manner of permutations in between – and the challenge of singling out a single theoretical framework or position becomes nigh on impossible. Original sources might include anything from folklore, transcripts of sixteenth century witch trials, medical and psychiatric case studies, gothic literature or the latest cult television series. Certainly, the project was feminist at its core, but no single 'brand' of feminism seemed to adequately encompass such diverse female histories over such an extended span of centuries, or what it was I was trying to uncover through my portraits.

The lack of a key theoretical position or argument proved a sticking point for two of my three examiners (although, interestingly, not for the third examiner, who was the only theorist of the three). This was not entirely unexpected – I had read enough doctoral theses and academic papers by this stage to be aware that I was leaving my research vulnerable to criticism. With that in mind, I did make a genuine effort to engage with theory. Really, I did. However, it virtually always felt retrospective, applied after the fact, and never served as the key driver for any pursuit of enquiry, which is theory's proper place. As I blew out word count after word count, it was the theory that inevitably felt superfluous and that ended up on the metaphorical cutting room floor, in favour of the stories and histories of my female werewolves. Not that I recommend this approach to others; indeed, the inverse. If there is a theory or philosophical position that might act as a lens through which to channel your research, grab it with both hands and don't let go. It will make your life as a PhD candidate much, much easier.

Even so, writers rather than visual artists offered the best model for how I might go about structuring my research and studio practice, even if the writers were not theorists as such. One such writer was Marina Warner, who not only researches women in folklore and fairy tales within their social contexts but also writes her own fiction. It was through Warner that I first became aware of the term 'mythographer' and the possibility of applying the term to my own research methodology. However, Angela Carter's subversive re-telling of the Red Riding Hood tale in her collection of short stories, *The Bloody Chamber,* came closest to my aesthetic aspirations, in that she drew on archaic and largely forgotten motifs from the popular tale, and resurrected them into a contemporary re-imagining of a young woman's encounter with the wolf. Carter's characterisations were infused with a gothic sensibility that was both seductive and dangerous, refusing to ascribe innocence or victimhood to either the girl or the wolf in their shameless carnality, respectful of and informed by tradition yet breaking new ground. These were all qualities I aspired to in my own portraits.

Carter has stated, 'My intention was not to do 'versions'… but to extract the latent content from the traditional stories and to use it as the beginnings of new stories.'* In the same way, I was not looking to simply illustrate existing narratives or bring to light earlier representations of female lycanthropy, but rather to construct new mythologies and new possibilities for imagining the female werewolf. Carter's further statement, 'For me, a narrative is an argument stated in fictional terms,'† also resonates with my own work, albeit substituting

---

* Cited in Haffenden, John (1985), 'Angela Carter', *Novelists in Interview*, New York: Methuen Press, p. 80.
† Angela Carter (2013), *The Curious Room: collected dramatic works* (Appendix: Preface to *Come unto These Yellow Sands*), London: Chatto and Windus.

imagery for narrative fiction. In hindsight, I might have made things easier for myself had I developed a new philosophical position centred on the Carter's and Warner's mythographical approach to feminist narratives, but that simply didn't occur to me until after the fact. And perhaps I might not have had the energy to do so anyway.

When I initially began my research I also underestimated just how many female werewolf narratives I would find, as well as how many new narratives would be generated in the course of my study. Stephanie Meyer's *Twilight* saga had not yet been published, *True Blood* had not hit our screens and the blazing popularity of paranormal romance had not yet been kindled. But werewolves, both male and female, suddenly became flavour of the month, crowding our screens, dominating our cinemas, overrunning the pages of juvenile fiction and choking the internet. Internet lists of 'best' werewolf fiction or werewolf films appeared with exponential regularity, featuring ever more titles, and ever more female lycanthropes. Indeed, as I performed a quick scan just today for 'best werewolf books' on *Good Reads*, of the top fifty titles only three are written by men (the first male author appearing at nineteen on the list), with the remaining titles almost exclusively featuring a female werewolf as the main protagonist.‡ A mere four of the fifty titles were published prior to the commencement of my candidature. Likewise, the female werewolf has acquired a correspondingly stronger visual presence. A Google image search for 'female werewolf' in 2005 barely revealed a handful of results. By 2014, there were pages of them.

Suddenly, my obscure niche research topic was catapulted into the mainstream. At first, I made a conscientious effort to acquire and watch every DVD in which a female werewolf might appear, to acquire and read every new novel but I soon became overwhelmed by the task, not to mention the expense. Also, I feel compelled to say, a lot of this new material was unmitigated dross – poorly conceived, shoddily executed and contributing little to re-imaginings of the werewolf persona or my field of enquiry. The same could be said for the flood of female werewolf imagery online – most of it in the realm of 'fan art' or conforming to very limited stereotypes of lupine femininity. Conversely, however, just as more and more contemporary female werewolf narratives were emerging, more and more historical material was also becoming readily

---

‡ www.goodreads.com/list/show/8321.best_werewolf_books, accessed 15 November 2016.

available as libraries and archives digitised their collections.

Not anticipating such a large pool of candidates, I was not especially discriminating in my early choice of 'inductees' for my Hall of Fame. As the PhD progressed, I had to become increasingly discerning not only in which material I would pursue, but also in my selection of subjects for my portraits. I had to ensure not only that significant female werewolf narratives were represented in my Hall of Fame, but also that I included representatives from each 'strain' of female lycanthropy, whether it be the witch werewolf, vampiric werewolf, suffragette werewolf, cinematic werewolf, medically anomalous hirsute werewolf, PMS werewolf, eco-werewolf, etc.

Due to the labour intensiveness of my medium, I was forced to exclude potential subjects if their flavour of lycanthropy were already represented, even if the new candidate were a worthier subject than the existing 'inductee'. The increasing access to information also meant that I was uncovering more details about individual narratives (some of which I only discovered after a portrait had already been finished) building a more complex repertoire of motifs that I could incorporate into the portraits. If I were to embark upon my Hall of Fame anew, it's highly likely that the final configuration of inductees and the manner in which they were depicted would be very different.

Ironically, as I was uncovering a broader spectrum of lycanthropic narratives, the demands of the reduction linocut medium increasingly precluded the possibility of including other mediums and methods of representation. My original proposal had included, among other things, an updated video compilation of existing female werewolf footage as well as some original video work, and sculptural elements such as costumes and action figurines, such as one might find in a conventional Hall of Fame. One by one, these other mediums were abandoned as too ambitious and too disruptive to the core business of producing the portraits. I had also grossly underestimated just how much time and emotional energy would be required for the exegesis.

I am not alone among artists in finding the exegesis the greatest challenge of my PhD candidature. I had not deluded myself that it would be easy, but I could never have anticipated the sheer, oppressive magnitude of the task. There were stretches of time, particularly in the final two years of my candidature, when I seriously doubted my capacity to deliver the goods, and when the light at the end of the tunnel seemed to be receding further and further into the distance. This was the rudest of awakenings. Putting aside due modesty, I had always performed well academically and am regularly applauded for my writing ability, so it came as a shock to discover that I was not as academically proficient, nor inclined, as my vanity had led me to believe. If I had been presented with an opportunity to quit in the final year of my candidacy without losing face or compromising my supervisors, I believe I would have taken it. I still feel self conscious calling myself 'Doctor' and harbour doubts as to my legitimacy to the title. Apparently, this is normal, so take comfort.

I believe it is, or at least was, common for visual arts PhD candidates to leave their writing to the end of their candidature. I do not recommend this. I wrote throughout my candidature and still found it challenging (to say the least) to finalise my exegesis. Since commencing my PhD, new milestone requirements have been introduced for candidates, which I believe are a useful tool in ensuring that studio research *and* writing progress in tandem. I was not required to present a mid-candidature review, nevertheless I engineered writing deadlines for myself by applying for symposia and conferences where I might present my findings. At the first few conferences I attended, I essentially presented information I already knew and the papers tended to be broad introductions to the female werewolf phenomenon. After effectively regurgitating updates of the same material, I came to realise that it was more useful to structure my papers around what I still needed to find out.

My strategy was to construct a chapter outline for my exegesis, breaking down the specific topics I wished to cover in the course of my research. One chapter might be dedicated to werewolves and witchcraft, for example, another focussed on Suffragette era werewolves, another on hairy women, etc. When applying to conferences, I would determine which chapters still needed to be written, and structure an abstract around the topic that was the closest fit for the conference. I found this a very effective strategy for ensuring that the writing progressed throughout the candidature. Presenting at conferences also introduced me to new ideas, new knowledge, new networks and academic publishing opportunities. In the course of my candidature I managed to publish three book chapters and two journal articles based on content within my PhD exegesis, with a further book chapter forthcoming. Scrivener word processing software was invaluable for organising and re-organise my notes and structuring my exegesis, and in recognising the gaps in my research. (I wish I'd known of it at the beginning of my candidature.)

The uncompromising rigours of the academic peer review process can be confronting and exhausting, but they are invaluable in refining writing and ideas, and in gaining a deeper appreciation of what constitutes academic research and original knowledge, as opposed to the natural development of studio practice. This is a distinction many artists grapple with when undertaking a PhD, reflecting the relative infancy of practice-led doctoral studies within the visual arts, as well as the uncomfortable fit between an artist's studio practice and the traditional parameters of academic research.

While the two are by no means mutually exclusive, it took me some time to fully understand that taking my studio practice to the next level in and of itself did not constitute original research, at least not within conventional institutional parameters. Research has historically been geared towards answering new questions with replicable answers; that is, anyone else asking those same questions and following the same logic will end up with the same answers. The aim of the artist, however, is to come up with answers that are unique to themselves, that no one else can or will come up with. New knowledge was not recognised through my creation of new portraits per se, but rather in the novel insights these portraits offered into female lycanthropy as a culturally gendered phenomenon. It was not sufficient to simply illustrate my subjects and findings; I was also required to offer novel understandings of how individual lycanthropic identities had been formulated, and how they were positioned within broader constructs of woman as other. It remains up for debate how successfully I managed to achieve these goals, nevertheless such considerations did shape my decision-making when constructing my portraits. It became important to me to explore different ways of depicting female lycanthropy, to imagine different manifestations as well as different degrees of transformation and hybridity, to acknowledge existing traditions without simply regurgitating them.

The need to provide answers also impacted on the final presentation of my portraits and the structure of my writing. The prescribed directive for documenting one's studio practice is to present it in chronological order of output, which makes sense in traditional research. One performs an experiment, analyses the results, and modifies the next experiment accordingly. However, the order in which I made my portraits was not necessarily predicated by the portrait that came before it. External professional practice demands might require me to focus on a particular type of female werewolf, or work to a particular scale, in order to fit the theme of an exhibition or the dictates of an exchange portfolio (i.e., a group print swap between a pre-determined number of printmakers). It might be necessary for me to follow a portrait of a contemporary PMS werewolf with a sixteenth-century hairy marvel, then an eighteenth-century vampiric werewolf, then a twentieth-century comic book heroine, then back to a sixteenth-century heretic werewolf. Chronological output did not necessarily serve to contextualise individual figurations within the broader lycanthropic tradition. In my instance, it made more sense to base the order of my exhibition, documentation and writing on the chronology in which the species of female werewolf appeared in the popular consciousness, that is, by the era in which the subject of the portrait manifested herself. Presenting my portraits in this manner enabled me to chart evolving figurations of female lycanthropy over the centuries, as well as to identify recurring themes and motifs. This latter aspect was also aided by the development of a series of illustrated wall texts to augment the portraits.

The wall texts were important in realising the overall premise of the Hall of Fame, providing biographical details of my female werewolves as one might expect to find in any Hall of Fame, rather than the artwork details (title, medium, year, etc.) one might expect to find in a gallery or museum. The wall texts were also important in decoding some of the motifs appearing in the portraits – for example, plants attributed with lycanthropic properties – contributing towards and allowing access to a visual vocabulary of female lycanthropy. This is a new development in my practice, stemming directly from my PhD project, that has become an integral feature of subsequent solo exhibitions. It has also forced me to consider how I might defer the artwork details elsewhere, in a manner that is still immediately accessible to the gallery visitor, and compatible with Hall of Fame conventions. My solution to date has been to provide a separate illustrated list of works in a 'souvenir' zine or brochure format.

As with most doctoral candidates in the visual arts, my project walked the line between 'pure' research and my professional practice as an artist. For the nine years of my candidature, I effectively did not undertake any exhibition or art project unless it contributed to my PhD in some way, while simultaneously exploiting opportunities for my PhD research to generate an income – albeit modest and erratic – from art sales, as I simply couldn't afford a nine-year hiatus from the gallery circuit. The labour intensiveness of the process also forced me to develop a more strategic approach to artwork production and editioning, especially in the case of exchange portfolios, which generally required that I produce large editions of small scale works. I might adjust my image or registration method, for example, to allow myself to utilise a section from a larger work for the exchange edition, or make two versions of an edition by altering the colour between the two. Serendipitously, these different state editions also fitted conceptually with the different states associated with a lycanthropic transformation. External deadlines ensured I maintained momentum with my portrait production, which was critical for professional survival, but also served to offset to some degree the countless unpaid hours taken up my PhD and taken away from my marriage and personal life.

While balancing my research with my professional practice was relatively straightforward, finding further space in the mix for family and friends proved a far greater challenge, particularly with teaching commitments thrown into the bargain. I am not surprised that many relationships do not survive a PhD and am eternally grateful to my husband for not abandoning me over the course of nine years of shoddy housekeeping, social withdrawal and emotional and intellectual preoccupation. I can't imagine how anyone with children makes it through a PhD intact. A number of friendships fell by the wayside, simply through lack of regular contact. I missed countless birthdays, parties, family events, dinners, openings and other key celebrations due to a never-ending tide of pressing deadlines and sheer exhaustion. I also missed the opportunity to say goodbye to my very dear mother-in-law, who died while I was in the UK presenting at a conference. I don't think my father-in-law will ever fully forgive me for this. Nor I myself. I put on weight, especially when a writing deadline was imminent, that has become increasingly difficult to shift. There were moments towards the end when I seriously feared for my sanity.

It can be difficult to justify one's PhD to others; I know that my husband questions whether the rewards of postgraduate study were commensurate with the level of commitment and personal sacrifice (his as well as mine) I invested in my PhD. Being employed on a 0.5 contract, I am allocated a half-day each week paid research time from RMIT, but this did not come close to covering the time I dedicated towards my study, or even the minimum 20 hours a week expected of part-time candidates. There is no automatic promotion or pay increase on completing a PhD (at least not at RMIT School of Art). A PhD will not increase the likelihood of selling your artwork, being selected for a prestigious exhibition or winning an art prize, although of course one would expect an increase in the level of sophistication of one's work. It may increase your chances of getting lecturing work at a University, or of keeping the position you already have. A PhD will also increase the likelihood of refereed publications, which your university will love you for (on account of the funding they receive) but which do not pay. In fact, they may even cost you money, especially if you wish to include illustrations, as academic publishers expect their authors to cover any copyright release fees. While at least my artwork production offers some possibility of financial remuneration, albeit speculative and long term, the same cannot be said of the writing.

Investing so much in something that delivers so few tangible rewards can appear selfish and self-indulgent to those around you who are constantly put upon to take the back seat, even if it feels far from self-indulgent to you. Undoubtedly, my perfectionism and workaholic tendencies make me my own worst enemy when it comes to negotiating a work-life balance, so my experience may not be representative of the norm (although anecdotal reports suggest that it is far from unusual). The question 'why would you do this?' is a very valid one, and one which I advise all potential candidates to consider very seriously.

Of course, there have to be some rewards otherwise no-one would even bother. The physical writing of papers for conferences may have been torturous, but the travel experiences these enabled were certainly among the highlights of my candidacy, not least because I could share them with my husband. I presented papers on female werewolves around Australia and in Philadelphia, Budapest and the UK. By good fortune, a couple of the international conferences corresponded with non-teaching times, so I was able to use these opportunities to travel more broadly, in trips I like to call European Werewolf Odysseys. Destinations were chosen according to their significance to werewolf lore: for example, the Werewolf Pines in Latvia (where, legend has it, one might transform into a wolf by crawling through the exposed roots of particular trees); the castle ruins of alleged serial killer/female werewolf Erzsebet Báthory in Slovakia; a provincial museum dedicated to the Beast of Gevaudan (a wolf that terrorised the French countryside in the eighteenth century) in central France; or the Ambras Castle in Innsbruck, Austria (where one can find sixteenth-century portraits of genetically hirsute celebrities, the Gonsalvus family); and, naturally, Transylvania. Most of these places are well off the beaten track, none of them were places we would have travelled to otherwise, all of them were absolutely glorious. I have to say, werewolves inhabited some rather fabulous parts of the world.

These trips were real adventures of discovery and delight. They enabled me to immerse myself in the landscapes and sample the local cultures of my research matter, gaining inspiration, re-invigorating enthusiasm for my subject, serving as motivation to endure further slogs of academic writing, and allowing my husband to share in the rewards of my labours. (He took perverse delight in informing others that he was heading overseas to hunt werewolves.) I was able to get some funding from RMIT to attend the conferences, offsetting travel costs, from which my husband also indirectly benefitted. Such moments were critical to sustaining my commitment to postgraduate study, and to keeping my husband onside, over such a long term.

I am also fortunate in that my chosen subject matter was and remains a lot of fun. At moments when I simply couldn't face wading through a Deleuzian treatise on 'becoming' or another eco-feminist manifesto, I could watch some meritless B-grade schlock or read some trashy paranormal romance and still lay a legitimate claim to be undertaking research. I had never been a fan of horror but, through conscientiously watching every female werewolf film that ever was, developed a sentimental appreciation for the genre – something my husband was happy to indulge, developing a rival soft-spot for zombies in response. I could talk about my PhD at parties and social gatherings, sharing my latest lycanthropic discovery without boring everyone senseless with impenetrable theory or bamboozling them with abstract concepts they had barely heard of, and cared even less about. Mildly apprehensive enquiries into my PhD research topic, asked only out of politeness, transformed into visibly relaxed fascination on learning that the answer was a Hall of Fame for female werewolves. It served as a terrific ice-breaker.

Am I glad that I undertook a PhD? Yes. Absolutely. My research uncovered fascinating female narratives and histories I might never have known of, deepening my passion for and understanding of my subject. Having to articulate my practice in writing revealed unexpected correlations and insights into my subject matter, as well as women's place in the world historically, and my place in the world today. Following the werewolf's trail has revealed hidden gems of Europe that I would never have discovered following the standard travel routes. Intense focus over such an extended time has added a depth to my work I doubt I would have been capable of otherwise. It gave me a real sense of purpose. Would I ever undertake another? Not on your life. The emotional and physical toll extracted by the PhD is simply too great to pay twice. It came perilously close to extinguishing the very passion that it ignited. Plus, my husband would divorce me. Would I recommend doctoral research to other artists? Only if they have an utterly compelling reason for doing so and even then I would advise extreme caution.

If I had my PhD time again, there are a number of things I would do differently, with the benefit of hindsight. Rather than exploring the full spectrum of female lycanthropy throughout the ages and providing a broad overview of the phenomenon, it would have been much more sensible, and manageable, to focus in on one particular aspect or type of female werewolf: the hairy woman, perhaps, or the suffragette werewolf, or the menstrual werewolf. By narrowing my scope, I could have increased the depth of my study and analysis, and maybe even formulated my thesis around a specific theoretical premise; I understand now why most PhD dissertations follow this model. It would also have enabled me to complete my PhD in four years instead of nine, placing less burden on my friendships, my marriage, my health and my emotional wellbeing. I might also have been eligible for a scholarship, which would have enabled me to make a greater financial contribution to my marriage, and cast my candidature in a less self-indulgent light to my husband. I would have determined which style guide I was going to follow and formatted my footnotes and text accordingly from the word go. I would have used Scrivener from day one to organise, filter and refine my research and my writing. I probably wouldn't have bothered with Endnote, although I know others who sing its praises, however I suspect they use in-text citations rather than footnotes. I would not have used my precious and hard-earned long service leave to complete my PhD, instead keeping it for its intended, and much needed, purpose. (Fortunately for the current generation of researchers, PhD completion leave has recently been introduced to RMIT School of Art, but was not available at the time I was studying.) I would have ensured that I had a well-established fitness regime in place prior to commencing my research and I would have engineered strategies, for example, committing to exercising with a reliable friend, to stick to it. I would also have been more active in engineering opportunities for sharing my research with my husband, my family and my friends. And I would have missed that last UK conference and flown home a day earlier.

I am glad that I was in regular contact with my supervisors throughout my candidature as they are the ones who kept me in line when I might have gone astray, and reassured me that I was on track to complete on time, when I suffered the gravest doubts about my ability to even finish at all. I am also glad that I had a regular social and creative outlet through my membership of the Lost Clog Lithuanian folk singing group. The regular rehearsals ensured that I had at least some social interactions outside my candidature or teaching, while the performances and marketing gave me an alternative creative outlet that had nothing whatsoever to do with my PhD, and which have opened up unexpected new possibilities for my art practice in the wake of the inevitable post-PhD slump.

For those considering embarking upon the PhD journey, my best advice is to maintain perspective and be realistic about what is achievable. Aim for full-time study wherever possible, to minimise the impact on your personal life and maximise the likelihood of maintaining momentum, and of gaining a scholarship. Remember that at least half of your time will be taken up with writing, which will effectively only give you two years in the studio so formulate your project accordingly. Develop strategies for progressing your studio research and your writing in tandem. Don't underestimate the influence of visuals in shaping an argument and embed images in your writing as you go. Keep a methodology diary, noting the decisions you made and why, that you can include as an appendix to your thesis. Certainly engineer exhibition and publication deadlines for yourself, but don't forget to also engineer regular social and creative outlets for yourself that have nothing whatsoever to do with your PhD. Remember a PhD represents four years of your life, not your whole life, so make sure you leave yourself a life to go back to, once your candidacy is over. And don't be afraid to have some fun.

JUGGLING ACTS

Rhett D'Costa

Title of study: Shimmering spaces: Art and Anglo Indian experiences
RMIT University, 2016

Abstract

The primary research for my PhD is a series of artworks, which seek to contribute to current discourse relating to culturally composite ethnicities, specifically, the Anglo Indian[*] community, in the context of place, belonging and identity. The artworks draw on my personal experiences as an Anglo Indian, and may be described as auto-ethnographic, highlighting the often precarious shifting social and political circumstances and predicaments associated with mixed race communities. A range of attitudinal and creative strategies, including the poetic, ironic, ambivalent and humorous, are used to develop a series of multidisciplinary artworks that utilise a wide range of materials and forms.

The research explores the Anglo Indian's dual ethnicity, revealing uncertainty contained in the indeterminate space occupied by the Anglo Indian and the conflicting and often discursive position of being both compatible and incompatible with aspects of Indian and British cultures. Place and home, particularly for the Anglo Indian has often been contested in terms of belonging and being, by Anglo Indians themselves and by the British, Europeans and Indians.

Given that Anglo Indians are a direct consequence of the British imperial

---

[*] Please note that I deliberately removed the hyphen from the name of the community in my research referring to the community as 'Anglo Indian'. For a rationale as to the reasoning behind this decision please refer to my dissertation, pp. 151 & 281.

encounter in India, the research draws on early historical colonial encounters, to present postcolonial discourses particularly in the humanities and social sciences, and on future considerations, imaginings and possibilities for the community. Rather than being subsumed into European and Indian history, misrepresented, or worse, being written out of history altogether, members of the Anglo Indian community have maintained a strong desire and conviction to narrate their own stories to determine and engage with their developing and evolving sense of a cultural identity in a global and cosmopolitan world.

The word 'shimmer' in the title (*Shimmering Spaces: Art and Anglo Indian Experiences*) examines this space of instability, fracture and unsettledness, as both material and metaphor in the artworks. Rather than determining the space Anglo Indians occupy as binary or oppositional, I claim this unstable space to be an ameliorative, shimmering experience: one which is mesmerising and optimistic, and simultaneously precarious because of its state of fracture. It is in this very state of unsettledness and fluidity where the third space of the Anglo Indian can be inscribed, enunciated and articulated, in spite of their complex history, which brought together in union, coloniser and colonised, sometimes deliberately, sometimes antagonistically and sometimes strategically.

This research puts forwards its primary enquiry of how a space of 'in-betweenness' can be encountered through ideas of place, belonging and identity in contemporary fine art, and how Anglo Indian identity emerges, evolves and shifts in the context of nationalism, culture, community, history and location.

--

Personal reflections on my doctoral journey

It could not have been more timely to write reflectively on my doctoral journey, as I have just recently completed. It felt appropriate to write of this experience at this point, as I had been internalizing reflections as I was drawing to the end of the research and was keen to share these experiences with others considering doctoral studies, particularly the processes I underwent and decisions made accordingly. The accounts I write should therefore been seen in this context; as someone who is writing reflectively on his experiences as the ink still dries on the submitted dissertation and the artworks having recently been removed from the final exhibition.

The choice to undertake doctoral studies

In the late 1980s and early1990s there was an impetus for academics to upgrade their qualifications by undertaking a Masters degree by research. At the time I was half way through an Honours degree when I was offered the opportunity to transfer to the Masters program. I was one of the earliest candidates to complete a Masters program with the School of Art at RMIT University. I recall there being so few models (if any), for studio based research degrees in Australia at this time. In hindsight, it felt as if we were all making it up as we went along, figuring out what was best and most appropriate for studio based research, where the artworks were seen and acknowledged as the viable outcome of the research, and at the same time meeting the scholarly orthodoxies and academic requirements and expectations of the university for postgraduate studies.

Doctoral programs were the natural logical next step in the evolution of studio based research programs. Again there was tremendous momentum from the university and external accreditation bodies to ensure that staff held the appropriate qualifications for supervisorial positions. I resisted applying to a doctoral program for a long time, for a couple of reasons. I had progressed from an undergraduate program directly into postgraduate studies, only taking a year off between the two, to travel on a scholarship. I wanted to make sure I was 'ready' to undertake doctoral studies and that I could identify meaningful research to undertake in studio based research and which also challenged the often narrow doctoral frames in more traditional academic research. When I talk of being *ready,* I mean that I was in a strong space mentally and academically, consciously prepared, to undertake the task at hand. I also wanted to harness more experience in my studio practice, without the constraints of academia. I wanted it to be my choice to enter a doctoral program and to do it on my terms. In hindsight, I suspect I just *fell* into my undergraduate and prior postgraduate studies, without really giving it much thought. The 'readiness' for doctoral studies I refer to also takes into account full-time workloads with the university I work at, and my personal and family commitments. At all stages of these deliberations, RMIT University and the School of Art, was very supportive and encouraging, as was my partner and family, as I was about to juggle life, study and full-time work.

Choice of university

I decided on RMIT University because of their reputation in the field of postgraduate practice-led research, and for more pragmatic and logical reasons. I felt the familiarity and engagement between work and study would be an easier transition, if my place of work was also my place of study. As well, there were particular supervisors I wanted, not necessarily because of their expertise in my theoretical field, but rather because of their research knowledge, supervision experience in studio practice and their own art practices. I also wanted supervisors who understood me, and that I trusted, so we could work well together over the duration and longevity of the program. Naturally, the relationship between candidates and supervisors is very important, not just in terms of their expertise but also that there is a mutual and respectful understanding between them. I did consider if being too close to them, as peers, would interfere or negatively influence their supervision. I questioned if they could maintain objectivity and be rigorous with their feedback and at the same time challenge and stretch my ideas further. These initial concerns I had, were never a problem. I can say it was a pleasure and great learning experience working with all my supervisors through the doctoral journey.

The process of selecting and scoping the research project

It was necessary to recognize and understand what 'new knowledge' my research would bring to my field. Therefore at the initial stages it was important to understand what work has already been undertaken within the scope of my enquiry to see if there were any gaps or further advancements I could make by reevaluating or recontextualizing existing knowledge. It was also important to find which other fields or disciplines research existed in to draw from, remembering that my research was fine art based. Developing a form of literature review helped tremendously in identifying key artists and writers and the chronological advancements in theories and ideas within my field of enquiry, so I could position my research accordingly.

I do recall when I started the research, I told my supervisors that I wanted the research to mean something to me. I did not fully understand what I meant by this comment, but I figured that if I was going to spend this amount of time and energy in something, it had to matter. I had to care about it deeply. In hindsight this thought must had influenced the decisions I would make regarding my field of enquiry. It did *personalize* the research, which added another layer of complexity as I had to explain, rationalize, validate and negotiate, objectivity and subjectivity and their roles and place in my research. But I was determined from the start to use the personal within the writing, ensuring at the same time that there was a balance struck between the personal and the scholarly in the writing. For me, this position felt more authentic and necessary for the research I was undertaking.

My PhD began with a very different research focus. It commenced by reviewing a career that spanned over twenty years as a practicing artist working primarily within the area of abstract painting. I wanted to explore alternate models of abstraction, which did not sit within the dominant Western model, by drawing on and reviewing existing research.[*] The rationale for opening up this enquiry stemmed from my dual Eastern and Western ethnicity, as an Anglo Indian. However, in the process of examining my relationship to Western abstract painting, it was the very idea of an East–West distinction that pricked my attention. As a result, it would be ethnicity/race/culture and its impact on an evolving sense of Anglo Indian identity (always in formation), that would become my focus. My research began by asking, what appeared on face value, to be simple questions about identity. What does it mean to be, live and experience the world as an Anglo Indian and how does being an Anglo Indian impact on or influence how I make artworks? Questions, surprisingly, I had previously not thought about critically in my life or artistic career. However, these questions (and many more) sat like a soft ache in my consciousness.

---

[*] The research I refer to includes: Mercer, K. (ed.) (2005). *Cosmopolitan Modernisms (Annotating Art's Histories: Cross-Cultural Perspectives in the Visual Arts)*. Cambridge, MA: The MIT Press; and Mercer, K. (ed.) (2006). *Discrepant Abstraction (Annotating Art's Histories: Cross-Cultural Perspectives in the Visual Arts)*. Cambridge, MA: The MIT Press.

These questions expanded to further questions; How did Anglo Indians evolve as a Indian minority group? How did historical events such as colonization, India's independence, and migration, impact on the Anglo Indian community? How is the Anglo Indian community perceived and represented, both within and outside of the community? How have these perceptions been created? How did having a dual ethnicity impact on the way I engaged my art practice? These questions would eventually lead back to asking how Anglo Indians negotiated the in-between space created by their dual ethnicity and how this impacted on art practice. These series of questions became an initial framework to guide the studio research. They also helped scope the theoretical research in terms of guiding which fields and disciplines I would need to draw on that were relevant to my enquiry. As importantly, it helped establish which areas I did not need to focus on, therefore helping to set parameters to contain and focus the research, which was always in danger of being too far reaching and expansive. I wanted to develop a project which was multi-dimensional and discursive and at the same time create a research terrain that was also carefully crafted. This was important not just at the start of research but throughout the journey. It was often so easy to go off into a variety of tangents and convince myself that it was relevant to my research. It was crucial to keep front and center the fact that my research was practice-led and studio based, so that other forms of knowledge from diverse disciplines could be considered and examined through this lens.

What was also really important at the early stages, was to maintain a flexible working model to fine-tune the research enquiry as the studio work developed and the theoretical research evolved. I say this because at the early stages of the research there was this overwhelming desire to lock down and fix the research in a stable, logical and coherent way. But in fact, I found that the opposite is often necessary.

Eventually these early guiding questions and the evolving studio deliberations around these enquiries would play an important role in determining the over-arching research questions, which were tweaked, massaged and adjusted throughout the journey, right to end of the process, where it eventually makes sense and seems obvious. But only because of the complex process, time and hard work you have gone through. It is indeed an emerging process. At the commencement of my candidature, I heard an ex-head of our school comment on how he believed that research questions come at the *end* of the process and not the beginning. I remember at the time thinking about the oddness of this comment and that if there was any validity to the comment, then how meaningful are these questions and why are they given signification so early in the journey? I can fully concur with his observations, now that I have been through the process. The initial iteration of the research questions steer and guide the process of enquiry. Their final form frames the overarching enquiry. This can only happen near the end, as I found out.

Determining emerging methodologies, processes and strategies

Establishing a series of methodologies for the research helped navigate discursive and non-linear processes for both the studio practice and the writing process. I spent a significant amount of time pulling apart the different components of the PhD and their orientations, to find connections, divergences, and relevance to each other. I devoted a chapter in the dissertation to the discussion of the nexus between writing/reading/experiencing/thinking/making/exhibiting/reflection and their roles in the PhD as cyclical, tangential and discursive. I wanted the relationships between studio practice to run parallel and link to theoretical methodologies; each guiding the other at different times throughout the research; one informing and expanding the potential for the other. It was this back-and-forth between visual (studio based) research and more theoretical research, which was important. I find a natural convergence and sympathy between the notion of art practice and research. Practice by its very nature implies a desire to reach a level of expertise through the process of repetition. (Re)search is a rigorous, focused and organized process of looking (repetitively) for the answers to a set of propositions. Both can be calls to action (as verbs).

I was very specific about what I wanted the writing to feel, look and sound like. I wanted it to carry three distinct styles (voices); that of the artist, academic and Anglo Indian. I was determined to bring forward narrative through the adoption of a personal voice from personal experiences, in the dissertation, as a valid form of academic research. So that the writing (dissertation) became a different (not more or less) modality of knowledge to the artworks, but always in sympathy.

I knew I was taking risks in the way I was writing and structuring the dissertation. This was acknowledged by the examiner's reports, which noted that I had taken risks (and that I was aware of it). One of my examiners described my dissertation as a 'distinctive exegetical document', which was 'fluid, boundary-crossing and methodologically complex'. The success or failure of the dissertation was very much hinged on determining and finding validation for the methods I wanted to use in the dissertation and across the studio practice. Because my research was spread across diverse disciplines in the social sciences which included, ethnography, geography, histories, anthropology, as well as literary criticism and art theory (the list goes on), it was crucial that I never lost sight of the fact that all the knowledge and information gleaned from these other disciplines were deliberated or translated or interrogated through the model of practice-led research. Meaning, that the studio and art practice was central to the enquiry and outcome. The research used a thinking through making, or practice–thinking nexus, where thinking is intricately embedded in the making process (practice); as well as, practice–writing and practice–reading, where writing and reading influenced the studio deliberations, which then opened up wider reading–writing fields of knowledge and enquiry. I found Bianca Hester's writings in her PhD on this subject invaluable.

Throughout the concurrent research processes and activities, I employed two key methodologies: heuristic and auto-ethnographic. A heuristic method is a way of finding or discovering that allows for possibilities. This permits speculation and informed guess-work, rather than following established formulas as a process, to gain an understanding of information. It incorporates experience-based techniques for learning, utilizing intuitive judgments. A heuristic methodology embraces a trial and error and a sometimes *working backward strategy*, as a way of discovering and allowing for adaptive ways of negotiating decision-making. Working in a creative arts practice is to recognize and value the importance of such methods, processes or strategies in one's art practice. I used these strategies in all aspects of the research. Since the research was close to being autobiographical and therefore intimately aligned to my own (the researcher's personal) lived experiences, I utilized auto-ethnography (as distinct from an ethnographic qualitative research method) for both the writing and creating the artworks. This method permitted more reflexive investigations in the context of the experiences had and the experience gained – with storytelling being a valid way to operate in the research as it embraced and foregrounded the personal, experiential and anecdotal.

Auto-ethnography validates the researcher (myself) as the primary subject of the research and because personal stories were crucial in the research, it allowed the research(er) to use feelings, emotions, ambiguities, stories, reflections, emersions and observations (in my case) as ways to understand the social and cultural in the context of being and belonging. Consequently, auto-ethnography disrupts the binary distinctions between objectivity and subjectivity, researcher and research, and therefore ideas of neutrality itself. As an *artist–researcher,* employing an auto-ethnographic method aligned seamlessly with methodologies I was employing intuitively in my studio practice.

Using heuristic and auto-ethnographic methods, I highlighted and drew on the method used by Tacita Dean for the exhibition she curated at the Serpentine Gallery, 2005, titled *An Aside*; a method closely aligned with the principles of a heuristic method.

I also drew on creative writer and academic, Francesa Rendle-Short's, writing practice and research into the relationship between *exegesis and eisegesis,* as forms of writing, theorized in an article, 'Loose thinking': Writing an eisegesis (2010). I first heard Rendle-Short deliver a paper, 'The drawing, breathing, writing body', at the Drawing Out conference (RMIT University, 2010), where she offered so seductively eisegesis as opposed to exegesis, as a more appropriate form of writing which aligned more sympathetically with creative practices.

Shifting practices as propositional

I came into the PhD primarily as an abstract painter. By the time I completed the PhD, the practice had expanded in terms of processes and methods, and materials and forms, which included video, photography, site-specific installations, object, and ready-mades. The diverse range of materials extended to Swarovski crystals, fabric, spices, threads and tree branches. The biggest shift in my studio method was to allow content to determine form and material. That is, the idea often dictated the form the artwork would take and the materials I would employ. What motivated these changes was not a conscious decision. What I did consciously do was to allow a coalescence of experience from past and present situations, to be *performed* through a process of experimentation. Throughout this process I stayed opened and attentive to the outcomes from the experimentation, to determine where or what the final resolution of the artwork would become. Form, content and methodologies throughout the PhD were kept in states of experimentation and indeterminacy for as long as possible before deciding on resolution.

This shift in studio methods, from a fairly conventional painting practice to more open and discursive practices, occurred almost incidentally near the commencement of my candidature. I was struggling with an idea for an exhibition I had committed to, at the very early stages of the candidature, which I felt had nothing to do with the research I was to focus on. The curatorial premise of this exhibition started to almost 'play out' in real time and experience as an unfolding, serendipitous narrative. The work I finally made for this exhibition* set up many of the conditions that I would harness throughout the PhD, allowing narrative, an openness to the artwork and idea evolving, drawing on the personal and anecdotal, looking forward and backward simultaneously, and most importantly, staying attentive and noticing throughout the experimental process. The space or division between experimentation and resolution therefore collapses in this context, or certainly gets lodged in proposition rather than fixity. Often an experiment became the resolved artwork. I found this form of art practice liberating and exciting, but also fraught with anxiety and uncertainty. I am not saying that painting is any easier as a form or process, but at least it fixed, to a degree, material, technique and form so that the experimentation and uncertainty sat inside these parameters.

---

* The exhibition I make reference to is Secret Files from the Working Men's College (2010), Project Space School of Art Galleries, RMIT University in conjunction with Midsumma Festival, Melbourne. This exhibition included my work *Brad* (2010). For a more comprehensive discussion on this exhibition and artwork see Chapter two in my dissertation *Shimmering Spaces: Art and Anglo Indian Experiences*, pp. 207–10.

Juggling a PhD and full-time employment ...

Anyone who is working in a full-time position already knows about life/work balances and the need for parameters. This was the biggest struggle and which required the most discipline. I undertook the PhD in a part-time capacity. I attempted to work a four-day week and have between two and three days for the PhD. I took almost six years to complete, because of workload commitments at the University. In hindsight this was not ideal as it is a very longtime to maintain cohesion, relevance and stamina. I would love to have devoted more concentrated time to the PhD and reduced the length of time of my study. Perhaps oscillating between part-time and full-time modes of study could have been a good option. But then this would have to be negotiated again with work commitments, leave opportunities and financial resources to support these decisions.

I thought I was proceeding well in the research having only ever seen the study in fragments and chunks, fitting it in between life's other commitments. I didn't have a chance to see or hold its totality until nearer the end. It was as if I was only seeing a close up (microscopic) form of my research at any given time, rather than a distant (telescopic) lens over the whole picture. I was very generously granted three months study leave from the School of Art at RMIT University near the completion of my PhD which allowed me to concentrate full-time, seven days a week, on the research to pull it together. Even then it was still a rush. Looking back, six months would have given me more time to redraft and be more judicious in the editing process. I don't think there is a perfect model for everyone. Certainly if I had to do it again, I would devote concentrated time (3 months) at the beginning of the study to get a solid start and direction, and a longer period at the end (6 months) to complete the project.

Juggling a PhD and life ...

When I commenced my studies, my peers did tell me that you never see your friends and partner. Thankfully I have a very understanding partner and friends, who gave me the space and time I required. I am sure he and my friends, who were so supportive throughout the candidature, were as relieved when I finally completed, as I was. If I had one more person ask me if I had finished *yet*, (which I took to implying it has gone on long enough), I would have strangled them!

You have to be both resilient and slightly circumspect about it (life and study). There are compromises and priorities, which I had to constantly juggle, as we all do. How do you *organize* your life in terms of risk, responsibility and the pursuit of happiness. It is a juggling act. What I did do was absorb life into my PhD and my PhD into my life. Because of the nature of my research I found relevance between life experiences and the research. They occupied and influenced this same space, rather than being compartmentalized. What really made this relationship between life, work and study operate smoothly, was learning to relax into the moments. A PhD can be very stressful at different stages. Staying opened to the idea that there is an accumulation of knowledge and experience throughout the PhD was important in helping me stay more relaxed throughout the process, rather than being uptight and stressed, trying to figure it all out at the start.

Difficulties and pleasures

Writing seventeen drafts of my proposal in preparation of my confirmation seminar and to convince a committee there was research, and that I knew what I was doing, was the most torturous, difficult and uncomfortable experience of the PhD. I struggled through this process. Each time a draft of my proposal, covered in question marks and challenging red highlights, was returned to me by my supervisors and the readers from the approval committee, I felt deflated. I doubted myself at every point. When my proposal was finally accepted and approved (I think they all just got tired of reading it), I could not look at it again. My supervisor very wisely told me to leave it alone for a while to settle, that is how affected I was by the process. I just needed to get in the studio and make work, to help sort out what I was trying to do. The work I produced at this stage seemed to signal my intentions for the research, I obviously could not find the words to articulate it in the form of the proposal, at this early stage.

I wish I had realized earlier (despite the sound advice of my supervisor), that I wasn't going to work it all out at the start, which is what I wanted, so to remove the high levels of anxiety and doubt I was feeling at the commencement of the program. Am I capable of doing this, at this level of study? (A PhD is after all at the apex of academic qualifications.) Can I write 40,000 words? Where will they come from? Can the art practice really address the research is a way which constitutes academic research. Describing the PhD as a 'doctoral journey' is apt, as it is a journey; a journey, which you attempt to map out and organize logically in terms of a proposal, a rationale, a description, a methodology. However it is important to understand it is a proposition. The best laid plan rarely goes to plan. The journey itself will throw up situations and circumstances that shift, extend, or even obliterate the best laid plan. You have to do the work to find out what the plan might be and revise it accordingly.

Finding focused time was the biggest challenge throughout my studies. Time is both your friend (when you have it!) and your enemy (when you don't have enough of it and there are deadlines!).

At the final stages of the PhD I worked with both a designer and an editor. File management across drafts and clarity of communication for associated changes to drafts is very time consuming and detailed. At this point I realized I had to 'let go' of the dissertation. It was so easy to keep finessing the document for conceptual changes (rather than editorial changes). I made this process far more complicated than it needed to be because I kept making changes, beyond the editorial. I should have followed logical rules: work through drafts with your supervisors, get the document to a final draft for editing, confirm/accept the editing with the editor, send the document to the designer for layout, get the document from the designer to the editor to make sure the designer hasn't missed information in the formatting process, then back to you for approval, any changes then goes back to the designer, then editor, until the document is fully approved and proofed for publication. Staying organized and staying on top of the process is really important. Thankfully I had a very understanding editor and designer who generously compensated for my own inadequacies through this process.

Despite all the difficulties I faced during the journey, there were pleasures. I learnt so much about my area of investigation, about my art practice and the writing process. The first time I held a hardcopy of my dissertation and when I put my final assessment exhibition together, I realized just how much work

I had done and what I had achieved. Of course when this was validated so generously by my examiners, it was a humbling experience.

The most memorable time during my research was the excitement I felt when I realized I could actually do it, and all the doubt and anxiety I experienced particularly about the writing, dissipated and I actually enjoyed the process. I thought writing would be my biggest difficultly and challenge – it was. But it also turned out to be a pleasure and a process I enjoyed (and according to my examiners, I was apparently good at. Who would have thought …).

If I had the chance what would I do differently?

Having only recently completed my PhD, there are a range of thoughts which sit front of mind: relief, exhaustion, doubt, excitement and the overriding thought which is, now that I have completed it I know how to do it *properly*…. I have been told by many peers this is a common response.

As mentioned previously, doing it over four years rather than six would have made more sense. I wish I could have had the luxury of more time near the end for a more judicious editing process. I would have loved the time to edit, edit and edit again.

I had an extensive bibliography, however there were so many more texts I would have liked to have read. At some point you realize that you have to stop. But there is always that nagging doubt that you have missed an important text, artist, book or paper which the examiners or someone else will question.

I published a catalogue to accompany three preliminary exhibitions during the doctoral journey. I wish I had delivered and published a series of conference or journal papers as well. There just wasn't enough time. I made exhibition a priority. In total there were six exhibitions I showed in during the research, but I could have and should have published conference papers in conjunction with the exhibitions.

Final thoughts and advice for prospective doctoral candidates

Getting the opportunity to undertake doctoral studies is a privilege. If you are fortunate enough to be accepted into a doctoral program, than do it. I found the experience valuable on many levels; professionally, academically and personally. Understand that the process is challenging and the learning curb very steep. Make sure you are ready to undertake the commitment. Most of us will probably only do one PhD in our lives. It may sound obvious, but I was aware from the start, that I really wanted to do it as well as I could.

Prepare your application well. Again, I think the more work you can do at the start of the process holds you in a really strong position to begin the journey.

Choose your supervisors carefully. I found it essential that I had supervisors who guided me but who also trusted me. But most importantly that they would give me permission to find, loose, pause and accelerate as fitted the moment. They did this. It was this guidance and care, which ultimately made the experience rich and meaningful. It will be your PhD in the end, so find a way to do it your way.

Give yourself reflective time to let the writing and the artwork sit for periods of time before you publish.

Get a good editor you can work with. Relax into the process and try to enjoy it. It is daunting, but it is a mountain that you don't leap to the top of, but rather, plan and undertake one step at a time so you can enjoy the pleasures of the journey along the way, even with detours and dead ends.

In this piece of reflective writing, I am aware that my responses are a combination that are both philosophical and pragmatic. I hope it provides an honest and heartfelt account of reflection on my doctoral journey. When I completed, people naturally congratulated me on my achievement. I took this as politeness, underestimating what I had achieved. This is only now slowly sinking in. It *is* a fine feeling of achievement.

References

D'Costa, R. (2016). Shimmering spaces: Art and Anglo Indian experiences. PhD project, RMIT University, Melbourne, Australia.

Dean, T. (2005). *An aside: Works selected by Tacita Dean*, exhibition catalogue, 18 February–1 May, Camden Arts Centre, London. London: Hayward Gallery Publishing.

Hester, B. (2007). Material adventures, spatial productions: Manoeuvring sculpture towards a proliferating event. PhD project, RMIT University, Melbourne, Australia.

Rendle-Short, F. (2010). 'Loose thinking': Writing an eisegesis,' RMIT University, *TEXT, 14*, (1), retrieved from www.textjournal.com.au/april10/rendleshort.htm

I JUST HAD TO DO IT

Lesley Duxbury

Title of study: Exposed to the elements: Representations of atmospheric phenomena and the construction of a cultural psyche

RMIT University, 2004

Abstract

By referencing images and texts of selected 19th century artists and writers, I investigate the ways in which experiences and representations of atmospheric phenomena have permeated the English cultural psyche and become a significant element in the definition of Englishness. The inherent properties of printmaking, such as sameness and difference and repetition and reproduction are investigated, properties that also underpin our readings of atmospheric phenomena. The main emphases of this research are the elemental forces of the weather, the transitory effects of light and atmosphere and their influence on the psyche.

The weather has long been a topic of speculation. From the beginning of recorded history to the present, atmospheric phenomena continue to have an impact on our lives. Among the burgeoning scientific discoveries in 19th century Britain were those relating to natural phenomena, such as meteorology and is a focus of this project. This scientific progress fired the imagination of the age and had a significant impact on the work of many artists and writers, in particular, the quintessential English artists, John Constable and J.M.W. Turner, and poets such as William Wordsworth and Samuel Taylor Coleridge.

As the end of this millennium approaches there is an ever-increasing emphasis on the definition and construction of personal and cultural identities. We are inevitably a part of the atmosphere or air; it surrounds us and we breathe it in. One's air, or temperament, is the point at which the self meets the world, and it can apply to the self or the way one exists in the world. Our unconscious responses to the atmosphere are taken for granted, including simply breathing in and breathing out and the body's ability to maintain thermal balance. This project examines the cultural psyche in response to a quotidian experience over which we have no control.

The research expands awareness of new interpretations of cultural identity through an investigation of the impact of the varying manifestations of atmospheric phenomena on the individual psyche.

--

The writing on the wall

My colleague turned to me and handed me a piece of paper saying, 'You should do this too'. In early 1997 I had arrived in Melbourne fresh from a three-month residency in Paris and travel in the Middle East and had 'walked into' a position as lecturer in Printmaking in the School of Art at RMIT University with few formalities. I was well respected as an artist and had a Master of Art under my belt but I had little experience as an academic having had only short-term contracts or multiple sessional jobs in the recent past. By 1998 I had an ongoing position coordinating printmaking and a future in academia, but what exactly did that mean and how did it affect me? The Royal Melbourne Institute of Technology had become a University a few years earlier in 1992 and when I arrived was still coming to terms with what that meant, especially the role of research alongside teaching. I had joined a team of highly regarded artist/lecturers – painters, gold and silversmiths, sculptors and ceramicists– who held exhibitions in the most highly-respected public and private galleries and had good reputations in their chosen fields, however in the university these achievements were not counted. Exhibitions were not recorded and certainly they did not count as research. Research meant writing; journal articles, book chapters and conference papers were the accepted forms but it did not mean making art or holding an art exhibition. Only art history staff in the School of Art had the potential for research it appeared. At the same time the university was being more open about what was expected of its staff and especially those who had transitioned from technical teacher to university lecturer. Everyone was expected to have a MA at least and while we were not openly encouraged to undertake a PhD but it was obvious even at that point that nothing less than a doctorate would suffice eventually. In 1998 in the School of Art one art history lecturer had a doctorate and one candidate was enrolled to undertake a PhD by creative project. This was the same year that Denis Strand released his report on the controversial subject of 'Research in the Creative Arts', the first time in Australia that so-called research outputs in creative art, music, design and writing had been named and studied and a set of performance indicators developed (Department of Employment, Education Training and Youth Affairs, 1998). The School of Art had neither experience in supervising doctorates nor what was expected of a doctoral candidate, especially a PhD by project in which any new knowledge created resides in the artwork itself. The form my colleague handed me to apply for a PhD was unexpected, however she was more astute than me and had already seen the writing on the wall.

I grew up in the UK and went to Art School there in 1968, a tumultuous year across Europe and the year of the Art School Revolution at Hornsey College of Art. I completed a BA at Maidstone College of Art and continued on to the University of London to undertake an Art Teaching Diploma. In 1983 I came to Melbourne, later moving to Perth where I undertook a Master of Fine Art. That I chose to undertake a PhD at RMIT University and as a lecturer in the same institution was not a problem for me as I had not been a student in that university previously.

Musings on John Constable

Having an application form thrust to me and completing its general details was one part of the consideration of doing a PhD. The second part–the topic– was quite another thing altogether. In 1991 I had relocated to Perth in Western Australia. I knew nothing at all about the west but because of its perceived remoteness (from the Eastern states) I had the impression that somehow it might be 'more Australian' than Melbourne where I had lived for eight years after emigrating from the UK. Knowing no one in Perth I enrolled in a Master of Fine Art program at Curtin University in order to meet like-minded people and to have access to the facilities I needed to continue as a printmaker–the research topic at that point was a secondary issue. Until I moved to Perth I had practiced steadily as a highly skilled printmaker, exhibiting in solo and group exhibitions and submitting my work for print awards. My interests had always been in landscape and I made prints of the landscapes I remembered from the UK and the new ones of the country around Melbourne, always with a 'romantic' sensibility. I was aware of the great differences between these landscapes on opposite sides of the world; the intense greens and rolling hills of my birth country and the drier, harsher landscapes of my new country. However when I began to explore Western Australia it quickly became obvious that I would never see landscape in the same way. Beyond the wheat belt that surrounds Perth, especially to the North and East the country transitions into desert – salt lakes, eroded rock formations, vast tracts of sand and dirt and sparse, spiky vegetation that over millennia have adapted to take root in such places. My perspective on what constituted landscape was completely undermined. Not only the landscape floored me but also the conditions under which I viewed it – the sky and the weather.

I arrived in Perth in early November and I am convinced I didn't see a cloud until the summer storms of January. There were only clear, impossibly blue skies from one side of the horizon to the other. A bright, strong sun cast sharp dark shadows until the middle of the day when it seemed there was no respite from the sun at all. I was completely thrown. At the same time in the city of Perth I heard many English accents, 'traditional' English food was served in cafes and streets recreated the medieval thoroughfares of the more ancient English towns. These new perceptions of place had quite an impact on my own understanding of Englishness, which became the focus for the MA and through which I attempted to discover what precisely was unfamiliar (Oerlemans, 2002). During the two-year program I became particularly interested in the nineteenth century artist John Constable, the quintessential painter of English landscapes and his observations of the sky and the ways it affects how we see the landscape. My prints and photographs changed substantially. From creating pictorial representations of landscape I began to use more minimal, more abstract ways to critique landscape, using text and innovative techniques of traditional printmaking. My work expanded like the desert landscape I was intrigued by becoming inordinately long, stretching away like the horizon and endless in form with no identifying features. I was excited by the work I made and it led me to projects beyond printmaking. Using a similar way of thinking I could adapt it to encompass public art projects and exhibitions in spaces other than galleries.

I brought these considerations to thinking about my topic for a PhD. I continued to be interested in exploring what I had started in Perth; what it meant to be English, especially in a place of immigrants where 'new Australian' artists were addressing their own cultural identities. However that there may be something to explore in being English did not seem to be an issue, the English were after all the dominant population. Although the impetus for my research was an increasing fascination with my own responses to aspects of being in a 'foreign' land and a growing interest in what it meant to be English, afforded by distance from my country of origin, I also wanted to explore my interests as a participator in the landscape and my enduring occupation with its representation. Being back in Melbourne I became aware again of its more English climate, albeit more extreme in summer. Thoughts about the weather came to the fore, as did its preoccupation by the English. All these things considered I still could not begin to see my way into a PhD without a strong title; titles are important to me and most of my artworks are inspired by a word or a few linked words. According to John Armstrong (2000), 'We are among other things, associating machines. Feed in an object (a smell, a word, an image) and it excites in the imagination a corresponding item (a feeling, a recollection, a hope)' (p. 62). This strategy also works for me and a good title might sustain an entire exhibition of work or a substantial text. I use the image-making capacity of words in my work to trigger the imagination, to evoke an image in the mind of the viewer (Duxbury, 2008, p. 22). Once I had a title that included such evocative words as 'the elements', 'atmospheric phenomena' and 'psyche' I felt I could begin.

I had already referenced John Constable during my MA. Adding the other quintessentially English artist, J. M. W. Turner, to my references caused me to wonder and question what happened in 19th century England to produce two such enduring artists and what the conditions were at the time that provoked their work. This starting point led me down the fascinating paths of discovery and inspiration that constituted my PhD.

Walking, thinking and making

On reflection I see that I did not declare a Methodology in my research proposal, instead I included a section on Studio and Technical Research in which I said I would employ a diversity of media to investigate the potential for printmaking to enhance representations of atmospheric phenomena. I would include traditional printmaking techniques alongside more contemporary means of reproduction and replication and I would encompass a range of formal vocabularies from minimalism and photography to text-based conceptualism in the production of the work. Practice-based research was a new concept across the country. In many ways we who enrolled in a PhD by project in 1998 entered unknown territory. We knew that during the PhD we would create artworks and that those artworks should result in new ways of making and resolving work that we could not envisage at this early stage. We also knew that we would write a long text to accompany the exhibition of art, an exegesis, which would be between 20,000 and 40,000 words. However we had no guidelines as to how the creative work related to the textual exegesis and had no precedents.

I had become aware of the concept of thinking through making and doing. After all as a lecturer it was advice I gave my students; that they should not sit looking at a blank wall for inspiration, they must begin some activity to be able to activate thought processes. Strangely, this became a central focus of my PhD research when the realization that my own activity of long distance walking initiated many of my artworks. According to Rebecca Solnit (2001) who has drawn extensively upon the experiences of writers and artists, walking stimulates a certain 'rhythm of thinking' (p. 5) and the mind becomes a landscape traversed by thoughts stimulated by this physical act.

Walking was not the subject of my project and not even a consideration as a methodology when I applied to undertake a PhD, but the experience of the long, isolated walks I engaged in during my candidacy drew together a number of strands of my research. Some pieces of work came directly from experiences of the walks, not as documentary photographs or images of what I had observed, but partly that and partly other input, from bibliographical, historical and scientific sources. My main 'inspiration', if it can be called that, was the natural, atmospheric environment that enveloped me and became a part of me, simply by breathing in and out; the activity of walking had the potential to unite the landscape, its atmosphere and my imagination (Duxbury, 2008).

Between two worlds

I had a full-time academic position, which allowed me one day a week for research or 7.2 hours. I enrolled in a part-time PhD, which meant putting in the equivalence of 23 hours per week and so I had to 'find' a further 15.8 hours a week to do justice to the PhD. Weekends, it seemed would give the most opportunity for dedicated time. However I spent my weekends with my partner who was employed 230 km from Melbourne in Gippsland. While I worked Monday to Friday in Melbourne I lived alone and rented a studio. Either I travelled to Gippsland on a Friday evening, returning Sunday night or my partner reversed the process. This left me four evenings a week to dedicate to my PhD along with my one research day. It should never be underestimated how dedicated one must be to undertake such a period of study while trying to maintain a normal life. I quickly fell into a routine in which I worked at RMIT during Monday to Thursday and spent Friday in my studio. At the end of each day except Friday I left my office and walked to my studio in one of Melbourne's busiest, most centrally located laneways. I etched a wallaby track down Swanston Street, through the Daimaru department store that existed then, through the Myer department store, across Bourke Street resisting the temptation to jump on a tram that would take me home and onward through a couple of lesser-known laneways to my studio in Flinders Lane, picking up a coffee from one of the many cafes close by. When walking through the department stores I gradually sloughed off my academic life and mentally prepared myself as an artist. Once in my studio, as the light outside faded, I engrossed myself in what I came to call 'mindless' printmaking. It was at this point and the consequence of my circumstances that my work practices began to change.

At the beginning of my project it seemed that there was little time for thinking, let alone doing and making work. I spent any quiet time, time when I was neither working, nor in the studio nor with my partner or friends, in the library or reading at home. This quickly led to wanting to experiment with some new ideas related to my project but my usual work practices were very time consuming and laborious. I had to develop new ways of making work to accommodate my working life. And to add to the urgency I had committed to a solo exhibition of new work in Perth the same year. The gallery was very large and quite daunting from this distance. Any new work would have to be made quickly and on a larger scale than normal. One of the methods I developed to achieve this was to create a number of matrices, either through etching or relief block and print them in a random way on small sheets of paper. I found I was able to sneak an etching plate with a photographically generated image into the acid bath in printmaking between consultations with students or between meetings. I was fortunate to have a technician who would keep an eye on me and remind me about the progress of my plate. Down in my studio, exhausted from a day of teaching and administration, I would mindlessly cut many small sheets of rag paper and print them with a flat colour. When I arrived at my studio exhausted the following evening, the ink would be dry and ready for a second printing, this time using the etched plates. Again the process required little thought, simply just enough energy to finish the process. And so I continued to overprint each image three times followed by a flat colour printing on the back of each. The paper was smaller than the etched plate and so registration was not an issue. Eventually I created four grid-like, large-scale prints. A random process resulted in extremely organized installations that changed the way I worked from that point on.

In addition to printmaking I had always taken and used photographs in my work. When I began my PhD it was right on the cusp of a revolution in communication. In 1998 only 16% of the population had access to the Internet and the School of Art was not part of that 16% and neither staff nor students were connected to each other by email. I had requested to be connected to the Internet when I arrived at RMIT and eventually a modem was installed in my office and I had a personal email address, not an RMIT one. The ways we took photographs were also changing and while I was the coordinator of printmaking I ordered our first digital camera and slide scanner. Until this point I had taken only photographic slides of landscapes and of my work and it continued to be the way I documented my project throughout the PhD. However, in 1998 an artist-in-residence from the UK introduced a select few staff to the production of large-scale photographic prints using a large-format digital printer and I was eager to be part of this transformation of photographic practices. It was a complicated and challenging process to convert an image on slide film to a digital image. I had to learn a new language of megapixels, input and output and much technical jargon that is unnecessary today. I volunteered for the second round of experiments and spent many research days learning the basics of Photoshop—and I loved it. In those days it took all night to print a photograph 100 cm square. Although I was enamoured of the technology I missed the hands-on processes of traditional printmaking and started to overprint the digital image with analogue methods, with screen-printing or relief printing. Until this time it was 'the hand with its unique digital capacities' that had been linked to creativity not 'the unease that the bringing together of digital imaging and art evokes' (*lightfingered*, 1999). But now I had found a way to combine old and new technologies to create work that resonated with my aesthetic sensibilities.

The large-scale multi-part prints and hand-printed digital images were the main repertoire of the work I produced for the PhD. I acquired more skills in Photoshop and I used traditional printmaking techniques on non-traditional materials such as aluminium. During my candidature I held nine solo exhibitions of my work and was curated into more than 22 exhibitions in public, state and university galleries, nationally and internationally, including the Metropolitan Museum of Art, Seoul; Art Gallery of Western Australia and National Gallery of Australia.

The lows and highs of candidature and beyond

The main issues I encountered through the period of study occurred right at the beginning and they were in relation to supervision and what was actually required of the PhD. When I enrolled in a PhD in 1998 along with several of my colleagues only one candidate preceded us and he was approximately half way through his research project. Therefore experience in supervising PhDs was minimal to say the least. At that point the university did not have regulations regarding who could be a supervisor. The majority of academic staff in the School of Art had undertaken a Masters qualification and were quite used to supervising such candidates, however the MA by Research at RMIT University was unusual in that it did not require an exegetical text; the research was carried out through the practice and making of art and the understanding was that it did not need a text to explain it. No one therefore had experience in supervising the exegesis that was required for the PhD. The temptation was to split the research into two parts to be supervised by one supervisor for the writing and one for the practice. I selected my supervisors based on their experience. One was an art history and theory lecturer in the School who had a PhD in Art History, who became my senior supervisor. My second supervisor was an active artist, a prolific painter who exhibited in a well-respected gallery in Melbourne and had some international reputation, however he was not particularly 'sympathetic' to my work having quite a different aesthetic and focus in his own work. My senior supervisor helped in the writing of my research proposal, which was enthusiastically approved by an independent committee but she had little to offer my work practices and rarely visited my exhibitions. My second supervisor did visit my local exhibitions but somehow managed to turn any discussion about my work into a story about his own. Inevitably I found myself working on my own on both the text and the creative work apart from conversations with my colleague who was experiencing similar problems. We learned how to be researchers through being researchers; we made it up as we went along, without a clear idea of what we were doing. However, according to Grete Refsum, 'The feeling of not-knowing is familiar to anyone who starts working on a new project and may be understood as a necessary condition for creators' (2002, p. 1). I did take my project very seriously. The work progressed and I became very aware of the ways I was thinking, reflecting and making; how what I was reading encouraged the creative work and how that in turn led to further library searches. I was excited by what I found, what I read and the new work I made.

Although I knew I would be writing approximately 40,000 words I had no idea what form my exegesis would take or what I would actually write about. There were no guidelines as to the format of the exegesis, nor what the content should be. According to Jan Svenungsson (2007), 'The thesis written by an artist doesn't know what it is supposed to be: scholarly or artistic, or both' (p. 62). The word 'theory' loomed large and it was tacitly agreed that theory would somehow make what we did a PhD, but the meaning of theory was not universally accepted. In early 1998 my university had no examples in its research repository and it was impossible to find any in other university archives. Any completed PhDs by project were hard copy only and retained in special collections in university libraries. Unless one knew someone who had undertaken such a PhD there was no way of knowing what was out there.

Initially the issues of supervision and lack of guidelines were frustrating but conversely they also gave me an extraordinary amount of freedom, freedom from the pressures of oversight from a supervisor and from the expectations of the formalities of the text. The PhD drove some extraordinary ventures such as extended walks in Tierra del Fuego and Newfoundland. I felt confident with the new work I produced during the PhD and was eager to exhibit it. This subsequently led to pieces being acquired by state and national collections and my project becoming known. In the early days of the PhD I tended to keep it quiet but once I started to tell friends about it outside the institution I had some remarkable experiences. At one point in my research I had read about the 19th century chemist and amateur meteorologist, Luke Howard who went on to invent the names of the clouds. He published the first seminal text on clouds in London in 1803 and I wanted to read it but no matter how I tried I was not able to find a copy of it. However, one evening a friend knocked on my door and suggested I might like to see what she had found at the Theosophical Society in Melbourne; she held out an original copy of Luke Howard's essay, *On the Modifications of Clouds* for me to borrow; it was the text that I had long searched for.

Given the period that I undertook a PhD there is little I would do differently. If I were to rewrite my exegesis today I would tackle that in another way. At the time I wrote it I didn't want to explain anything in terms of how certain readings might have led to making particular artworks. I wanted to avoid description and elucidation but had no help as to make it otherwise. Today with the benefit of hindsight and after supervising more than 24 doctoral students and having examined 20 PhDs I am clearer about the exegetical text or dissertation. I encourage my candidates to be as creative with the text as they are with their practical work and I have supervised some beautifully written and intelligent dissertations that avoid simplistic description and overwrought theory.

I undertook a PhD at a time when it was apparent that it would be a mandatory qualification to be an academic. I was an established artist and doing a PhD over six years changed my work practices and gave me more confidence to write and I went on to write numerous journal articles and book chapters. Becoming a Doctor of Philosophy improved my prospects for promotion within the university and my positions on committees. It was a necessary undertaking given my ambitions but I do wonder about its relevance today. Of course it is still a requirement for any academic position, however I now supervise PhD candidates who have come through undergraduate courses, undertaken a one year Honours program and been accepted to do a PhD. Such students have few life experiences and no record of exhibitions, some having only exhibited in end-of-year graduate shows. They write badly and rely heavily on supervisors to put it right. A PhD completed in three years by such a student does not produce a better artist and it does not produce an academic. I wonder what the PhD is about today.

References

Armstrong, J. (2000). *The natural philosophy of art*. London: Allen Lane, The Penguin Press.

Department of Employment, Education Training and Youth Affairs. (1998). *Research in the creative arts*. Canberra, Australia. Denis Strand.

Duxbury, L. (2008). The eye (and mind) of the beholder. In L. Duxbury, E. M. Grierson and D. Waite (eds.), *Thinking through practice: Art as research in the academy* (pp. 17–27). Melbourne: RMIT University.

Lightfingered, (1999). Exhibition catalogue. RMIT University, Melbourne: Sophia Errey.

Oerlmans, O. (2002). *Romanticism and the materiality of nature*. Toronto: University of Toronto Press.

Refsum, G. (2002). Contribution to an understanding of the knowledge base in the field of visual arts. *Working Papers in Art and Design, 2*. Retrieved from https://www.herts.ac.uk/__data/assets/pdf_file/0014/12308/WPIAAD_vol2_refsum.pdf.

Solnit, R (2001). *Wanderlust: A history of walking*. London: Penguin Books.

Svenungsson, J. (2007). *An artist's text book*. Helsinki: Finnish Academy of the Arts.

'DID WE GET AWAY WITH IT?' OFF STAGE AND BANTER: MUSICAL AND VISUAL PUNS IN A PHD STUDY INVOLVING A HYBRID ART PRACTICE

Phil Edwards

Title of study: Audio CD production as a contemporary hybrid art practice

RMIT University, 2003

Abstract

This PhD project, Audio CD Production as a Contemporary Hybrid Art Practice, now situated in an historical context, explored how a hybrid art practice based on the production of music and images and resolved in the production of audio CDs might be used to explore the impact of new technologies on a contemporary art practice.

During the two years of this study, 2001–2003, I completed a series of art projects that involved the production of audio CDs – regarded as contemporary technology at the time – in a Fine Art practice. These projects included a series of installations, performances and collaborations that were intended to expand the boundaries of what was, in my experience in Australia, usually considered contemporary Fine Art practice. Often the outcomes of these projects took the physical properties of conventional pop art products of the time, such as the music poster, CD cover art design and pop music. The performances on the audio CDs are not strictly traditionally defined music, however, as I was – and am not – in the traditional sense a trained musician. The art products made use instead, the semblances of music structures but involve many strategies of construction employed in a visual art practice such as, use of historical references, chance discoveries, collaboration and other process-related production methodologies.

This study was completed at a time when the Internet was only becoming a commonplace domestic tool and Audio CDs were the latest technology. It was completed in Melbourne, Australia, when hybrid art forms, though historically ever present, were becoming more commonly accepted within the study of art especially since the general acceptance of post-modern theory. The study reveals both the exciting possibilities and limitations of using the term 'new technology' as a term to justify the validity of an art practice seeking to be hybrid in discipline and philosophy and contemporary. The outcome of the study was series of projects and performances undertaken, recorded visually and sonically and resulting in the production of a set of audio CDs whose accompanying visual artwork was presented for assessment.

--

The past is a foreign another country: they do things differently there.

L.P. Hartley, *The Go Between*, 1953

These opening lines from L. P. Hartley's novel seem a very apt platform from which to write a personal review of my doctoral journey. This is the first time, 13 years later from the completion of the doctorate – coincidentally the same age of the novels main character, Leo – that I have had occasion to open the pages of my hard copy exegesis and read what I wrote at that time. It is with some trepidation that I began to do so.

Leo as a young boy in the novel was the interlocutor between to two tragic lovers whose respective social classes at the turn of the nineteenth century in England meant they were unable to meet except in secret. Leo at the age of 60 finds his childhood diary, from those years and begins to reminisce about his past.

I found parallels in reading my old exegesis with Leo's experiences reading his old diary. Both, incidentally, recovered again in red coloured cardboard boxes. I remember discussions as to whether it was appropriate for me to use such a colour to enclose the documentation of my project. I have read many

PhDs since in the last 13 years but never revisited my own.

The aim of my study, titled *Audio CD Production as a Contemporary Art Practice*, was to help me to continue to understand my already existing expanding hybrid art practice, through the strategy of making audio CDs and their accompanying visual packaging in order to explore the spaces and theoretical links between the cultural and historical sources of consumer Pop Culture and Fine Art Practice. In a sense I wanted to act, in an academic context, as a go-between between those two worlds as I saw them then. I no longer think of those differences as being relevant to my continuing practice.

I was, I believe, the first RMIT School of Art (SOA) student to come through from TAFE to PhD graduation. There had been one other RMIT SOA PhD graduate before me but they had done some of their studies at another institution. As such, there did not exist in 2001–2003 the current PhD system of checks and balances that exist to help a candidate with their studies. There was no one on staff in the SOA with a PhD, and the experience that goes with that. There were, however, very well informed and experienced artists from whom I received appropriate guidance as supervisors. In particular I wish to note the excellent supervision of David Thomas who helped me a great deal in developing an ability to identify more clearly the content of my often erratic and haphazard study methodologies.

There is a background to my art studies which I wish to present here as I think it is relevant not only to the understanding of my journey as an artist and academic but important in situating that journey in its times. It is relevant to this essay as I believe that all candidates bring their past to their studies. I already had two qualifications before I went back to RMIT TAFE to study art. One was a Bachelor of Education (Environmental Science) from which I developed an interest in the organic structures of the natural world and a Masters in Educational Studies in which I continued my interest in the history of English literature – both of which became important elements in my research for the PhD. I must also confess here that I do appreciate how some young undergraduate students may behave as I failed my first course twice due to an over indulgence in extra curricula activities, most of which revolved around my interests in pop culture, rock and punk music. It seems inevitable to me now that my early youthful experiences would find resonance in my later more formal studies.

I decided to do my PhD in 2000 after completing my MFA at RMIT. I was unsure as to whether not I would be able to financially afford the time it takes to do a PhD in the future as the government of the time was considering the raising of university fees. RMIT University supported me by giving a Post Graduate Research Scholarship for both the MFA and PhD programs for which I am still grateful.

My MFA studies were relevant to my PhD as it is in those I began using aspects of sound in my installation practice, mainly by incorporating Op Shop vinyl record covers and playing their music in exhibitions. I had, for all intents and purposes, stopped using traditional painting media and sought to use furniture, hard rubbish and detritus as the main media of my practice. I sought to employ what I had learnt in formal terms about the poetics of painting and its history in, what I saw as, punkier and grungier presentations.

The PhD was an extension of my MFA studies.

The activity of audio CD production by local artists, both in terms of limited production runs on a home computer or commercial scale print runs, was becoming an increasingly common phenomenon at the turn of the century in Melbourne. Mindful of the history of art over the last one hundred years, many Fine Art trained artists were taking advantage of the new technologies available and producing sound art in an audio CD format as well as producing accompanying visual art.

My understanding of post-modern art practices suggested to me that I might make a hybrid art product that overlapped ideas in a range of media and had multiple points of departure into the community. I seemed to me that increasingly as traditional artforms become intermeshed with contemporary digital technology, hybrid artforms were arising and the relationship between high art and pop art commodification was constantly being challenged.

I was not used to writing academically at length – that is probably still evident – and only my first research question holds partial legitimacy for me now as I review my PhD exegesis.

Research Question 1. What strategies can be developed to integrate sound with a visual art practice to create a hybrid art forms within a Fine Art practice? (It is important to note here that as I revisit my PhD journey in this chapter I note to myself that I would be a lot more rigorous with my writing of the exegesis and its premises now that I am much more experienced.)

Research was two-fold.

I examined theorists and critics such as Roslynd Krauss, Hommi Barber, Douglas Khann for ideas about post-modernism, cultural hybridity and the relationship between technology and art but more importantly for me I became involved in the local Melbourne sound scene as an observer and performer.

I was a constant visitor to sound activities and sought them out at Pop Music venues, ARIs and alternative sound events such as the 2001 'What is Music Festival?' and 'Liquid Architecture'. I became familiar with the performances of Anthony Preteros, Robyn Fox and Michael Greaves.

There has been a strong link in the visual arts and pop music historically. To this day many a young visual art student is also a member of a music group. It is not uncommon to find students in an undergraduate painting course also involved in a band and performing about town at local hotels or bars. I wanted my studies to reflect and critique this situation.

I have always suspected that, at some point and in some context, art inevitability fails to communicate what it aims to. This became an integral subtext to my art practice and both my MFA and PhD research studies. It still is.

This subtext is also the reason the music group *AND* was formed that became pivotal to my PhD project. *AND* is still an ongoing activity I use to explore sound, installation, performance, co-modification and to explore the slippage between pop culture and Fine Art. Preliminary variations and models of *AND* commenced immediately prior to the PhD. Many of the *AND* experiments used pop conventions in the making of the music and the design of the cover art. The pop conventions included the use of guitar, keyboards and drum machines and the use of visual puns in the graphic design of the cover art.

Initially *AND* was formed pre-PhD – from an improvised keyboard (me) and saxophone (John Aslanidis) performance organised by Platform Art Space in the Degraves St railway subway in 1998. John and I performed together a couple of other times but it was through my collaborations with fellow artist Peter Ellis that *AND* took on the significance for my PhD studies that it did. The other two bands at the 1998 Degraves St event had names and were listed on a poster accordingly. Like an afterthought we had been listed as '*And*'. It seemed a perfect name as it suggested an afterthought – incomplete and unresolved.

AND used as its manifesto a poem, titled 'How to Play Piano', I had written in 1997, during MFA studies, for my first improvised solo piano recording and CD titled *Murmurmania*. It was intended as an allegorical instruction for the making of art in a hybrid art and performance practice.

'How to Play the Piano'
think about it
don't practice
don't stop
if you find something you recognise abandon it and
move on
don't do it again
always play seriously

The making of the *AND* recordings with Peter were the most enjoyable aspect of my studies and his input as a mentor and collaborator cannot be underestimated. Put simply, it was fun and rewarding to participate in making music and CDs in which we exchanged musical and visual puns through our playing and cover art.

AND recordings resulted from extended jam recordings in various locations over extended hours. A clichéd sample beat taken from a programmed keyboard such a 'rhumba' or 'waltz' or 'march' was set to a usually slow rhythm while we both collaborated on our respective instruments – me on keyboards and Peter on electric guitar.

The aim of *AND* as it developed into an extended series of collaborative interlinked works rather than one-offs. It involved the making of music that was played as seriously as possible, evoking resonances between retro-pop culture and the music of the op-shop – lounge and garage artefacts. It also involved more severe editing of the sound components than I had previously employed and a careful consideration of the collaborative nature of the accompanying visual imagery on the packaging. The packaging and titling involved a lot of deliberate punning on pop music and painting culture from the 1960s, 1970s and before. as this was a common interest of both collaborators. This series of *AND* artworks explored how CDs and their accompanying images could be presented in art galleries in a Fine Art context. It may have been the most focussed aspect of my studies.

Other collaborations occurred during the PhD but this is the only one that, because of its ongoing nature and the number of CDs that came out of it, even after the completion of the project, that allowed a definite evolution to occur within the one exercise, thus it needs to be considered here as one exercise. Although each of the six CDs that resulted from our association was discussed in this exegesis separately I see the collaboration as one evolving experiment in the making of hybrid artworks.

Other visual artists were involved in AND collaborations in subsequent years including Louise Weaver, Andrew Seward, Richard Holt, Peter Henderson, Bill Cobbett, Stuart McPhee, The Gentleman's Record Club, David Haines, Michael Graeve, Ben Harper, Nick Jones, Sue Dodd, Brett Jones, Dave Collins,Peter Henderson, Guyver the Third, Kristian Brennan, Peter Jones, Angus BlacKburn, Tony Woods and Jon Cattapan

The social context for collaboration in making performances and CDs was an aspect of my exegesis I recognise now could have explored. More and could have been the topic of a study on its own.

Concurrent with my collaborative works (all without the consent forms or ethics forms needed in these times) was another solo music Cd project titled *SOSO*. These recording were made alone or from collaged sound field recording which allowed to take on the persona of a mythical or fantasy personality. They could have been developed into a PhD study on their own also but I began to develop problems in identifying both the content and scope of my studies within an Academic structure. I had not identified these quantities enough early enough in my methodological structure.

The methodology for this project was always a work in progress. I did not pre-determine the individual events or think until afterwards how I might link projects together. If I was to conduct a research project like this again, and being mindful as I now am of the current structure of PG studies, I would plan more carefully because the lack of planning led to an inevitable confusion when it came to finalising my studies and writing my exegesis. I am very aware of the shortcomings in my exegesis now but upon reflection of the documentation realise just how extensive the whole project had become. Reviewing my exegesis in a contemporary context I can see approximately three (or even more), PhD projects that could have been made from it. This is a condition I am acutely aware of now when I am supervising current candidates.

Eventually it came to the time when I had to edit, organise and present my findings. It was then that I realised the extent of what is required at this level of Academic study. I had many hours of recordings, 26 CDs and hundreds of images (on slides), but no real sense of how of how to write the exegesis. The inadequacy of the premises for my research became apparent and this was without doubt the most debilitating time I experienced in the program.

I did have a lot fun making the art though and still enjoy them as an outcome even if the final stages of putting it all together was unpleasant experience. I found out that I didn't have the time I thought I had to write the final draft. I had only a few weeks, not a few months. I remember spending nearly nine days straight staying awake and nearly having a physical breakdown, working on putting the exegesis and documentation together. It is one of the reasons I have not looked at my exegesis until now because I knew it should have and could have been better. I would be able to do a better job now.

The final exhibition had not been thought about in depth either and was what I now recognise a continuation of the documentation. If I had to represent I would create an event similar to the one that occurred in one of the last projects in 7th Gallery, an ARI in Fitzroy in 2003. During the period of invigilating and organising that event I invited other artists and members of the public to come into the gallery to collaboratively record sounds, discuss and argue about the project and make visual art. Each day something improvised, new and different happened. The resulting seven CD box set of chaotic recordings and dozens of slide images were a much more suitable conclusion to research questions revolving around hybridity in social, media and cultural contexts than the traditional painting based display of the CDs on coloured tables in a white gallery space that was the actual final outcome for assessment.

After the PhD exegesis and assessment experience I felt deflated and decided that I was no longer interested in being an artist. Having convinced myself that I was not interested in art anymore I left with my family to work overseas forever teaching English as Foreign Language – I completed a Cambridge TEFL course via snail mail in Istanbul – but returned some months later after realising that I was still making drawings. On return I stopped recording for a short while and returned to daily abstract painting and figurative pencil drawings from observation in notebooks. On weekends I joined a crew of *pleine-aire* painters and became a landscape painter for a few years. My association with Academia was, I thought, over.

Upon my return I have continued to make *AND* and other recordings and visual artworks.

What I learnt from my PhD journey was to make sure that as a candidate was the difference between a personal and internal art practice and an academic exercise is immense. They are not mutually exclusive ways of working but they are not the same thing. One remains an artist in-spite of the demands of Academia.

I would advise beginning candidates to be fully aware of the structure and demands of the course they are enrolling and stay aware that the PG studies they are undertaking do not define their total art practice. Ask why you are doing it, what do you want from it and what can the institution do for you. PG levels of study DO help an artist become more informed about their practice but they do not define them. It most important that the demands of this level of study empower you as artist and the analytical skills you develop never leave. Nothing beats hard work though and I know many artists who make wonderful work without the experience of PG studies. I also know many artists well qualified whose work does not interest me.

In short, my advice for new candidates is be clear about your goals, work hard and plan.

My PhD experience was a positive one overall, which I appreciate even more in hindsight. I was fortunate to be part of the initial and developmental implementation of this level of studies at RMIT in an almost pre-digital age. There are so many avenues for research available now and candidates should take advantage of them. With regard to the claim that each project should to add to body of knowledge, that is something I am still suspicious of, agreeing as I do with Voltaire that 'History is a lie commonly agreed upon.' It is more important that the studies undertaken by a PG candidate add to that candidate's accumulated personal knowledge and help them develop their understanding of their personal practice in a wider world sense than the ideals agreed upon by any formal institution. When their formal studies finish what they take with them to the studio is of the most important legacy.

Remember: 'The past is never dead. It is not even the past' (William Faulkner, *Requiem for a Nun*, 1951).

IT'S ALL ABOUT ME

Julian Goddard

Title of study: Democratising art

Curtin University, 2012

Abstract

Through a narrative *Democratising Art* reconstructs my 30 year-plus contribution to the production and discourse of art in Perth. The document chronicles this engagement through an explanation of exhibitions, writings and organisations I have created over that period. It argues that this contribution demonstrates a consistent body of creative production articulating political, Indigenous and aesthetic concerns evident in Western Australian art. And that this engagement has affected the understanding, reception and production of art and art history leading to an expanded idea and experience of such in Western Australia.

--

> *There is more potential in Perth than anywhere else I have been, for making art and exploring possible audiences. It is less explored than anywhere else I have been.*[*]

My PhD experience was a little different than the usual trajectory. In 2009 I was working at Curtin University in Perth and took the opportunity to enrol in a PhD by supplication. This award allows for Curtin staff members to undertake a 'Doctor of Philosophy by Submission of Published Work' and is open to continuing staff members who can demonstrate a sustained and significant

---
[*] Alan Vizents (1986). Quoted in David Bromfield *Gone West. Essays and Criticism 1981–1992*. Perth: PICA Press. 1993, 46.

research record. This involves the presentation of a body of research that after the completion of an appropriate exegesis can be assessed for a PhD award. It has been a long-standing incentive for staff at Curtin and over the years many have successfully taken this path to Masters and PhD; including a small number of Art and Design staff. I completed my PhD by supplication titled *Democratising Art* in 2012 after previously twice giving-up on traditional PhD enrolments – once in the mid-1980s and later again in the 1990s. Both times I wasn't able to give the required attention needed because of family, work and career commitments. Also both were conventional art historical projects that did not relate clearly enough to what I was actually doing which was more like a practice than research. And very much in the spirit of what was in the 1970s and 1980s known as 'political art'.

In those decades the idea that practice could be considered research as such was not part of academic thinking. The shift of ideation to 'practice-led' PhDs only occurred after a major political and social change in Australia's tertiary education system in-line with the reformist Hawke/Keating government of the 1980s and 1990s. The emergence of practice-led higher degrees by research awards after the 'Dawkins Revolution' in higher education in 1987, was a great opportunity for people conducting 'making' as their research, such as is the case with artists, designers, craftspeople and most importantly in my case curators. But it was also vexed with problems of how to legitimately use the word research given its traditional text-based/science format. This dichotomy continues but given the sustained efforts of arts academics over the past 30-plus years, we now have our own conventions and history of legitimacy.

While the PhD by supplication has been a feature of Curtin's higher degrees by research program for decades – the acceptance of practice lead-PhDs within this initiative did not really kick-in until such PhDs became more common within academia in the first 10 years of the new century. However a PhD by supplication presents a significant variation to the now conventional practice-led award. The major difference to a standard practice-led PhD is the allowance of research outputs that predate enrolment to be considered as part of the research project.

In my case I was able to present a record of curation, writing plus the formation of organisations* reaching back to the early 1980s as 'practice', along with a 30,000-word exegesis.† I did not include other activities or outcomes – such as art works or films and their associated exhibitions or my academic achievements – but chose to concentrate on my work as a curator and writer directed at articulating Western Australian art history and contemporary practice. But most significantly I argued that my work in establishing organisations was a nescient form of what is now called 'social practice', especially my work as a galleriest. Including these three fields of endeavor allowed for an extended perspective by which to review my practice over more than three decades. While this gave me a great opportunity to reflect on what I had achieved over that time it also presented a number of problems.

The most difficult part of the project was developing a coherent narrative (or explanation, i.e., exegesis) for my various activities over the extended 30-year period. Finding an ongoing and consistent driver or motivation for my practice/research required having to reflect and question why I had taken such a path and how the practice/research made any ongoing sense. Doing this type of PhD, while different, forced me to assess the value of what I had done over the greater part of my adult life. This is not, in any way, the usual outcome of a PhD but more like an assessment of a career. It was challenging, requiring me to reconstruct past ways of thinking and personal motivations.

As a student in the 1970s I was part of a generation of first-in-the-family university students and coming from a family that was politically active I gravitated to left-wing ideas and thinking spurned-on by such things as the Vietnam War and later the overthrow of the Whitlam Government. So in a sense the script was written early in terms of my personal motivations within the field of art. I had started going to art galleries when I was a teenager having been at a high-school that encouraged such activities – especially one teacher who was also the house-critic for the *West Australian* – Murray Mason, who was for me at least, the epitome of cool. For whatever reasons I drifted

---

* These organisations included: Parameters (1978–1979), The Dispossessed Artists' Collective (1979), The Artworkers Union (1979–1981), Praxis Inc. (1980–1990), the journal *Praxis M* (1983–1997), The Beach (1987–1990), Australian Centre for Concrete Art (2001–) and the Bureau of Ideas (2004–).

† Since 1980 I have produced over two hundred exhibitions, two books, over twenty journal articles and newspaper reviews and some thirty catalogue essays, and have given numerous public lectures/papers, all on aspects of Western Australian art.

towards Art and English at school and combined with the politcalisation of my peers and friends – I started at University with a left-leaning attitude to all things worldly, including art. So while the retrospective narrative I needed for my PhD exegesis was set way back in the 1960s and 1970s when I was beginning to move out into the wider world, I like most young people, had no real ideological position, plan or training that would guide that trajectory. However writing the exegesis required me to make some sense of what I had done over the proceeding 30 years. And to consider what sort of cohesion there may have been (if any) that glued together the various and somewhat scatological activities that had produced a considerable amount of outputs.

The second problem with piecing together this effort was to actually remember what had been done and what evidence existed (collateral materials, documentation, reviews, etc.) that could substantiate the projects discussed in the exegesis. Given that the notion of 'research culture' is a relevantly recent idea, for most of the period covered by my PhD I was not thinking that what I was doing was research as it is considered today. It was just what one did. Even the word practice was novel when applied to the arts in the 1980s. You just did it without thinking about what you were doing in terms of it being part of personal research trajectory, a career, an academic pursuit or even as anything of any real consequence outside of its immediate reception and experience. Consequently a major part of the exegesis – almost ironically – required significant research to track-down appropriate documentation and other relevant materials to support the veracity of the projects presented as part of the PhD. This took time and considerable primary research in libraries, archives and museums, as well as tracking down and working with people who had kept such materials.

A third problem was in validating the projects presented within the PhD. Again this required primary research in locating reviews, citations and commentaries that confirmed the projects (writings, exhibitions, organisations) historically and also pointed to their value. Where they successful? Did they have an impact? Were they of quality? This validation was critical in assessing the research. Without it the list of events and outputs, was just that – a list. For instance a book (*Organise. Labour. A Visual Record*) I co-wrote with a colleague, Lenore Layman, won the 1988 Western Australian Premier's Book Award. This type of validation was necessary to give weight to the research and justified the projects in terms of their social value and consequence.

One of the three areas I put forward as practice/research was the work I had done forming art organisations. The idea that an organization could be an artwork was not prevalent when I became active in forming groups that could foster a positive intervention in Perth's art scene. The first group was Parameters that I started with three colleagues in 1978 and the most recent The Bureau of Ideas that I began with a friend, the French sociologist Marie Bonnal, in 2003. As a student I was inspired by Joseph Beuys' 'social sculpture' initiative that included the formation of the German Green Party and the Free International University. A little later I became aware of the Western Australian writer and political activist Katharine Susannah Prichard, who helped establish in Perth in the 1930s at least three organisations as means to effect her ideas and beliefs.* I always considered my work in establishing groups and organisations as a way of building a stronger art scene in Perth and argued in the PhD that this should be accepted as a type of 'social practice'. While writing and making exhibitions are more accepted practices, for the formations of organisations to be seen as an activity that could be consciously practiced did require a strong demonstration of a long-term commitment to this endeavour. My supervisor agreed that this could be seen as a part of the research or creative practice and I proceeded to include the initiation of these organisations as part of the research outputs.

Once I had established exactly what I was going to use as the 'published works' as per Curtin's guideline for submission for a PhD by supplication, I then began developing the necessary historical narrative to explain the research through a kind of reverse engineering exercise. That is I worked backwards trying to find a logic or sequence. When doing this I realized there was an apparent lack of coherence and understanding of how the list of activities knitted together. I further realized that the difficulty I was facing was due to a lack of a proper research question that could drive the project as is the case with conventional PhDs. There was no singular research question as such that had driven my project over that long period. Instead I formulated an overarching, extended statement that tried to explain the practice as a continuum:

---

* These were: The Modern Women's Club (c.1936), The Movement Against War and Fascism (c.1936), and the Workers' Art Guild (1934).

For the last thirty-odd years I have been engaged with both historical and contemporary art in Western Australia. The products of this engagement include publications, exhibitions and the formation of public organisations, all directed towards the articulation of art within the larger social formations of Western Australian history and culture. While these activities can be broadly broken down into two major areas of research – post-colonial Western Australian art history and Western Australian contemporary art – there are also three dominant interests that have shaped the direction of this production. They are my political convictions, my interest in the aesthetics of minimal (neo-concrete) art and my engagement with Noongar art. My research and production has explored the possibilities for art to engage new audiences by constructing contexts wherein people can relate to art beyond the usual conventions of simple enjoyment. By extending the experience of art to include practices at the margins of art, such as trade union banners, community art, naive art, Aboriginal art, and advanced art practices that push the boundaries of what art might be, I have consistently worked to expand the contexts within which art may be accessed and experienced. In the broadest sense, my work has been about democratising art and expanding aesthetic experience in the ways that art may be conducted and engaged with. Much of this has been underpinned by using Structuralist and Marxist models of analysis that I embraced as a student in the 1970s, and have continued to use, more or less, since then.

While my practice has been to expand and reveal deeper understandings of the way art has and does operate in the local context of Western Australian society, this has been done through an analytical lens firmly held in place by a political agenda.

That was the easy part. I then had to demonstrate if and how this had been achieved.

The role of the exegesis in my PhD was similar to that of most practice-led PhDs. It set the background and context of the research and articulated the statement above. Despite not having a research question as such the exegesis did give me the opportunity to construct an argument through a narrative that would hopefully convince the examiners that the practice/research mounted to justifying the award of PhD. I did this through organizing the material both thematically and chronologically. I designed the exegesis around the three types of activity: writing and public lectures, exhibitions and organisations. This was set in a chronological frame that was modulated by periods of interest, namely: political art and activities from 1970s – 1990s; a period in the late 1990s (which continues) when I spent much time and effort working on neo-Concrete/Minimalist art (with a major consideration of aesthetics) and the 10 years leading up to the time of the PhD submission centred on activities to do with Noongar art from the south-west of Western Australia. This was all qualified by another statement:

> In reality, these periods and interests are not dry demarcations, but an overlapping, porous and continuous set of research foci, and all are directed towards constructing a context in which local artists and their practices can be located.

This rather complex structure gave me the architecture to build the exegesis. Without it the amount and variety of material I had to present would not have been manageable in any way that could have made a convincing argument or a sense of cohesion. Indeed working this out was probably the most difficult part of the whole process and required a few different permutations. As I have said above not having a proper research question to drive the overall project and direct the exegesis required a retrospective narrative that could not only pull the whole exegesis together but give the overall project (30 years plus) a sense of direction and substance. In a way the process compared to a conventional PhD was back-to-front, requiring a re/evaluation of material, some of which was over 30 years old.

One of the most enjoyable experiences in writing the exegesis was discovering that there really was a semi-coherent narrative to what I had done over the previous 3 decades. Just the sheer act of re-discovering material and events that I had forgotten was in itself a treat, but to be able to plot a meaningful narrative over such a long period was very gratifying. I would say this is a distinctly different experience than working through a conventional three-year PhD that sets a durational parameter around the practice. To be able to have such a large scope of practice to recount and reconsider was, while a management problem as described above, a real luxury. And to have had that luxury (almost indulgence) to write about myself in this way, was a privilege. Not many people have the opportunity to look back at what they have done in the manner that this PhD allowed. I am grateful to have been given that chance. It certainly gave me to the chance to evaluate what I had done and to appreciate how fortunate I had been.

As I say this evaluation was as much a personal experience as an academic one. In the introduction to the PhD I wrote:

> In no way does this exegesis suggest that the research and scholarly work I have produced over the last thirty years can be considered disinterested. Quite the opposite, for at times my scholarly research and production have been coupled with my political agendas. Indeed, there is little distinction between the layers of my intentions. My active use of political models of interpretation, such as Althusser's Marxist Structuralism, and my activities in writing about art, making exhibitions and starting organisations such as Praxis and The Bureau of Ideas, are differing layers of the same practice aimed at the democratisation of aesthetic experience. I see my research and production as an ongoing political practice.

As such writing the exegesis was basically autobiographical and in retrospect, prone to emotion and at times exaggeration. However in writing the exegesis I did monitor my responses to critiques of the projects that ranged from embarrassment to pride. I tried not to let these emotions colour the writing too much; but this was sometimes a problem – especially dealing with projects in which I had invested so much time and energy. I was also aware of the difficulty any hyperbole (whether positive or negative) would present to examiners when having to assess what I was saying about the success or otherwise of a project. Similarly having had several ongoing close working-relationships with people mentioned in the exegesis such as artists and writers over a long period, I also had to monitor my opinions and comments that could have too easily have become overly personal. It is impossible to speak objectively when writing in the first person but a PhD exegesis is not the place for personal opinion and expression but rather a place for considered argument supported by factual material.

A PhD by supplication is not the usual way to gain a Doctoral qualification but it does have a place. For a generation or two that started their academic careers and practice before HDR awards were a part of the art school landscape it gives an opportunity not only to gain a higher qualification but also to look back and make a timely assessment of what has gone before. This can have some very practical, as well as academic, outcomes. There is now a document that, while it reads like an autobiography, also scans a period of art history in Perth that was for me at least, exceptional. This document can be used in the future by other researchers and historians. As Alan Vizents' opening statement above says of art in Perth – it's unexplored territory and unfortunately this goes for much of its art history as well. My PhD, while written as a personal account, does at least chronicle much of the art activity in Perth over the period from 1980–2010 and hopefully it can be of use in the future as one record of that period.

'CROSSING NO-MAN'S-LAND AND BACK': A DOCTORAL JOURNEY THROUGH ART, WAR AND THE TOPOGRAPHIES OF EMPTINESS

Paul Gough

Title of study: Painting the landscape of battle the development of pictorial language in British art on the Western Front, 1914–1918
[2 volumes]

Royal College of Art, London, 1991

Abstract

Within months of the outbreak of war in 1914, the landscape of Flanders and Picardy had been divided into two fixed zones: a zone of known ground occupied by the British troops, and beyond, the enemy-held territory. By daylight the battlefield was deserted, combatants were hidden in a labyrinth of trenches and subterranean passageways; only at night could the strip of land that acted as a buffer between the two armies be explored.

This thesis examines the effects of a war where the landscape, rather than the figure, had to convey the omni-directional face of conflict. It looks at a wide range of paintings and drawings produced on the battlefield, and the development of a pictorial language capable of describing the unique conditions of trench warfare.

The appraisal of the battle landscape fell into two distinct categories: one, that prioritised command and control of a hostile terrain by a method of fragmentation and analysis; the other, that revelled in the violation of the landscape and was fascinated by the destructive capabilities that were unleashed by fixed warfare.

From these two appraisals came two very different aesthetics: the first (argued in Part One of the thesis) was an aesthetic of reason and control – imposing onto the battle landscape a number of immutable directional laws, reducing the environment to a matrix of datum points and co-ordinates, unifying the terrain under the systematic spatial framework of one-point perspective.

This rational and objectified examination of terrain was possible only as far as the front-line – the furthest edge of known and secure land. Understanding the territory beyond gave rise to a very different aesthetic. This response (which comprises Part Two of the thesis) was based on an Intuitive reading of the battlefield. It required the combatant to become an explorer of a realm that was mysterious, in a state of flux, and not bound by normal laws of space, time and pictorial order. On the deepest tracts of battlefield in the later stages of the war, combatants experienced a range of phenomena that could only be expressed in the language of Romanticism. The paradoxical nature of trench warfare saw the re-emergence of the 'Tragedy of Landscape' as a major genre, and the combination of vastness, power and exhilaration stimulated the revival of The Sublime, or more properly a 'negative sublime' as a means of understanding and describing the 'empty battlefield'.

Motivations

I studied Fine Art to degree level in England graduating with a first-class honours degree and a distinction for my dissertation. The written components of my degree, including an extended tract of written research on youth subcultures, had been stimulated by the teaching of one of the tyros of British cultural history, Dick Hebdige. It was he that aroused a passion for deep reading and systematic enquiry, but also an interest in exploring archives and collections. This would eventually re-surface in my doctoral work eight years later.

In between times and following my first degree I was accepted to study painting at the Royal College of Art in London. My master's journey was largely studio-based but my practice was informed by a wider range of reading than I had first anticipated. Under the professorial guidance of such eminent narrative painters as Peter de Francia (who had known Beckmann and Guston) and a group of younger painters familiar with the new spirit of painting in Germany and Italy – Michael Heindorff, Graham Crowley, Stephen Farthing,

Ken Kiff, Mario Dubsky – my studio work was enriched by current fiction, film-making and theatre.

Herzog and Tarkovsky's new films were being shown in London; Beckmann's exhibition of all his triptychs went on show at the Whitechapel; Immendorf, Baselitz, and Marcus Lupertz visited the School of Art; during one summer recess Francis Bacon used the professor's studio; John Berger was a close ally of several staff, and Ron Kitaj was a correspondent to several students.

The inter-relationship between the written word, poetry, rich narrative and image-making was core to the School's pedagogies. New figuration abounded; in Scotland young nationalist painters came to the fore; new galleries opened and the Arts Council promoted festivals and new public galleries.

Politically it was a tense period: the Miner's Strike was followed soon after by the Falkland's War, Margaret Thatcher's eminence aroused political and creative counter-reaction; anti-racist rallies and marches were standard. My time on the master's program was book-ended by the Iranian Embassy siege and the Brixton Riots at one end and *glasnost* and the Polish shipyard worker disputes at the other. Somewhere in between British painting took on a rich polemic that was at its best compelling, urgent and politically theorised.

As a master's student it was the company one kept that was as telling as the work produced: the Royal College of Art is the ultimate meritocracy; a playground for some 500 ambitious postgraduates drawn from a global elite. The race to exhibit, to publish, to be connected and collected was intense, although performed within an arena of studied indifference. Reputations were made and lost in a week; contact lists and friendship groups fiercely guarded. Although trends and fads were omnipresent; niches were keenly sought; whether they be the articulation of Po-Mo Memphis in the School of Architecture or the surface design and fabrication of state of the art SLVs in automotive design. Of all postgraduate schools in London the RCA set the pace; the YBA's and *Frieze* years of Goldsmiths were a decade distant.

My painting became a deeply informed practice; everyone's painting had to be. Not so much saturated in literary or filmic references as enriched by allusion and knowing. R. B. Kitaj's deeply layered historically enriched figuration was the paradigm.

As a painter I was reading widely around the subjects that fascinated me:

contemporary and recent British military history, the aftermath of European conflict; the commemoration of war in all its forms; the many means of remembering; war as dis-membering; peace and recovery through re-membering. Much of this was palpable and actual, not historic; the Iranian Embassy siege had taken place two blocks away from my north-facing College studios; the Brixton Riots took place on the doorstep of my ungainly student squat behind the prison; the victory parade of the Falklands War took place only a mile from the College; every morning the mounted troops of the light cavalry would be exercised in Hyde Park; the Remembrance Sunday parades lined up on my cycling route home.

As students we were encouraged to embrace our contextual roots, to pay homage to the past not as a deadweight or as a drag anchor but as a way of helping position our practice. Adorno was at a premium; Beuys visited the School; Calvino became an influence. Embracing Italian medieval mythologies as a way of understanding current political behaviour set a rich benchmark; hearing contemporary music as part of the Royal Albert Hall Proms – held a few hundreds away from the studios – merely compounded the many moments of serendipity; all these influences found their way into my paintings.

We were encouraged to travel; scholarships and grants were offered. The Royal Academy Schools awarded me an overseas travel scholarship to the Prado; I was encouraged to visit France and Germany; to see the RCA painting studio in the Ile de France in Paris. Having been an ERASMUS exchange student to Metz I visited the lines of the former battlefield that run through Belgium to Verdun in France and then onto the Swiss border. My large-scale work grew richer through these geo-political references; I started writing about the historical dimensions to the work. My weekly model – the redoubtable 'Bruce' – dressed in military uniform and struck martial postures which I translated into a *dramatic personae* of large, well-rounded and individually striking portraits, which were joined into complicated multi-figured narratives. I was exhibited, selected by curators, featured in glossy magazines. Although 'Cool Britannia' was another government away, British figurative painters, venturous young tyros were being sought, promoted and bought. In central London the creative glue was electric: post-punk music, east-end fashion design, textile artist-entrepreneurs, anti-Thatcher renegades created a potent creative cocktail that knew few boundaries.

I became lucky. The new – and ambitious – Curator of Art at the Imperial War Museum, Dr Angela Weight, took an interest in what I was painting: a large work was purchased for the permanent collection. As a master's student it was a tremendous fillip. It opened other doors: I was commissioned by several units of the British army – the Royal Marines, a cavalry regiment; a Royal Artillery Unit that had been in the Falklands. It was a curious turn of events. I had to paint tanks, landing craft, gunners laden with surface-to-air missiles; I had to paint on location, on training grounds, in barracks, on the parade square, during live firing and noisy practices. It meant adjusting my pictorial language, recalibrating my 'personal' vision, and – above all – understanding the nature of a commission. Without knowing it, I was laying down the habits and lines of enquiry of my future doctoral research.

Although they were done largely to 'earn a crust' these commissioned paintings introduced new forms, shapes and texture into my practice; they required me to read around a topic, to locate the historical dimensions, to take bearings that were not always rooted in art history. Engrossed by the writing of Paul Fussell and Susan Sontag; the films of Tarkovsky and Herzog, I began exploring the persistence of memory and the ways in which nature dealt with the aftermath of trauma. Keifer's work and that of Jochen and Eva Gerz seemed extraordinarily relevant.

Ironically, the act of painting could only ever target one dimension of these concerns. The arena of interest was so multi-faceted that many of the questions aroused by this *nexus* of interests could simply not easily be addressed in charcoal or paint. The prospect of a doctoral journey lay head.

'The why' and 'the where'

Finishing my master's degree in London brought one period of study to a close but it left a large part of my enquiring mind unrequited.

A few years after leaving London (to pursue paid employment) and not long into a full-time lecturing position my ambition to revisit the intellectual fields re-surfaced. Although I was practicing, exhibiting and my paintings being bought, studio work could not satisfactorily answer the questions that had been prevalent in London, and stayed afire in my imagination.

My practice had begun to focus on the voids of war; the interplay between geographical dimensions and historical under- and over-lay. While the male figure still played a substantial part in my painting I was drawn towards the appearance of land in and after periods of distress.

New writing by psychologists such as Eric J. Leed provoked thinking around liminal experiences and indeterminacy; a wave of cultural geographers were driving lines of enquiry about 'space benevolent and malevolent'. Reviewing the representation of war by British and other European artists I began to frame up a series of questions focussed on the role of the battled and embattled figure in the militarised landscape. I started to imagine a lexicon of emptinesses, and thought more about how and why we choose to commemorate, remember and forget.

The urge to study a PhD emerged from this rich – but loosely formed – bed of enquiry. It lacked at this stage a goal, a shape, and a sense of the rigour required by such systematic study. My main motivation was deceptively straightforward: how to address a series of questions that simply could not be addressed through studio practice, but might be informed [perhaps tangentially] by my experience as a painter, practitioner and also as a painter who had been commissioned via the Imperial War Museum to work with the military.

During that period I was teaching in a post-1992 new university in England. At the time I was a lecturer of only a few years service. I took advice from colleagues and created a case for funding. It was extremely unusual at that time for a practitioner lecturer to embrace PhD study; very few nationally had crossed that divide. I imagine that my case was so compelling [or so unusual] that the rationale for funding [fees only] was accepted. I committed to undertaking the doctoral study in my research allocation as part of my academic workload.

I applied and was accepted to study at the Royal College of Art, London (RCA) in the Department of Cultural History. I did not want to undertake the higher degree in an art history department: I was looking for something rooted in a broader reading of visual cultures, more closely aligned to the teaching I had experienced in my first degree, which nurtured a sense of urgency, relevance and timeliness in one's chosen topic. The RCA had the best combination of tutors and supervisors, and the departmental chair, Professor Christopher

Frayling, had a strong record in the field. The college also combined practice and theory in its range of programmes and departments. In addition to my eminent supervisor Dr Frank Whitford, I met my fellow students, many of them studying for masters degrees, and was encouraged by their range of contemporary interests, their sense of urgency and their commitment.

Deciding titles and topics

The working title of my research focused on a comparative history of the commissioning process for German and Allied war art from the First World War. But after a few months of exploring the topic in broad terms and scanning the existing literature it became clear that the topic was simply too vast; the British holdings of art, correspondence and other primary material alone were simply enormous. I renegotiated the scope of the research, eliminating the German lines of enquiry, and started to bring my painter's eye to the material most of which was held in the Imperial War Museum's vast collection of commissioned war art.

Method in the 'mid-ness'

A methodology emerged gradually; at the heart of the enquiry I had to explore the holdings of the art collection at the IWM; this took the best part of 18 months working part-time. I travelled to London (from Bristol in the West Country, about 120 miles away) weekly and spent a day working my way from A-Z through the drawings and prints in each of several hundred large archive boxes in the Department of Art. After twelve months I worked my way through the racks of the basement, making thumbnail sketches of each painting as I had done for each drawing and print.

This may sound rather long-winded but the surprising truth was that there was no systematic record of the collection; the last published record was from 1963 and was outdated and misleading. The collection of war art from both world war and many conflicts since 1945 forms a unique body of work and rivals Tate Britain in terms of its coverage of the greatest national artists of the 20th century; the collections spans Henry Moore to Paul Nash, Laura Knight to Eric Ravilious. A programme of recent acquisition has brought many contemporary artworks into the collection including Lubaina Himid, Gilbert and George, and Deanna Petherbridge.

As I started to systematically explore the archives in the museum (and increasingly from other regional UK museums and some selected galleries and museum in the Commonwealth) a number of themes and lines of enquiry emerged. Over time these became the outline of the eight or so chapters that formed the heart of the dissertation. Given that there were 130 official war artists from the Great War and scores of non-official artists I knew that a second volume of my dissertation would take the form of a biographical and bibliographical database of war-related artists in practice between 1914–1919.

By the time I had worked my way A-Z through the archival boxes, and across the stacked racks in the basement I realised that I knew the collection possibly better than anyone, even the assistant curators who had to make an inventory periodically. Over the course of my studies I was able to re-attribute one or two pieces, including one that had been left in the 'anonymous' box (a battle scape of the Ypres Salient by W. Mears).

Following my systematic audit of the paintings, drawings and prints I worked my way through the correspondence and committee files in a room of crammed filing cabinets. I spent many days making transcriptions of relevant extracts. Note-taking and copying was an exhausting aspect of the work; it required diligence and patience; as did the organisation of file cards under a complicated matrix of subject, thematic and artist's headings.

Practice suspended

My studio practice ground to a halt during the four years that I was registered to compete the PhD. At the time though I recognised that my future studio work would be deeply informed by my lines of enquiry; my doctoral research also exposed me to scholars and curators who were interested in the inter-relationships between practice, deep reflection, and contextual enquiry. This was another of the beneficial by-products of my research; it also gave me an unusual edge as an artist (at that time anyway, but has largely become the norm today).

Organising time and distance

I travelled to London (from Bristol) weekly and spent a day a week working my way A-Z through the drawings and prints in each of several hundred large archive boxes in the Department of Art. After twelve months I worked my way through the racks of the basement, making thumbnail sketches of each painting as I had done for each drawing and print.

My family accepted my weekly trip to London; despite the strict and demanding routine it fitted in reasonably well with family life, but it was the nightly reading and note-taking that impacted most. During the four years of my doctoral study I was also teaching full-time as a lecturer in a large school of art, media and design. Towards the close of my study (the writing up period you might say, though in truth I was writing up various sections of the dissertation after 12 months) I would work until very late, sometimes until one in the morning, at least four nights a week. The demands were significant though my family supported me (or at least tolerated me!) during this time. Deadlines were important and there came a decisive point where I simply had to close the books and concentrate on 'writing up.'

My teaching and administration work continued apace. Indeed I was promoted during the course of my studies, becoming Programme Leader and head of the department during my days as a PhD student.

Significant issues

Despite the high wire act of balancing family, work, and the doctoral study there were no significant issues. My work was steady, studious, rather solid; there weren't that many moments of imaginative breakthrough – a few, but realistically doctoral study is much more prosaic. One has to draw long-term satisfaction from the entire project, not quick fixes.

One of the challenges perhaps I ought to have embraced more readily was taking my work-in-progress into the scholarly community. My supervisor strongly recommended that I used the conference network to make my research known, to enter the debate and to hear from others in the field. I was reluctant largely because as a practitioner I felt at a slight disadvantage; I lacked the confidence that others seemed to have. Furthermore, the networks were less varied and widespread than they are now: the conference scene now gives much more opportunity for HDR candidates to talk at conferences, to co-publish and to have their work tested in public scholarly arena.

Difficult memories?

I always knew that doctoral study was a task that required diligence and fortitude, with the occasional moment of luck and serendipity. I felt supported by my place of work (although at that time it did not really enrich or inform my teaching). I felt very supported by my supervisors (though by the middle of my four years understandably I had outstripped their knowledge and relied more on their impressive ability to help edit and shape my lines of enquiry). There were family crises (the death of my father) and moments of delight (the birth of my first child, a daughter) but significant though these were, I knew I could not be deflected from the daily and weekly grind of doing the doctoral work.

Most memorable time? Drawing connections between various bodies of work that I was looking at in the archives; chasing up leads in obscure regional collections; meeting visiting curators in the reading room of the IWM some of whom became life long allies; sitting next to the Marquis of Anglesey in the Reading Room of the British Library as he was researching another volume in his history of the British cavalry.

Possibly the most memorable day was one of my weekly visits to the IWM in Lambeth, south London the day after the great storm in UK (1987) when all the trees in the park around the museum appeared to have simply toppled over.

Finishing the PhD was a singularly satisfying period, a mixture of suspended elation and exhaustion. Subsequently my most memorable moment was seeing a large art work of mine (which had been purchased by the Imperial War Museum in London for its permanent collection) hung in an exhibition of drawings and other piece alongside the very soldier-artists that I'd been writing and researching for so long – to the left of my large piece was work by Stanley Spencer and Wyndham Lewis, to my right Paul Nash and C. W. R. Nevinson. If ever there was a defining moment in my post-doctoral life that fused theory, practice and context it was then.

My dissertation was awarded a university prize too 'the Penguin Publishers award for best thesis in the Humanities', which was an added bonus on top of the rather grand graduation ceremony in the Royal Albert Hall.

What would I do differently?

I would not have done much differently. In my first study group seminar the Head of Department said to us all that once we'd handed in our dissertation we might be on the road to being cured. I'm still not certain of that.

I would have bought a more powerful PC, a lighter laptop, learned to type properly, taken better advice on how to organise the thousands of record cards that I diligently wrote up each night.

I ought to have joined a more lively and rigorous 'learning group' who might have tested my ideas more deeply, although the two or three colleagues who helped do so made an incalculable impact on my thinking.

I should have published more as I was 'writing up' or at least soon after. But this was a confidence issue, as mentioned above, and the opportunities seemed far fewer; the approach to treating doctoral students as junior researchers simply did not apply then.

It took me some time to re-arrange the narrative into a form to be published but the resulting book – *'A Terrible Beauty': British Artists in the First World War* – did justice to the years of PhD study and all those late nights, and the publisher was very generous with colour images. Having sold out, it went to a revised edition in 2016.

WALKING (WITH YOUR LEGS, IN PARTICULAR) WHILE LOOKING AT YOUR LEGS WALKING (BUT NOT WITH A MIRROR): ACTS OF BALANCING IN DOCTORAL RESEARCH IN ART

Michael Graeve

Title of study: Celebrating the crisis of representation: Foregrounding conjunctive and disjunctive relations in painting and sound installation

RMIT University, 2015

Abstract

Painting and multi-channel sound composition are combined in this practice-led PhD to generate installations that foreground an ongoing oscillation between conjunctive and disjunctive relations. While interactions between painting and sound practices have contributed to advances in their respective fields, the creation, analysis and curation of such work has often emphasised causal relationships. This study offers an expanded focus by bringing together painting and sound in ways that acknowledge equally the junctures and disjunctures between the mediums.

The practical and theoretical considerations of this study are framed by concepts drawn from the work of Friedrich Schlegel, Novalis and William James. Initially this study is informed by the Jena Romantics' response to the crisis of representation brought about by Immanuel Kant. It uses Novalis' proposition – to study foreign systems to better understand one's own – to interpret conjunctive relations between painting and sound through the lens of transcription. Such conjunctive relationships are then rendered complex in installation, following Schlegel's questioning of the possibility of representation and proposing instead endless deferral of resolution, ongoing contradiction and free play. Finally, James' argument that experience consists of what he terms both conjunctive and disjunctive relations, brings to prominence a complex understanding of the conceptual and experienced in installations.

The exegesis provides an overview of five key projects through which the practice-led research has developed. The philosophical and conceptual frameworks are used to interrogate these projects to allow consideration of sound and painting installation within the context of specific art historical and philosophical sources dealing with representation and experience in installation, painting and sound art. In developing a complex interplay and understanding of spatio-temporal and audio-visual fragments, this study seeks to celebrate the free play of experiencing suggested by the crisis of representation.

--

Who meddled with my curriculum vitae? There must be a misunderstanding. It states I've spent 13 years at art school? More than primary and secondary schooling put together? Bachelor, Honours, Bachelor, Masters by Research, Masters by Coursework? All those double-ups, and the odd order of degrees, surely it must be enough?

It is mid-2007, and having completed a MFA at the School of the Art Institute of Chicago as part of my Samstag International Scholarship, and returning to Melbourne after two and a half years living in New York and then Chicago, now was the time to leave studies behind. The Americans didn't call the Master of Fine Arts a terminal degree without reason. And despite returning to the little pond of Melbourne's arts ecosystem, my exhibition practice was keeping me busy. Rather than living overseas, I was now travelling overseas from Melbourne to ply my trade, with five overseas journeys for performances and installations in 18 months over 2007 and 2008. All the while I was building a teaching portfolio across RMIT, Victoria and Monash Universities. Not being a student seemed so grown-up.

But the simplified duo of practice and teaching was short-lived. The MFA a terminal degree? My foot. I had after all settled back in Australia, where we are way ahead in the degree creep curve – ahead even of the United States. The PhD for artists was the next must-have.

Two years of generous conversations with many doctoral supervisors and students followed, and I started sketching out in my mind a cartoon version of a doctoral journey – that journey I am here reflecting on in turn. Thankfully it wasn't just a need for another terminal degree that drove these early discussions. I first formed, and then paraded increasingly grand creative challenges past current candidates and potential supervisors. Out of these sketches formed a picture of what might be involved, and the picture looked exciting. I trusted being able to build on my different experiences inside and outside academia to answer all the component parts of such an impending journey. But what impact might such a new focus have on my artistic career? And what of all the aspects of the doctorate that I didn't know about?

Central to my developing understanding of the impending doctoral journey was Professor David Thomas, from whom I had already experienced fifteen years of generous mentorship, starting in my undergraduate studies. Is there a glass-slipper story in doctoral land? If so, then that person able to persistently ask fresh, challenging and revealing questions of your practice for one and a half decades shall be your dream supervisor. (And so it turned out.) Nevertheless, I was sufficiently reluctant to press the start button on such a big project that I had to be threatened by scarcity: Some of David's students were completing, making space for new students; if I didn't make a move this application round, then he'd not be available for supervisions again for some time.

I booked a Japanese dinner with a wise friend and colleague, Dr Bruce Mowson, who'd been through the doctoral process recently, and helped me corral my notes and intentions. He had already counseled me on the topic for some years, and over this extended dinner I had only to consolidate into simpler wordings the six or seven ways in which I was going to fundamentally rewrite the history of abstraction and non-representational painting by revealing how painting and sound and audiovisual histories had interacted in ways that somehow no one else had ever noticed before. Oh, and even the word 'transgression' figured in there somewhere, too.

The balancing act between ambition and reality, between over-reach and plain pedestrianism had commenced. It was only the beginning of many such negotiations, but I had by now gained a sense of hunger for this process. I submitted my doctoral application with anticipation.

In choosing to study at RMIT University I was primarily focused on the prospective supervisory team. Their active encouragement during my 'I'm interested' stage certainly played a central role in my choice. A scholarship offer from another university might have snatched me away, but I didn't apply elsewhere.

As such, my due diligence investigations into other universities as possible study venues was cursory. I do remember being struck, though, both by how specialised many academics' interests were, yet how wide also their academic expertise were. Likewise it was clear that the collections of key words indicating research areas revealed nothing about anyone's potential enthusiasm, critical thinking, ability to question, and to generally be able to support my own journey.

That means that much must be gauged outside the formalities of the application process and little of this is contained in websites or brochures. I am reminded of enquiring about applying to John Armleder's Meisterklasse in Germany, years earlier when applying for the Samstag Scholarship. It was hard enough to get through to his secretary, who then told me that I had to be invited into John's class. I was sufficiently confused by this esoteric form of application system to ask how I might be invited – surely there was an application form and guidelines and deadlines and timelines and course guides and learning objectives and glossaries of terms and summaries of summaries and hidden web-links to be found. A pregnant pause of appalled silence cut through the flow of our phone conversation, before she answered in only somewhat clearer terms: 'What do you mean with your question of 'how can you be invited'? I do not understand. In order to be invited, you have to be invited.' Stated this way, I do think I finally understood. There really were no forms for me to fill in, I would not be given a login.

Similarly, when looking into the PhD before enrolling, the process even of applying appeared absolutely opaque. With my PhD now complete, and my details appearing on a register of supervisors, this disjuncture is in turn borne out in the emails I receive. Often from strangers, they purport that it might be a simple step for both the student and the potential supervisor to say 'yes' to the academic marriage of research supervision. I suggest it is not.

Deciding on my topic, project and thesis was revealing, and from course commencement to confirmation of candidature took a little over the first year. Three intersecting storylines framed articulation of my topic.

The first storyline commenced with an invitation to participate in *Sight & Sound: Music & Abstraction in Australian Art*, 2010, curated by Dr Steven Tonkin, exploring 'the intersections between music and abstract art in Australia from the early 20th century to contemporary practice.' Invited just before commencing the doctorate, the curatorial discussions and development of the installation spanned the first six months of my doctoral studies. The exhibition itself provided a local community of practice second to none. I'd previously exhibited with Robert Owen and John Aslanidis, but seeing works by Roy de Maistre, Roger Kemp, Yvonne Audette, Ludwig Hirschfeld Mack and Donald Laycock in the one room with my own installation provided a deepened sense of the histories my work participates in. The catalogue essay detailed an Australian microcosm closely related to my own developing literature review. Even more timely were the rich conversations with the curator. Tonkin curated a narrative through the artworks by having a light and sound sequence programmed to literally spotlight one artists' work at a time, and at that same spot-lit time then diffusing a sound composition that had informed, or was composed to accompany, that artists' work. The sequence concluded with my installation, deliberately located in the centre of the gallery. A similar sequence ensued in Tonkin's catalogue essay, which considered my installation as providing a possible 'foil to the parameters established, ... pos[ing] critical questions about the pictorial representation of music, and broaden[ing] the parameters of the exhibition...' (Tonkin, 2010). Thus, while my work was clearly placed within a lineage of relations between abstract art and music, the curation also revealed how my work questioned the traditions and assumptions that that field has established. This written statement was the first of a series of external and independent acknowledgements of the contribution of my doctoral research, which in itself addresses one of the assessment criteria that PhD examiners need to take into account.

The formation of my topic was also strongly influenced by an exhibition I developed in Italy, simultaneously to *Sight & Sound* premiering in Melbourne. *Spatial Choreography*, 2010, was created nearly entirely in situ at blank, the gallery of e/static, curated by Carlo Fossati in Turin. While two mid-size canvases were sent ahead of time, and I took an archive of sound recordings to compose from, the majority of visual elements and the four-channel sound composition were conceived and executed in the gallery over seven days. Work progressed in a concentrated but playful manner. It turned out to be an exhibition project that asked more questions than I could answer at the time. An improvised process of working was heightened by material and time limitations. For example, in *Sight & Sound* I tried to reveal an improvisatory aspect of the work by visibly pushing and shoving parts of the work around, ripping panels off the wall and placing them in other locations. In Turin, *Spatial Choreography* increasingly put the viewer into motion, explicitly developing a variety of viewpoints and hearpoints for the work. Both the similarities and contrasts between these two showings allowed me to articulate a series of research concerns.

While these practical projects narrowed in on my subjects of research, my reading sought to widen my thinking and writing. Teetering stacks of books graced my desk, and more and more ways to contextualise my work beckoned. But I gained particular energy from two authors. Firstly, I encountered the comparative criticism of Daniel Albright, whose *Untwisting the Serpent: Modernism in Music, Literature and the Other Arts* (Albright, 2000) provided for me new languages to understand the visual and sound relationships I was seeking to articulate. If the author Daniel Albright provided me with a sense of methodologies for writing and understanding the visual and aural disjunctions I was exploring in my work, a specific book by another author allowed me to better approach issues of meaning and philosophy implicit in my work. Azade Seyhan's *Representation and Its Discontents: The Critical Legacy of German Romanticism* had been sitting abandoned on my bookshelf for fifteen years. I had purchased it purely on account of its title at a time when I hoped to better understand my discontent with representational art. I got none of what I wanted from it at the time, but it survived multiple cullings of my library, I suppose until I was ready for its subject matter in a new way. In the long run I framed my doctoral dissertation with three philosophical fragments by Friedrich Schlegel, Novalis and William James, the first two indeed featuring in Seyhan's book. Between two simultaneous practical projects, and the appropriate readings, I felt my project galvanising, my questions clarifying.

An art methodology is a multi-channel mixing desk with all the channels engaged. While you could (and do) occasionally listen to the individual channel paths, it is in their cacophonous interaction that research functions. You make art, you write, you make more art, you revise the writing, you find new sources, which make you realise new contexts, which makes you ask different questions, which changes your understanding of the artworks, which changes the writing, which changes the artworks, which changes the enquiry, which... Thus, the methodology is the work, is the making, is the reading, is the writing, is the interrogation. As I went, I understood more and more of the ingredients. And the mix, also.

It's not easy finding your research feet. Keep talking and listening to yourself at the same time, and what happens? You may well become self-conscious, tilted, strained. I had a sense of this happening in the middle of the program, where some projects became stiff and literal. I have come to liken research to the process of walking (with your legs, in particular) while looking at your legs walking (but not with a mirror). You have to contort the top part of your body to see the bottom part walking. And then try to be athletic with your walking at the same time, let alone with your thinking!

The demands for innovation, new knowledge and explication are the forces that end up making this way of making art into a unique kind of methodology. And it is a methodology that isn't as accountable to the artwork as a discipline, as it is to the academic context that gives research its' wings. The beauty, and mind-bending complexity, of the practice-led PhD is that in order to function, and to pass, it requires multiple redundant systems of activity and practice placed into coherent context. Originality doesn't count until its' contribution is articulated. Coming to understanding what a project might contribute to an area of investigation provides clues to what is at all possible, let alone original, long before the final conclusion of the project. I think of redundancy also in an engineering sense, where every perspective backs up another. Such a formalised process of networking is really the task, and a strange result is that matters at hand become simultaneously dull and exciting.

They become dull because this is how we might think about book-keeping and sorting. Dull also because nothing can sing on its' own terms anymore. Yet, for all the tension between a vibrant untamed artistic practice (those unkempt qualities we so often seek in art, or stereotypically associate with it), and the accountability of research, it was also exciting, because through it, so many parts begin to shimmer in relation to each. And having to define these shimmerings, their relationships, their powers over each other, to create inventories of these choruses and disjunctures, all of this fundamentally deepened my perceptions and understandings of my practice. I was able to get into one perspective or another by will, not just by accident.

Fellow PhD students and supervisors famously discussed the intangible scale of doctoral requirements, the myriad aspects comprising it, and the sense that one had to overshoot the mark on a lot of them, to make sure one didn't fail on one or another of them. The doctorate was indeed as insatiable as an art practice itself, and as insatiable as the sole trader business of an artist: One surely could always do more and better.

As such, I know of no elegant formula to organising the dance between doctoral focus, family time, money, life, friends, parents, employment and professional practice – let alone recreation. My exhibitions continued both inside and outside my PhD studies, locally and internationally, and while they gave me fodder for my research, the objectives and demands of curator and gallerist frequently departed from those of doctoral research, as did the running of a professional artists' public practice. And while the Australian Postgraduate Award scholarship was a boon, and more than appreciated, it wasn't the kind of money a young family could live off well, once the cost of an art practice was deducted, (an art practice which the more prolifically one produces, the more expensive it gets). So I couldn't but take the sessional teaching work offered along the way. Also less than convenient for doctoral studies, I continued to feel needed on the board of Liquid Architecture Sound Inc, where I had been vice-president for four years before becoming chair in the second year of my doctoral candidature, taking over the role from my research supervisor Associate Professor Philip Samartzis, spending a good half day a week on this voluntary but essential role.

Without doubt, my doctoral studies came on top of a fully lived professional life, and a fully lived private life. Add full-time study to a full life, and things get complex, no way around it. What are the limits to a workday or a workweek or a work year? I worked on art and teaching and PhD for six days a week for the majority of the time, and seven days a week for months and months. And long days, not every day, but regularly 12 or 14 hours, and often longer still in the lead-up to exhibitions. Indeed, family and recreational life suffered reductions in time allocations.

One of the most difficult challenges for me was negotiating the relationship between creative practice and creative research. Excellence of an artwork is not necessarily excellence in research, nor is excellent research necessarily what a curator or gallerist demands of an artwork or a project. These are fascinating demands to have competing in one's practices, and I never experienced them falling quite into equilibrium. Likewise, the equation between conceptual safety and danger. The higher the stakes, the higher the degree, the more a bind comes into play between danger and play, between predictability and reproducibility and creativity, between proving and doing. The management of this tension is the most difficult part of the whole process. You can't just go through the ropes to make good art, yet you have to go through the rules. Interestingly, we are also at a time where the seeds of intent for doctoral studies are revealed earlier and earlier: It's not unusual for the more ambitious of my first year undergraduates to be enquiring about what they have to do in order to progress through into a PhD. I've seen experimentation stop, and I've seen the flatness of artworks by students playing it carefully in order to achieve the right grades and to be able to clearly justify their outcomes. Surely I didn't fall into this trap?

Crowded timetables result in potential problems for creative thinkers: How to allow space for the important creative work to occur, when so much busywork seems to prevent it? How to keep a focus, for the busy work doesn't go away, nor can it be ignored. As an artist I am palpably interested in tools and systems of thinking, and I've studied my share of productivity models. I've come to use three interrelated methods that I have practiced for fifteen years now, though I keep engaging them in new ways.

In part, I use a slightly modified version of David Allen's (2001) *Getting Things Done: The Art of Stress-Free Productivity* system for tracking and planning within my projects, for keeping an overview of my responsibilities, for processing inputs, and for being aware of the difference between processing, planning and doing. It has been the most effective and intuitive way I've found for keeping dozens of balls spinning up in the air, and for me to not have them all mashed up indistinguishably in my head. It distinguishes between capturing, planning and doing mindsets. It encourages capturing all inputs and responsibilities in a system outside the head. I administer much of this through two tools: Omnifocus software and my calendar. My Omnifocus is divided up into roles and responsibilities, and under these headings I have sitting hundreds of projects, including project notes, references, links. Subservient to the projects then are actions I plan to take in order to make projects happen. It's a space for accountability as well as for capturing the outcomes of playful planning.

I've also found Paul Graham's distinction between maker's schedules and manager's schedules (Graham, 2009) useful, and I block out chunks of my calendar to be in maker mode. The interruptive nature of manager mode seems to take over any left-over times, anyway. Regardless, if in maker or manager mode, for getting actual work done at the computer itself, I often use the Pomodoro technique. The simultaneous urgency and expansive experience of duration it provides within a 25-minute period are a constant delight, and keep me more on track than any other technique I've used.

One last tool I'm surprised is so seldomly used: Scrivener. Given the non-linear process in which research writing accumulates, the linear writing mode of Microsoft Word seemed patently unsuited to my exegetical writing endeavours. No other tool or technique has so revolutionised writing for me as this software, which allows work at both the smallest detail and at the largest scale. It easily handles hundreds of chunks of writing, encouraging changes of hierarchy and outlining, and the way in which texts could be cut up, recombined, and reshaped was an unending delight.

Who meddled with my curriculum vitae? There must be a misunderstanding. It states I've spent 17 years at art school? More than primary and secondary schooling put together? Bachelor, Honours, Bachelor, Masters by Research, Masters by Coursework, Doctor of Philosophy? All those double-ups, and the odd order of degrees, surely it must be enough?

References

Albright, D. (2000). *Untwisting the serpent: Modernism in music, literature and the other arts.* Chicago, IL: University of Chicago.

Allen, D. (2001). *Getting things done: The art of stress-free productivity.* New York: Penguin.

Graham, P. (2009). Maker's schedule, manager's schedule. Retrieved from http://www.paulgraham.com/makersschedule.html.

Seyhan, A. (1992). *Representation and its discontents: The critical legacy of German romanticism.* Berkeley: University of California.

Tonkin, S. (2010). *Sight & sound: Music & abstraction in Australian art.* Melbourne: Victorian Arts Centre Trust.

PLEASE DON'T CALL ME DR

Ian Haig

*Title of study: Dirty bodies and clean technologies –
the absent abject body in media arts culture*

UNSW Art & Design (formerly COFA, University of NSW), 2014

Abstract

My research explores why the abject body is not conceptualised within the idiom of media arts culture. Why is it missing and often edited out of the framework of art and technology? While media arts often rethinks the body and its augmentation and enhancements through new technology, the abject body is often nowhere to be seen. It would appear that the abject body has been disqualified as an aesthetic from the post-humanist paradigm of art and technology. In its place appears to be the transcendence of the body through technology, rather than the base level everyday reminder of our meat bodies. I explore what cultural conditions have led to the erasure of the abject from media arts culture. In addition I look at the cultural history of abject art and the abject body's relationship to the emerging mediasphere. My own studio work attempts to reactivate, reinsert and reconceptualise the abject body within contemporary media arts.

--

Trust me I am a Doctor

In 2009, I wrote a piece for a now defunct online journal, it was called 'Please don't call me Doctor'. The piece discussed my general cynicism and criticisms to the lemmings like rush towards practice led PhDs, little did I know that a mere twelve months later I would be signing up to also do a PhD!

So why am I cynical of the practice led PhD? To be honest, my allergy towards the practice led PhD is probably more an allergy to the notion of credentialism (I still avoid as much as possible to use the title Dr on anything, though it will probably be inserted by the editor on this piece of writing). Also the idea that somehow the PhD was a validation and elevation of my practice, I have always found more than a little irksome. Along with the notion that the PhD was somehow going to ratify my art practice of twenty odd years. Finally now with a PhD I was a real artist?

I still have some nagging concerns and some of my cynicism remains, now on one hand this may be perceived as a negative account of my PhD experience, on the contrary, my critical take on the PhD space for artists is intended to be productive and are constructive criticisms. To see some of its shortcomings, some of its problems, as a way of moving forward. It took me some time to come around to the PhD camp, my cynicism held me back. However I can actually see the value in a PhD now, I can see how it can activate, modify and energise a practice and how it can allow for a valuable space to figure out what it is your art practice is really doing or not doing, just don't call me doctor.

I was late to undertaking a PhD, I commenced in 2010 and was in my mid-forties at the time. In retrospect this was the right time for me, as I figure one needs to generate a large body of work and have a relatively established practice before embarking on a PhD. The trajectory of undertaking undergraduate studies through to honours and directly into a PhD is, I think a little absurd and somewhat misguided.

In researching PhD options, as I worked in an art school, I knew I didn't want my colleagues to supervise me, that seemed like a no-brainer, so I looked further afield, and decided on what was at the time the College of Fine Art (COFA and is now rebranded as UNSW Art & Design. As my practice and research is largely centered around the body/technology and media art, COFA had a high-profile media art program, however to be honest that wasn't really what drew me to COFA it was more the idea that it was away from Melbourne and out of my comfort zone.

It was only after enrolling in COFA that I was told their practice-based PhD program required a thesis, opposed to an exegesis. At first this caused some anxiety, as I wasn't confident my writing and formulating my argument etc would be strong enough for a real thesis, actually it was more like a mini thesis I produced which ended being around 50,000 words. I also realised there is a great discrepancy between practice-led PhD programs in Australia. Some are exegesis based, some require a thesis, others require a final exhibition, others don't, some require a minimum of 25,000 words in an exegesis, others 40,000, many fly the flag of 'practice-led research' and 'thinking through practice' as it turns out COFA's approach was more in the form of 'research-led practice'.

The notion of 'practice-led research' has always troubled me somewhat, while I understand it's the dominant mode of art school based PhDs, for me it's far too entrenched in the precious idea of the conditions of 'studio practice'. The notion that one's research stems purely from one's practice and making (as is implied by the term practice-led research). I can't help think is a little problematic.

My research and my practice are situated in culture, just as the art world is part of culture, it doesn't exist in a vacuum locked away in isolation in a little white cube studio. Much of my research didn't really draw on my 'practice' but rather a discursive engagement with the culture around it: cinema, television, the Internet, YouTube, technology, the body. While my 'practice' synthesized and processed all these things, I really preferred the notion of 'research led practice', it was culture that was informing, driving my practice and research not my practice informing my research. Perhaps it's just a semantic difference, and maybe ultimately they are the same thing (practice-led and research-led) however I actually do think it made a fundamental difference in how I approached and thought about the PhD.

My practice has always been less a conventional studio based model, of working and experimenting with materials and processes, and developing ideas through materials, partly because of my background in experimental film and video, my practice has always been closer to the simple idea of executing an idea, and responding to something, it is more project based, as in the notion of writing a script and manifesting that work in a physical form. I don't work through things, I just make them. In addition a number of my projects for my PhD were outsourced to other people to produce part of, I've never had any problem with this (however I am sure others possibly do) while on one hand this method of working is part of the discourse of 'collaborative practice' or 'post studio practice' for me it's really following a film production model, of developing an idea/script and then working with others who have a particular skillset to realise those ideas, it seems entirely normal to me.

I too found the notion of a thesis, significantly different to an exegesis model. In the first instance I could situate my research within a wider cultural frame and write about the cultural context first and secondly write about how it impacted on my practice, this approach was more closely aligned with how I approached the production of my own artwork where my work is largely a response to various pre-existing cultural/technological narratives. While many PhD candidates have a final exhibition for their work to be examined. I didn't have an exhibition at the end of my PhD, as some of the works no longer existed, or had decayed or been damaged over time and only existed in video documentation, other works were Internet based pieces that only existed online. While I had many exhibitions throughout my PhD, the idea of having a final 'best of' exhibition of work at the end of the PhD I've always found a little odd. I always approached the PhD as 'research' first and foremost and less so about mounting an exhibition in a gallery as the culmination of everything.

I actually think this is where the practice-led PhD misunderstands the nature of PhD research in a way. While we have inherited the model of the PhD from the sciences, I don't think scientists are having a big experiment at the end of their PhD research, where the final experiment is the culmination of everything they have researched. While I understand the notion of a final exhibition is interpreting the PhD space for the discipline of fine art, it somehow implies works are resolved and exhibition ready and devalues research that wasn't resolved, or even failed. I know this happened in my own case, sometimes failed projects can be just as valuable as resolved ones. I also figure, galleries, funding bodies, curators often engage and assess one's work on documentation, it's actually a very familiar process for artists, but, for some reason, for a PhD, an exhibition is often a necessity. In my own case if I had mounted a final exhibition I feel many of the works would have been compromised through sound bleeding from one work into another, and presenting works that had decayed or fallen apart etc. A final exhibition would have given a very inaccurate way of viewing/hearing the works. In some respects the PhD exhibition is probably well suited to the disciplines of painting, sculpture, photography, but less so, I believe to video, sound, media art, technology based works.

However, having said that, I did notice a number of times during my candidature, at my PhD confirmation, mid candidature review and completion, the critical discussion which took place was invariably always centered on the writing and my argument and never the artworks I was producing. I found this a little odd considering the PhD was a research-led practice model, there was very little discussion of the artwork I was generating for the PhD. With such a focus on the thesis, I got the feeling my artwork was really secondary to the whole process. In this context there is a danger in the artwork becoming an illustration of the writing and not an extension of it.

In some respects writing all those words is a little odd for artists; we don't expect art historians or cultural theorists to produce art and have solo shows (though maybe we should!). Within the convention of academic discourse I too found it difficult to simply say something without having to base it within a framework of existing knowledge cannabilised from other critical positions. While on one hand I understand the convention of academic discourse, the artwork, I was producing as part of my PhD was just a complete outpouring of a messy, excessive, visceral aesthetic of the body, and, in a way was a nice balance to the rigidity of the writing, in some respects I also felt the art work took on more of an actual critical position, than the writing.

Institutional research is often premised on the idea of identifying a problem which, I have always found somewhat problematic, particularly from the point of view that often it is precisely the problem itself which is of interest and the idea of solving the problem, no longer makes the problem interesting or of value. The notion of problem-solving too has an element of the engineering imperative about it and the idea that art has some kind of instrumentality about it which is also a problem! Having said that my PhD topic did identify 'a problem' however it was a problem I had no interest in solving.

Within the academic institution and to an extent in the contemporary art world, there is a growing focus on art and research that is worthy, that is in some way value adding to culture. Where art and artists are seen as socially relevant, positive agents of enlightenment and where the art gallery and university function as a therapeutic institution. Often through themes of sustainability, the environment, globalization, climate-change, etc. Research centers in universities are based around such areas, and increasingly artists identify with such hot topics. My own practice has never looked to such themes or 'concerns' and I've always been deeply cynical of such things, I've always felt art should create problems, not solve them, to provoke, push buttons and to question things. I've always found it entirely odd that we don't expect other modes of cultural production; cinema, television, music, to have some morally profound ambition, but in contemporary art practice there is an assumption that art must be of 'value', that ultimately it must be serving something that is redeeming and socially virtuous.

In the current climate and paradigm of the academic institution and the drive for research 'to make the world a better place' along with the growing fraternity of artist's interested in improving the world (as if artists have power) I knew I wanted to take my practice and research in the complete opposite direction; to explore abjection, disgust, the use-less and the repulsive. So in many ways I saw the suffocating 'worthiness' and 'save the world art' of research in the academic institution having a profound effect on my thinking and my own research during my PhD. (This possibly was coming more from my experience as working in a university with its prescribed worthy research mandates etc and less so from other PhD students.)

The notion of doing a PhD which is clearly framed within the value of academic discourse and producing outcomes that were more aligned with non-value and disgust I found somewhat perverse. However it is precisely because of this framework of academic discourse that a viewer would have to see intellectual value in an aesthetic, that they would possibly have otherwise simply dismissed and avoided. In many respects, this has defined my practice and research; the refusal to accept that the base level is devoid of meaning and cultural value. On one hand the idea of non-value is of interest to me, but so too, is to find and discover value in the abhorrent, the repulsive, now that's real value; because you have to work at it to find it, it's not value that is presented to you pre-packaged as cultural value.

In some respects my PhD did actually sabotage my own practice, (in a positive sense) which I was very pleased with. I also believe a PhD should fundamentally modify one's practice in some way. Undertaking a PhD provided a framework to make work that I quite possibly wouldn't have made had I not been doing a PhD and exploring the theme of the abject body as my research topic. Much of my work has always had a degree of humour in it, the PhD provided an opportunity to take my practice somewhere else, to produce work that was darker, more visceral and which short-circuited the humour or at least reframed the humour with a more bodily and darker abject aesthetic.

My research topic was centered on the absence of the abject body from the framework of media art, the proposition was that technology has given us the rational, the clean, the logical, the inverse of the messy, irrational, visceral body, so much so that the corporeal, abject body and technology appears to be almost an incompatible aesthetic within the idiom of media art. So in some respects my research identified a gap in the existing knowledge. As part of the PhD I researched various texts on abjection and ideas of base materialism while lots of the critical voices in my PhD weren't specifically coming from continental philosophy, but framed more by a discussion of contemporary filmmakers and culture, artists, science fiction authors, cultural commentary, interviews, with a general framework around art theory some film theory and philosophy etc.

My methodology, which at times I have issues even articulating, as in some ways the methodology or process is a very organic one, it's also very much based around ideas of a film making model of pre-production, production, post-production, so my process consisted of watching and re-watching numerous movies (in fact I probably watched more movies in my PhD than anything else) particularly the genre of body horror, reading various key texts, particularly those on abject art, body horror, lots of Internet research, interviews with artists, filmmakers, art critics, this then led to ideas in the writing, which in turn resulted in various projects, but almost all of my projects came out of writing and the cultural research. In many ways the process of making the work I was less interested in, I was interested in what the work was doing, what ideas where underpinning it.

Others have expressed the increased academisation of the art world, as a result of artists undertaking PhDs.[*] I tend to agree with this to a degree. There

---

[*] Elkins, J. (2009). *Artists with PhDs: On the new doctoral degree in studio art* (1st edn.). Washington, DC: New Academia Publishing, LLC.

is something to be said for not understanding what it is you're doing as an artist, I can see value in that. At times I am still not entirely convinced that by drilling down into one's practice and arriving at a deeper understanding of it, that it automatically equates with producing more interesting art, sure it may result in a more intense engagement with the ideas underpinning the work, but that's not the same thing as producing more interesting art.

In some ways, artists have no control over the interpretation of their own work, once it goes out in the world anything can happen and often does. Artworks are liked for the wrong reasons, works are misinterpreted and misunderstood. I know I have experienced the reality of enjoying a piece of contemporary art only to then dislike it one I read what the artist has to say about it. However the creative-led PhD seems to avoid these ambiguous grey zones so common in the reception of contemporary art. I also wonder just how many artist-doctors who are experts in their own practice does the world really need? The cynical part of me also wonders how is being an expert in your own practice really contributing to new knowledge?

However for all my cynicisms (and there are many) I did enjoy the process of undertaking the PhD. I am too always a little surprised when I hear from colleagues or other artists just how grueling the experience of undertaking a PhD is, considering the PhD is about your own work. I never found that, I developed many ideas during the PhD for future works and can really say it profoundly alerted by art practice. I am careful not to say my work was 'improved' by my PhD, but clearly something happened in the process that re-wired my art practice and transformed it in some way.

I was a little obsessed by my PhD, in some respects I think to be obsessed by your research topic really helps ones motivation, it certainly helped drive my PhD. Weirdly I was slightly disappointed when I had to finish my PhD, as I really engaged with that intense research that was part of the whole process. I presented a number of papers at various conferences during my PhD, I actually found this really helped shape some of my chapters and various aspects of the research, I also found the deadline of having to write a paper worked well for me and it was another driving force for the research.

I think it's important to always question the PhD (as I have here) and not just accept it, but to undertake it on your own terms, to re-wire it, re-think its parameters. I also think it's important to rally against it in a way, to push at its edges, to explore what is acceptable, what is possible as academic research, to unpack it, have fun with it, to criticise it. If these things aren't considered or thought about I feel the result will be very dry, academic research and formulaic art which is the last thing we need.

COMING OUT ... AGAIN!

Richard Harding

Title of study: Juxtapose: An exploration of gay masculine identity and its relationship to the closet

RMIT University, 2014

Abstract

The study is a visual investigation based in studio practice and informed by theoretical exploration. The notion of visibility for gay men has changed dramatically since the advent of the Internet. Online platforms have spawned terms such as 'straight-acting' that privilege heteronormative masculinity above other forms of masculinity based in a hierarchy of masculine performance and identification. My proposition was that the more a gay male performs, simulates, or copies a 'straight' mode of masculine performance, the more his otherness is rendered invisible. Consequently, he builds a closet around himself. The research undertaken for this project employed various methodologies that focus on printmedia's inherent qualities of sameness and difference through collected found images and text. Incorporating questions of authenticity and the real, the print-based artworks interrogated heteronormative masculinity through mass media. My project combined the discourses and practice of printmedia with cultural and queer theory, to interrogate connections between heteronormative masculine performances by gay men and how this could closet otherness. The aim of this research strategy was to locate a psychological or actual space that was free of the homosexual closet.

--

The trigger for my PhD project happened sometime before my application in 2006. My art practice was and is based in the mantra of the 'personal is political'. At the beginning of the last decade or the turn of the century I was as they say, 'single and looking for love' ... some might say in all the wrong places. At this time a major social shift within the LGBTIQ community was occurring responding to the advancing digital technologies of the Internet. Even though this was a global phenomenon my community and specifically gay men, like myself, began incorporating individual online identities into their social arenas. These soon became large cyber communities where people could be whoever and whatever they chose to be. The fluidity of identity had joined the virtual realm of the Internet. This new mode of communication was transforming the community in numerous ways. These networks offered the opportunity of anonymity and safety while presenting many new questions of self-identification, naming and labeling that allowed people to be more open and out – virtually. Yet the Internet also set the scene for a more sinister outcome – the evolution of the virtual closet.

During this period my art practice alternated between analogue and digital production methods, so much so that I felt a need to consolidate my technical explorations and experiments through a focused project. The artworks I made at the time were responding to events around me in a way that was immediate yet there was a need to mine deeper into the concepts due to their ambition, demanding more complexity and nuance than the general artist activist mode I was operating within.

Even though I had conducted multiple projects around identity politics, gender and the homosexual closet I had not yet set a formal technical position within my practice that combined all these conceptual elements. This activated a more reflective position toward my own practice and the questions that were ongoing or that returned due to my personal and professional life. Questions of why and how artists and curators with established practices repeatedly returned to personally driven central concepts, theories and philosophies to address current affairs and concerns became more persistent.

Within the *Juxtapose* project my focus returned to concepts of visibility and invisibility of sexual identity that enabled or dissipated the homosexual closet through print process and production. The personal trigger for this was my discovery of the term *straight acting* on the Internet dating platforms which I engaged with. Here was a term that clarified and evidenced my concerns of the cyber world's anonymity that was going to prove to be a backward step for equality and liberation. My response to this term was one of disappointment that grew into actively opposing and discussing this term on-line. The online community was fractured over this term and the multiple issues it spawned. This led to growing discussions on notions of gay masculinity and its definition within queer culture at the time.

As an artist who had based his practice within the printed realm I had become more intrigued by how the theories and philosophies of reproducibility could assist the production and delivery of artworks. Within my doctoral proposal I began to formulate concepts that print production was based in otherness in some form due to the alignment of reproducibility to the feminine. I began posing questions of liberation or subversion with acceptance or conformity though print practices. This led to the examining of the edition, repetition and performance. How could gay men perform a masculine identity without closeting themselves when masculinity was measured against a heteronormative model? How could these concepts be explored and activated by the act of making and production of multiples?

While the technical research was driven by the paradox of the print original as an analogy for the terms gay and masculine the theories of sameness and difference were also activated to position sexual orientation and gender through the protocols of the editioned print. But why do this? What was my point or perceived outcome? Beyond simple awareness, or cautionary tales of the dangers of the closet I wanted to explore the possibility, through my art practice, of locating a space virtual or actual that was free of the homosexual closet.

In deciding to return to formal study I opted for a part-time load due to work and family commitments. The flow on effect was an elongated time-frame that had positive and negative attributes. Firstly, the lengthened time frame that part-time study offered allowed for an expanded reflective phase within the research project; conceptually and technically. One of the inherent qualities of a print based practice within its many steps of production are the forced waiting times that occur for drying, layering and proofing. This built in reflective time enabled numerous perspectives and adjustments to be considered during production. Secondly, the scope of the theoretical research benefited from this time frame in its depth and breadth. This became more evident in the writing of the exegesis in the final stages of the program while preparing for examination.

The negatives of part-time study were not evident at first. The main concern that emerged was the speed at which social change occurred from the advent of the Internet, this was unpredicted. Added to this was the Internet's rapidly expanding influence as it grew exponentially in a short time span along with the many permutations of hardware and software. We are still seeing how the Internet is reshaping the fabric of our many cultures locally and globally. In retrospect my project could have become obsolete before it was presented and published due to this. Even though some aspects did fall away such as notions of camp other components of my project expanded such as the acknowledgement of photography within my print practice and its position with my project. I now see these adjustments as part of the process of such a large undertaking within my practice and the doctoral program.

The choice to undertake my doctoral studies at RMIT University was based on the School of Art Higher Degree by Research (HDR) program's mode of delivery, emphasising the doctorate by art project with an adjunct exegesis–now a dissertation–to contextualise the project historically and theoretically while positioning it within contemporary practice. Added to this was RMIT University's School of Art acknowledged inclusive and investigative approach that encouraged candidates to explore and experiment through making. To test and trial propositions through various mediums and approaches. For my doctoral project this research approach offered a deeper priority that I anticipated would travel beyond the academy into arts industry and thus the general viewing public as it was based in studio practice.

Sameness and difference

Utilising my print based practice I pursued my research topic through examining the theories of reproducibility addressing the proposition that straight-acting was yet another form of closeting of and by gay men. As I interrogated my processes and ideas through trial artworks and discussions with my supervisor my research questions slowly reveiled themselves. This process was the beginning of a deeper understanding of the research project's purpose and my practice in general. I proposed that mediums of reproducibility, such as those within printmaking, are based in otherness and specifically in the context of my project a sense of queerness was present. This guided me to questions of gender and sexual orientation. Eventually I distilled the many questions down to two main points of endeavour for my project:

1. In what ways can printmaking's intrinsic nature of the multiple be employed to facilitate an analysis of sameness and difference in the construction and deconstruction of gender and sexuality?

2. How can the performative codes of posture, gesture, speech and costume be re-applied in a print based practice to explore proposed links between a gay masculine identity and the closet?

As my ideas continued to oscillate around the concepts of the closet and gay visibility within an era of supposed acceptance, a position I found artificial and imaginary, I began to align my ideas with notions of the 'open secret' and various hierarchies that I believed were at play within my practice and art practice generally. Concepts of liberation and freedom are elusive easily falling away within a dominant patriarchal system when not maintained. Through the vigilance of remembering histories of otherness and building on victories no matter how small are of great importance. This remembering combined with an ongoing vigilance against the closet reignited the activist within me. Thus, returning to questions of hierarchies of gender and sexual orientation through my chosen discipline of Printmaking.

At times merely asking questions of otherness can still raise eyebrows and sighs of, 'haven't we done that? All that gay stuff was done in the 80s – we need to move on etc.'. It was these very responses that sustained my interest and thus continue discussions on the silencing of otherness by a dominant heteronormative mainstream culture. It is interesting to note here that these statements came from gay and straight practitioners by way of various discussions prior to and during my doctoral candidature. Within my art practice I aligned this mode of silencing to the post-medium era put forward by the American theorist Rosalind Krauss. Through this configuration I began to unpack the sense of otherness I carried for print based production within art practice generally. In my project and exegetical feedback one examiner stated that this was an old argument and I agree it is. Yet the question remains, why are there still discussions on and in disciplines that are positioned as craft based or 'other' against disciplines like painting; which is still used as code for Art? This became part of my projects methodology; aligning the hierarchies of gender and sexual orientation with the otherness of printmaking. It was through the examining and questioning of my practice and of those around me that I expanded my understanding of the use of various mediums as vehicles for conceptual delivery.

Understanding your practice

My project used a combination of methodologies but began with using the central conceptual premise of sameness and difference to align the processes of reproducibility with gender and sexual orientation in the realm of printmaking. Over the course of my candidature it became increasingly evident that the project incorporated essential photographic elements, not as a separate fine art medium but as an integral component of an expanded print based practice. Being print based the project included multiple mediums with reproductive capabilities, hand stenciling, object based works, photocopying and high-end inkjet printing. The project interwove and embedded photography within the traditions of my print practice through the found image and analogue photographic processes such as photographic silkscreen printing. By using the concepts of reproducibility as analogies for otherness I then began to unpack how these operated within my studio practice.

Prior to my candidature my practice had operated with constructed archives for some time. However, the intuitive system I employed of collecting and sorting within my doctoral project was examined and analysed to assist the development and mining of the central concepts much further than previously. Due to the expansive nature of the project I began to set definite parameters to work within. One of these was the collection of primary research material. For the *Juxtapose* project the focused was on images from printed news media within the Melbourne geographic location: *THE AGE*, *mX* and *MCV* (Melbourne Community Voice) from 2006 to 2012. At times this expanded into the Internet through the gay website gaydar.com.au that triggered my project as a way of cross-referencing and monitoring the use of the term 'straight-acting'. As my candidature drew to a close the use of the term 'straight-acting' fell out of favour within the gay community. However, the use of terms such as 'no fems' and 'masculine only' grew in frequency online at the same time.

These parameters based my project's archived collection in notions of the everyday with ideas of a catalogue or cataloguing types. Thus creating a store of images that represented archetypal and stereotypical males to create new works from. At this point the projects methodology was still forming as I collected piles of image and text from the newspapers to sift through. The active looking that was being conducted through the process of collecting became more considered and directed through my research questions. At this time I re-read *Camera Lucida* (1980) by Roland Barthes and developed a personalised version of his studium and punctum within my collection. Barthes defined these terms through the process of looking and seeing particular images that are categorised as cultural or historical (studium) and individual or familial (punctum), a relationship that is established between the 'Operator and Spectator', 'Creator and Consumer' or for my purposes the Artist and Viewer.

Through my project's parameters the studium became the collection of male images from everyday printmedia to be archived, referenced and reused repeatedly. While the punctum was the selection of specific images based on my personal desire of body type, pose and attire. This method also resonated with Honoré Balzac's code system of self-representation that included four main signifying elements costume, posture, speech and gesture laid down in 1830. My research led me to questions of how humans identify each other through visual cues and sound.

My intuitive mode of working within the studio lent it self to and aligned with the cut-up techniques used by American writer William S. Burrows in his novels of the 1950/60s, and UK musician David Bowie in his song writing during the 1970s. According to Tim Head author of *The Art of William S. Burrows: Cut-Ups, Cut-Ins, Cut-Outs*. The cut-up method was a continuation of the ideas of Tristan Tzara, which he described in How to Make a Dadaist Poem (*Pour faire un poème dadaïste*, 1920). Burroughs acquainted Brion Gysin with this method, who accidentally discovered or re-invented it in Paris in October 1959, when cutting out passe-partouts for watercolours with a Stanley knife (2012, para. 4).

Through the selected and reproduced images or found '*readymade photographs*' I began exploring the performative notions of camp, the in between of the binary masculine and feminine. This pathway was abandoned because the outcomes did not address the research questions adequately. Thus, the project focused on what could be referred to as hypermasculine representations within the news media that determined medium and technical choices for print production. This direction was more purposeful aligning with the conceptual and political imperatives of my project. Due to this there were concerns at times, that my project could be seen as complicit with the heteronormative patriarchal system purely by re-presenting these found images.

Prepare for change

American cultural theorist Judith Butler writes of, 'Compulsory Heterosexuality' setting it self up as the original, the true, the authentic; the norm that determines the real implies that 'being' a lesbian [gay man] is always a kind of miming, a vain effort to participate' (1990, p. 312). Through this position Butler gave my practice-led project permission to move into a space, a studio space, that allowed for further questioning via the performance of image making, the found image and gender representation and repetition. I would say an ongoing queer performance that repeated itself in many guises of my candidature. Notions of authenticity played out in my project through the paradox of the original print, editioning and images of performed masculinity.

From the beginning of my doctoral program I connected with a supervisor who was open to alternative modes of practice and discussions in which nothing was off limits. This allowed for conversations that moved freely between practice and theory, philosophical conundrums and acknowledgements of yet to be resolved cultural dilemmas such as the 'closet', in its many guises. The supervisor/candidate relationship was enhanced through a balanced consultation schedule and maintained on both sides.

As my project developed, progressing sporadically at times, I garnered a deeper understanding of my own practice and my motivating triggers. Even though I was exempt from participating in the Research Methods course due to completing it previously I chose to take part. Aside from the obvious benefit of reviewing current research approaches my involvement assisted the fine-tuning of my methodology through the group workshops and peer-to-peer critiques I found invaluable.

In retrospect the milestone presentations, as stressful as they can be at times, aided in the development of the project. This was due to the requirement for the candidate to put their research up for public scrutiny. The lead in to these presentations allowed for a revision of the research questions and the project's methodology. I used these milestones as pauses to reflect on whether I was 'staying on message'. Did the research correlate to my objectives? Did the current output of artworks talk to my conceptual concerns? Did the technical experiments relate to my questions of studio theory and print philosophy and so forth? In a general sense the development of my practice, and thus my project, appeared to be a natural progression of active making and reflecting. I would add to this a maintained focus that occurred due to the rigor of the program and the academic support on offer.

Work life balance or we all have issues

As I completed my doctoral studies within the University I am employed by I was given a research allocation within my academic work plan. This time was added to through after hours and weekends. The ebb and flow of the project governed the input as needed. My time lines were broken into semesters with components of the project allocated through technical and theoretical investigations. I would use aspects of my annual leave at various points of the project allowing for an extended focus within the studio research.

As my doctoral project was triggered through gay dating sites one of the main elements I needed to shuffle was my romantic life. Work, studio and family were appropriately distributed and working well. It was through the cyber world that I found time to go on dates and in the process I met my partner Tad. Nine years on he and his son Simon have been incorporated into my extended family and I into theirs.

The main element of the study program that I found confronting was the scale of the PhD project. The personal perception of doing a PhD can become distorted and all consuming. The project at times seems to take on a gargantuan psychological space. This is a dangerous realm to dwell in as it can render a candidate inactive thus making the situation even worse through a state of stasis. No one project will, nor can it, cover every aspect of your topic. Within my candidature the act of coming out was entrenched through my project, conceptually and practically. At times the expectation to perform this act with each discussion or presentation became a burden that activated a sense of 'coming out fatigue'. This produced a sense of anxiety at times that was channeled back into the work and the accompanying exegesis.

Due to the elongated time frame of part-time, keeping the project on track or staying on message was paramount. At times I did stray from my initial purpose however I utilised my proposal to reinforce my intention and maintain direction. Added to this was the importance the exegesis played in unifying the studio production and reflection. The exegesis needed to be written as a stand alone document that lived beyond the examination yet was set within the framework of a practice led research project. In my project the exegesis operated as a conduit between studio methods, final artworks and theoretical discussions.

Another issue would be the ever-changing administrative components of the Higher Degree program. Even though most candidates understand this it is a frustrating element that needs to be monitored. I found this more frustrating then problematic and it was based again on my projects timeline more than anything else.

What if?

Looking back, if I had my time again I would be more proactive in making connections with my peer group within the PhD program. I would endeavour to allocate more time for participating in the extra curricular workshops and lectures offered by the School and University. Also, there are aspects of my project that I would have liked to explore further such as race or more specifically the notion of whiteness in relation to the closet. This aspect of identity recurred at several points during my research. This was especially evident when investigating artists and writers whose practices were also based in some form of otherness. Even though racial identity did not become a major research element of this project the combination of gender and orientation with race was acknowledged through the nature of invisibility that 'whiteness' allowed some gay men to utilise to blend in or pass as straight. I recognised this as an aspect of western gay male identity that required further exploration in possible post-doctoral research.

Choose your supervisors wisely. If the supervisor is not living up to your expectations discuss your expectations with them. Negotiate timeframes and consultation schedules. If this does correlate with your expectations discuss changing supervisor but be reasonable in what is required. It is important to remember this is YOUR project not the supervisors.

Be mindful of your time frames in all aspects of your life: as a candidate, a work colleague and family member. The people around you will usually be very accommodating however PhD candidates can be hard work at times … so I was told.

Do not focus on the fact you are doing a PhD project, work through your research questions and experiment and explore as much as possible.

Most importantly, enjoy your time as a PhD research candidate – professionally and personally – it can be a very rewarding exercise beyond your expectations.

PHOTOGRAPHING THE AUSTRALIAN LANDSCAPE THROUGH EXPEDITIONS

Shane Hulbert

Title of study: Photographing the altered landscape

RMIT University, 2012

Abstract

This practice-led research project is a visual investigation into the artistic, cultural and technological status of altered landscape photography in Australia. The outcome of the research is an exhibition of twelve digital photographic prints that consider the capabilities and limitations of contemporary digital technologies in the practice of altered landscape photography in Australia.

An altered landscape is positioned, for this research project, as one that evidences irrevocable change, the crafting of the land through construction and intervention, a system or process of modification that results in the making of something new or different from the pre-existing state. This is the land that has been disrupted, been made artificial and different from the what is on or above it. Humans mine for the resources needed to create new constructions, settlements and cities, shift the borders of the bush through removal and addition, and alter the environment to change its purpose to suit the expansion of civilization and the needs of our culture and economies.

The research investigated fine art landscape photographers from the mid-nineteenth century to contemporary times, and aimed to identify the conditions under which they photographed, their choices for subject matter, the type of equipment they used, and to assess their influence on the practice of landscape photography. The research also investigated the relationship between certain Australian sites and how these places are situated within ideas of nation, both historical and contemporary. From this, the research established a series of categories for contemporary altered landscape photography in Australia, as a way of seeing the land, and as a way of exploring the land to produce this body of photographic work.

Throughout this project it was always my intention to ensure that every fine art photographic print I made responded to the deepest traditions of the photographic medium, while exploring the capability and suitability of digital devices and processes for photographing the Australian altered landscape. As an artist and researcher I am consciously positioning myself and this research from the perspective of the producer, rather than the consumer, from the perspective of reflection on the altered landscape as subject matter, and the way technologies are suited to contemporary landscape photography and situated in my practice.

The project was ultimately a photographic study of human geography, of place and of landscape and through the lens of discovering, uncovering and revealing how the landscape is altered by human intervention, it contributes a new body of knowledge in the field of Australian landscape photography, and a way of approaching and understanding the Australian altered landscape.

--

I have been photographing seriously now for 20 years. I approach photography as way of exploring and understanding the world I live in, of taking the mystery of a moment or a place, and permanently recording light, detail and structure. This reveals how I see and feel about sites and places. I look on with interest at how photography has shifted over these last 20 years, particularly the democratization of photography due to the current dominance of smart phones as cameras[*]. Due to the nature of my subject matter, I am rarely, if ever, in a situation where 'the best camera is the one I have with me'[†], but rather the best camera is the biggest and most advanced camera I can carry. While I do not

---

[*] Dutch artist Erik Kessels cleverly interrogated this with his Photography in Abundance exhibition in 2011, in which he downloaded and printed every public image uploaded to popular photography site Flickr in a 24-hour period, and then 'dumped' over 1,000,000 prints at Foam in Amsterdam.
[†] Quote attributed to photographer and online educator Chase Jarvis, suggesting that equipment is secondary to the stories and moments that can be captured if you always have a camera with you. He is referring to his iPhone app, as mentioned in the YouTube advertising video, https://www.youtube.com/watch?v=0lotlwm38OM, accessed 26 September 2016.

pass judgement on the rise of versatile non-camera devices for photography, I do recognise that photography has a unique language that is intrinsically linked to the technology of optics and capture mediums. I prefer the tactile physicality of big cameras with nobs and dials, large and clear viewfinders through which to see and compose the 'messiness of the world' (Shore, 2007, p. 37), the weight of the machine, and manual controls that I can manipulate to capture expressive photographs.

I generally do not take pictures of people, but rather the evidence of people, and the mark of humanity on the Earth.

The photographs of Frederick Sommer, Stephen Shore, Andreas Gursky and in particular Emmet Gowin have influenced me. In his farewell lecture as Professor of Photography at Princeton University in 2009, Gowin eloquently spoke about his relationship with land, 'I love the hand of the human being on the landscape … The living landscape is a field of action, not stasis. It's constantly evolving and adapting … A field seen a second or third time is not ever the same' (Gowin, 2013, p. 19). Like the landscape of the human hand, the PhD is a process of evolution and action, and perhaps the most difficult part of this process lies in first deciding to undertake such an intense level of study.

I decided to undertake a PhD because I wanted to understand my relationship with photography and art in a more complex and meaningful way. I needed something new in my life that would help make me a better artist. I was also acutely aware, as are many artists, of the dangers of 'stasis' and repeatability in practice, or what one of my now graduated doctoral candidates, artist Mathew Sleeth, claimed in relation to his own practice, that there is a risk of 'swapping out subject matter and repeating the same projects with different content once you have an effective template' (Sleeth, 2013, p. 78). I did the PhD to discover and confirm my subject matter, but also to develop a more rigorous practice.

I often look back at images I never exhibit with a sense of curiosity. I keep them as part of the repository that is my conversation with photography. Sometimes I see something new in an old image. I looked at a lot of my images prior to undertaking the PhD and realized, somewhat reluctantly (an ego thing) that I needed help shifting my photography and practice out of what I considered the passive framing of the world, and into the more active position of responding to the world.

Parallel to my art practice is my academic career. It was clear to me when I decided to undertake the PhD that the relationship between the art schools and the academies had changed – the sector was being disruptive before 'disruption' was even a thing. I came to the understanding that a PhD was required for survival, but I realise now that was an easy out – it was not as simple as that, the PhD made me a far more conscientious academic, an ability to see the helicopter view on many diverse situations, a better citizen of the university sector and a far more effective educator at both the undergraduate and postgraduate level. I sometimes think the almost mandatory requirement for the PhD in academia is institutionally short sighted for an art school, then I remember how valuable the experience was for me.

The selection of an institution should be determined by a range of factors, and central to that is the supervisor. I chose RMIT not because I was employed there (it sometimes made things easy, it sometimes made things hard), but because the right supervisor was there. I often wonder whether a candidate can outgrow their supervisor, however, in the case of my primary supervisor, that certainly did not happen to me. The discussions, the ideas, the conveying of expertise and knowledge, this all meant there was a rich and valuable ongoing dialogue exchange. This exchange focused and supported my practice in ways that I value to this day. He left the university towards the completion of my study, and was generous enough to continue advising until the end.

Territory, influences and determining a topic

In the early stages of the project I became misguided into thinking that the proposal for the project had to be original, and that it had to set a course of inquiry that would be able to define the contribution to knowledge and the significance of the project in the field of study. This led me down several wrong paths, and the territory for investigation kept expanding, ultimately becoming too large to contain within the one research project. One very simple question from my supervisor, which has resonated with me ever since, put it all into perspective – 'what do you want to photograph and make work about?' The answer came easy, and the proposal was written, with the subject matter of my photography becoming core to my research and project, and approved within two months following that conversation.

Once I had finalized the topic, and the research questions, I took a break from writing, and spent six months photographing. It is inevitable that the project will change – change in the sense that it will evolve through discoveries, interests and contexts as they emerge, that one is simply not aware of at the beginning and thus the process of learning is revealed. It is expected and it should be encouraged.

What was also important in those early days was to find companions and friends, what is commonly referred to as a 'community of practice'. A community is of course important, but it is inevitable that certain people will emerge and stand out as being critical to the project. In today's global climate, those friends may exist in several forms, they might be local, they might be on the other side of the world, you might never meet them, they might even be deceased. The experience of their presence may be virtual, through their images or written thoughts, and they form a vital part of the researcher's community. Melbourne artist and educator, Dr Les Walkling (also my primary supervisor) speaks of this in a recent website essay 'On talking to dead people', in which he describes the value and experience of having conversations with dead people, not through their words, but through their artworks (Walkling, 2016). In addition to people, I also developed a particular fondness for places.

The journey from field trips and road trips:
Ideas, methodology and where they come from

For a brief period of time, when I was a teenager, I became obsessed with the cars from the Australian film *Mad Max 2: The Road Warrior* (Miller 1981), set against the backdrop of the expansive Australian landscape. In particular, I loved the way they powered around the desert, billowing massive dust clouds, while chasing down Max and his loyal blue heeler dog (named 'Dog') in his partially wrecked V8 Interceptor. I even had the pictures on my bedroom wall. When I discovered these car scenes had been filmed outside Broken Hill, in the western part of New South Wales, I knew that one day I would visit there myself. It is interesting how these memories fade over time, only to return years later.

Broken Hill became a place that I revisited several times during the project. On each visit, the harshness of the conditions reminded me of that wonderful

Australian colloquialism 'dry as a dead dingo's donga'. What I was looking for in Broken Hill was a site that 'represented' Australia, both geographically and culturally. What began as a childhood longing, shifted into more empirical research by way of identifying and breaking down the significance of the site in the Australian psyche for extended field work and imaging.

I fixated on Broken Hill due to its strong relationship to Australian outback culture and history, in particular:

> 1: The town of Broken Hill is one of the key physical and culturally representational sites for many Australian films and artists that use land as a central narrative element – starting in 1971 with Ted Kotcheff's *Wake in Fright*, a story about a disenchanted teacher who descends into alcohol driven violence and degradation after losing all his money gambling in a game of two-up. Violence, fear and difference become the central Australian motifs explored through Broken Hill, from over-sized, diseased, people-eating feral pigs (*Razorback* 1984) to drag queens on a journey of self-reflection and discovery (*The Adventures of Priscilla, Queen of the Desert* 1994). Broken Hill seems to be the place where as Australians we face our fears and find ourselves. Iconic Australian rock band Midnight Oil filmed their 1987 hit *Beds are Burning* in Broken Hill, car companies advertise indestructible 4-wheel drives and the Australian Tourism Board filmed the 2006 *Where the bloody hell are you* campaign there.
>
> 2: Broken Hill is also the only location on Australian soil that came under attack in World War I, when two Turks, (a butcher and an ice-cream vendor) fired into a crowded open railway car travelling to the 1915 New Year's Day picnic, in response to growing hostilities between the English and Ottoman Empires. The 'Battle of Broken Hill' had all the classic elements of a wild gun battle, raging for several hours through the outskirts of the town, onto a defensible hill top, with the baddies ultimately cornered and killed. When it was over and 'all-clear' six people were dead, the attackers, three passengers and a defiant pub owner shot by a stray bullet.

Sites were important to my project and research, and with Broken Hill I valued the way it iconically connected to Australian myths and culture. Broken Hill also represented a wonderful example of how this was uncovered through the research. In his seminal work on landscape theory and experience, *Landscape and Memory* (1995) writer and historian Simon Schama considers landscape to be a repository, the accumulation of the memories and experiences of humanity. Schama writes of landscape as being 'culture before they are nature; constructs of the imagination projected onto wood and water and rock' (Schama, 1995, p. 61). Schama succinctly traces the relationship between iconic aspects of the environment; river systems, mountains, valleys and forests, and the social systems that developed around them. He predominately investigates the psychological conditions of European cultures that gave rise to landscape, suggesting that they were not always associated with happiness, and that these projections of experience onto the landscape are informed by the linage of cultures and civilisations.

Broken Hill became a place I visited many times. Through revisiting this one place, I was able to explore its iconic environment through Australian landscape narratives. In a very non-empirical way, I knew that revisiting the same site was not simply 'swapping subject matter', but rather it was affirming my value in what I was doing, it was allowing me to explore a phenomenological relationship with practice and research, through a systematic process of repeatability and growth. This revisiting also enabled me to align my visits to Broken Hill to those of previous explores, and to position the site in the same way – as a point of departure into the outback.

Wandering

I mentioned earlier the importance of establishing conversations with other artists. German filmmaker and photographer Wim Wenders (b. 1945) had a profound impact on my methodology of travel and wandering. During the middle stages of the production, I made extensive use of the idea of road trips as being an important way of discovering sites and places. The advantage of the road trip is that it allowed me to explore multiple sites between a point of departure and a destination.

Wenders' extensive wanderings around the world, including the outback of Australia, formed a vital insight into how I considered the road-trip for my research methodology. Wenders utilizes the road-trip as a way to scout film locations, and has amassed a significant body of photographic work on landscapes that evidence the footprint of humanity on the earth.

The road-trip defines all of Wenders' films, however the one that most influenced me in the early stages of the project was his 1991 film *Until the end of the World* (*Bi sans Ende der Welt*), in which the concept of the road-trip spans continents and time. Set on the eve of the millennium, under the threat of nuclear annihilation, the main characters begin their journey in Europe, move through seven countries and fifteen cities, eventually concluding in a remote area of the Australian Outback (set in Coober Pedy in the northern region of South Australia, and Utopia Station, 350kms north east of Alice Springs in the Northern Territory). This is the ultimate road-trip: Sam, an American, searches the world for images to record on a new sight device, stolen from the US government, that will enable his blind mother to see again. His journey is interrupted and infiltrated by various characters, each on their own journey, including government agents and detectives, bounty hunters, Sam's father, his girlfriend, her boyfriend, a writer and various others. In the end they converge on a site in the remote Australian Outback, waiting out the nuclear blasts that will end the world. The blast never comes, and the characters become addicted to using the stolen device to replay images from their dreams. The irony being that the wanderers, trapped on the other side of the world, become imprisoned in their own minds and memories, through their dreams of sometime and somewhere else.

The road trip defined a large portion of the research, and several exhibitions were developed from these wanderings. Towards the later stages of the project I started to analyse and question the relationship between road trips and the Australian outback. During the many hours and kilometres on the road, I was developing an awareness of the outback adventure, by way of not only responding to sites I visited, but a more phenomenological way of experiencing the land, country and landscape. I ultimately redefined the framework of my travels with a methodology that was more scientific, yet more rugged, adventurous, dangerous and exploratory – this led to me abandoning the road-trip, drawing on Australia's own narratives and myths, and embarking on expeditions.

In settler Australian history, the expedition became the defining way of discovering the continent, claiming the land and opening up the unknown interior of the nation to development and industry. Australian expeditions to the central areas of the continent contributed to the discovery of river systems and mountain ranges, laid claim to farming lands and new settlements, and continuously pushed the frontier region of the country. Expeditions charted the unknown geography of the country, promoted the potential for expansion, while also reinforcing the belief of the hostility of the land. These expeditions, and the geographic, regional, anthropological and cultural discoveries attributed to them, can be closely linked to the formation of national identity and relationship with the land. Ross Gibson's *South of the West: Post Colonialism and the Narrative Construction of Australia* (1992), provides a provocative analysis of different systems of cultural representation through the land, and the desire to explore away from the coast and towards the centre:

> In front of them, immediately, was an enormity with which they felt compelled to relate. And because Australia is an island, regardless of where on the coastline the settlers stood when they pondered the island, they all looked toward one ultimate point of convergence – towards the centre. (Gibson, 1992, p. 9)

The concept of the expedition, following a long line of evolving ways of thinking about and photographing the land, became my primary method of discovery and collection. From field trips, to road-trips to expeditions, my methodology was, for me, intrinsically connected to the inquiry, to what I was making work about, and to how I made the work. Through this, my practice developed from being *in* the landscape, to being *of* the landscape.

From 'mighty blows' to 'critical hits'

A common reflection at the completion of such a life changing experience is to think about what should or could have been done different. Should I have spent more time on this, less time on that? I grew up playing video games, and at about the same time that I started the PhD, in 2004, video game company Blizzard released the ground-breaking massive multiplayer online game *World of Warcraft* (WoW). At the time, this was like no other game ever released, and I levelled up a character to 60 (when Level 60 was the highest). The average time for this was 260 hours (two hours per night, five days a week average, for six months), and I am a mid-level gamer, so assume more like 350 hours. Was this time better spent on reading or something more scholarly productive? I joke with friends (both real and online) that I would have completed my doctorate two years earlier if I did not play WoW. Truth is I do not believe this. I do not believe there is anything I would have done differently. I sometimes make a lame attempt to cite the amazing landscape in WoW as some kind of inspiration, and that it was research – and while it was at the time an impressive virtual landscape, it was not 'that' good. What the game did become, however, was a way of sensing the value in time and distance – the hours and hours of online gaming matched the hours and hours of physical road trips and expeditions through the desert, it also gave me a sense of space to process and reflect on the intense study in which I was engaging. Remembering back, I would read for some time, take notes, work on images – be a student. Then later in the night I would wait until the house went to bed, then log on and play. During that time, I would synthesize what I had read, then I would start to think about those things in direct relationship with what was happening in the game, the immersion into the game allowed me to process some of the thinking I was doing during the day in a different mental head space and context.

I was an unusual player in that I spent a lot of solo time in the world, playing alone and travelling alone. Journeying through the virtual landscape made me think about my journeys through the physical landscape. WoW was often criticized for the slow pace of travel through the expansive world(s), but for me it became an important part of the experience. One of the major outcomes from my project was a relational connection between Australian expeditions and the way I positioned my practice within the landscape. I know I made this connection late at night while playing WoW. Distance is distance, and after researching early journals on Australian expeditions, in an attempt to find places with historical significance, I realized, that it was not only about the place, it was also about the travel and the distance. I made this connection to my practice while travelling through a virtual world, realizing I was also on an expedition. My only regret was not writing about this in my exegesis.

Personal growth, or how I freed me from myself

Some time ago, at the beginning of my doctorial research, I was fortunate enough to hear Spanish artist Joan Fontcuberta talk about his art practice. He begun the talk with a simple, yet memorable line that has resonated with me ever since – all art is autobiographical. At the same time as this talk, my supervisor provided some advice on doing the PhD, he suggested 'Make sure your life is in order – avoid moving house, don't break up a relationship or fall in love … these are things that will distract you, and you really want to avoid distractions'. Naturally I did all of those things (some more than once!), however, rather than distract me from the research, it created a meaningful parallel through which to situate myself within the growth and personal development that comes from such a high level of study. It was sound advice; it just did not fit in with where I was in my life. A doctorial project might be about that research topic and it's elusive 'questions' but in art it is of course also about the development and growth of the researcher as an artist.

Something else was important to me about the possibilities of deep thinking and how a PhD would help me to realise how I engage with art, and who I am as an artist. The PhD helped to free me from myself. It made me more aware of how to live in the world and how to be a better, happier and more connected citizen. It also provided answers to something uncomfortable that was forming in my 'helicopter view' of myself – questions about how I respond to the challenges of life, and the way I was engaging with knowledge. English social scientist, and chair of the Refugee Studies Centre at the University of Oxford, Professor Alexander Betts, recently suggested that there is a 'gap between public perception and empirical reality,' and that we have 'moved to a postfactual society, where evidence and truth no longer matter, and lies have equal status to the clarity of evidence' (Betts, 2016). My capacity to live in the world is more enriched from doing the PhD, it has helped me to live a more fulfilling, examined and flourishing life. It made me a better artist and it made me a happier person. Towards the end of the PhD study I exhibited my work at the Centre for Contemporary Photography. In the year following the completion, I exhibited my work at the National Gallery of Victoria as part of their iconic *Melbourne Now* show. I attribute these achievements to having undertaken a PhD.

The PhD is one of the most profound experiences of my life, not only the eight years it took to complete, but the lasting impact it has had on me as a person and as an artist. The only thing that has affected me more is the relationship I have with my four-year-old son Emmet.

Despite that early caution from my supervisor about getting my life in order, and everything I learnt in relationship to that, like a frustrated parent I sometimes find myself repeating the very same cautions to my own candidates – I have to remind myself of everything I went through and learnt along the way, tell them to forget what I just said, that I take it back, and instead encourage them to embrace the mayhem and chaos – after all, it's only a PhD! …

References

Betts, A. (2016). TEDSummit: Why Brexit happened – and what to do next. Retrieved from https://www.ted.com/talks/alexander_betts_why_brexit_happened_and_what_to_do_next?language=en.

Gibson, R. (1992). *South of the West: Post Colonialism and the Narrative Construction of Australia*. Bloomington: Indiana University Press.

Gowin, E. (2013). *Emmet Gowin*. New York: Aperture.

Shore, S. (2007). *The Nature of Photographs*. London: Phaidon.

Sleeth, M. (2013). *Representation and Reproduction: A Love Story*. Melbourne: RMIT University.

Walkling, L. (2016.) *On talking to dead people*. Retrieved from www.leswalkling.com.

REVISITING RESEARCH

Ruth Johnstone

Title of study: Revisiting the print room
RMIT University, 2005

Abstract

The interrelationship of art to architecture was closely aligned in the second half of the eighteenth century and it is a major consideration in current spatial art practices. The aim of my doctoral research project Revisiting the Print Room was to investigate the cultural conditions that encouraged this nexus in the eighteenth century and how this information might inform contemporary art practice. Specific investigations were directed at the contextualization of the print placed within an architectural environment through a series of print installations and sculptural works. While my studio research and exhibitions complemented and responded to the largely historical content of the written research, the exegesis examines the eighteenth-century tradition of the print room, with a particular emphasis on the Castletown House print room in County Kildare, Ireland, supported by a survey of recorded and extant eighteenth-century print rooms in the Europe, Ireland and UK. Extensive documentation of the printed elements in the Castletown House print room and a detailed analysis of these components are documented and dispersed for the first time in this project. The historical research contributes to the body of knowledge and critical analysis of eighteenth-century interior design and the role of women in this discipline. The relationship of art to architecture in the eighteenth century provides a reference point for a reconsideration of current exhibition design and more specifically of contemporary printmaking as it relates to installation practice. The application of print media is broadly embedded in most forms contemporary art practice and my aim is to highlight approaches to print media that are not constrained by modernist codes of practice. My project takes the form of installation, architectural modeling with micro-installation and fragmentary sculptural works with the application of reproductive print media.

--

Having completed a Master of Arts in Dublin and finding it a rewarding process for my art practice as well as a broadening cultural experience, five years on I was keen to embark on a doctorate. In the late 1990s the Head of the School of Art at RMIT called for academics willing to undertake a PhD. New programs for post-graduate research were emerging in the School of Art and staff were encouraged to apply as there were few academics with doctorates and qualified doctoral supervisors would be needed in the future. I enthusiastically took on the challenge and was further supported with an RMIT post-graduate scholarship, generously allowing for release from teaching and enabling me to exclusively focus on doctoral research full-time for a number of years. I also enjoyed periods of lecturing part-time and researching part-time as each task offered a different kind of stimulation and provided a breather from the alternate activity.

I made extraordinary efforts to leave the country to study for my Master of Arts in order to give myself a very different kind of exposure to education and art practice. Having both studied and taught at RMIT I had this dual experience in an institution that had a national and expanding international profile. To contrast this with a different learning experience, I didn't want to go to another art education centre such as London or New York, but chose a peripheral location for my Masters. A former whiskey distillery repurposed into an art school in Dublin, on the rough side of town, but a swift walk to the intellectual and creative wealth of Trinity College, was a liberating place, a place for working hard in the studio. The National College of Art and Design closed its doors on Friday evenings and this forced me to seek out other aspects of culture and to make the most of my proximity to Europe. By the time I enrolled in my doctoral project, RMIT served as a base for me to make more new research and work in Ireland, to follow up on new research that I knew had gaps in knowledge with further opportunities for research incursions into the UK and Europe. RMIT was a platform for producing the desired intellectual property appropriate for a PhD but I was definitely not operating in an insular environment. I had to negotiate a number of languages and made several extended trips to the northern hemisphere where primary research material was housed.

Having spent intermittent periods in Ireland studying, returning for artist residencies, art commissions and exhibitions, it was natural to want to continue my association with Ireland. As my practice at the time of undertaking my Masters was the construction of architecturally-scaled printed paper rooms and corridors, Dublin studio co-habitant and friend Ciarán Ó Cearnaigh suggested I see the prints embedded in the walls at Castletown House, County Kildare. The room was prepared from the early 1760s and prints installed by Lady Louisa Conolly by 1769. Lady Conolly's heritage and life was as fascinating as her dedication to decorating her grand restyled Georgian house. Now the Irish Government's official reception site for international visitors, following a dramatic history of Castletown being saved from developers by the Hon. Desmond Guinness, my research assists in the process of restoration, care and education about works in the House. It was an incremental but a significant step to take from making paper printed rooms to installing prints by pasting them on pre-existing walls and making models of these installations. While the historical research was important to me, linking it to contemporary art practice was also crucial and opened up an extended spatial practice. The adventurous and deliberate inclusion of contemporary prints by Lady Conolly in the eighteenth century mirrors my own challenge to keep the nature of my practice current, even though my research is also immersed in history.

Perhaps unusually, the argument in my rationale was set from the start, with a firm understanding as to how my research could contribute. I was less sure how my practice would proceed, so I allowed for a methodology to form as early historical and theoretical research was undertaken. The sourcing of historical references also informed aspects of my methodology. While my knowledge of printing processes were able to stretch back to the eighteenth century because the fine art print processes essentially hadn't changed, identifying who made the historical prints and where they were made and the decoding of iconography was far more complex. The work of the detective became an attractive one and proved to be a positive, if obsessive, mode of operating. The close connection of the eighteenth-century Irish and British aristocracy to France and Italy, as major stopping posts on their grand tour led me to making several extended visits back and forth to collections in France (Bibliothèque nationale de France), UK (Public Records Office N. Ireland, Belfast, British Library and British Museum, Victoria and Albert Museum print collection, Witt Collection in the Courtauld Institute of Art) as well as back to Dublin's collections of the National Gallery of Ireland, National Library and the Chester Beatty Library. Sustained searches in these collections generated impetus, especially as I progressively connected fragments of information and came to the realization that eventually you rightly become the world expert in your defined research area. While the concept of delivering new knowledge as a condition of achieving a PhD is a confronting one, I knew that I could re-find lost knowledge and re-contextualise historical material for new purposes and of course make new artworks in innovative modes, resonating with new-found knowledge. The notion of an original idea in relation to genius as a model is difficult for me to perceive as a possibility, but perhaps my resistance to such concepts drove me harder in searching out innovative practices and to make unique linkages of ideas and draw together diverse contexts. Lesley Duxbury and Elizabeth Grierson support my intent in *Thinking Through Practice*, their book laying out the issues of art projects for doctoral research. The publication also addresses the position of art projects in the context of PhD research as art doctorates began to proliferate in Australia:

> When Johnstone brings her first-hand and bibliographic-referenced knowledge of the Castletown print room together with an installation art practice, she is most certainly transcending previous references to both history and practice of print to present us with new and original representations that engage the viewer both physically and psychologically.[*]

Making prints on paper was my background practice, albeit on an architectural scale, as I commenced my doctoral research. And while I had also made prints

---
[*] Duxbury, L. & Grierson, E. (eds.). (2007). RMIT Publishing, Melbourne, p. 12

on a miniature scale, the extent of scale was much expanded as I developed work in the doctoral program. By 2003 my work trailed through four floors of the Temple Bar Gallery and Studio spaces. Being on site in advance with a studio residency confirmed a need to understand a space by experiencing that space day to day whilst making work for that space. The same consideration confirmed my need to take on the whole rear staircase and its three floors as well as weaving work through the entirety of the top floor of the Gossard Building at RMIT for my PhD examination presentation. The Gossard Building was considered a rather unsalubrious site by one of my examiners, in contrast to having exhibited with a solo exhibition at NGV (International) in 1998 as well as at Temple Bar Gallery and Studios as part of my PhD program. While there was a contrast of these prestigious installation sites against my chosen examination site, the key driver was still to fully comprehend the uniqueness of the space in which I was operating and to find enough space to install projects made over a period of six years.

Thanks to an RMIT post-graduate scholarship I was able to make the most of full-time research periods. Time away from work allowed for extended visits to the northern hemisphere to research collections and undertake artist residencies. At times working full-time gave me the opportunity to work on detailed documentation for extensive appendices, from 7 pm to midnight for a couple of years. The extra discipline of working on research after academic work hours with a small break in between was also good training and experience for balancing studio research with dissertation writing when I had every day available for my PhD research. It is easy to underestimate the time it takes to write up research and to refine writing. While many artists can fall in love with writing during the doctoral process it is usually not our first talent over visual acuity. Nonetheless for most candidates working on art projects, myself included, dedication to research can lead to publications of substance. My chapter 'Lady Louisa Conolly's Print Room' was published in the lavishly illustrated book *Castletown, Decorative Arts* (2011) and launched by the Taoiseach of Ireland.* Elizabeth Grierson and Lesley Duxbury (2007) in their Introduction to *Thinking Through Practice*, lay out the positioning of art research and its status in doctoral research:

---

* Elizabeth Mayes (ed.) (2011) OPW, Trim.

This way of thinking about research is not without its dissenters however. According to the principles that determine what research is, artist-researchers are not counted as 'legitimate' researchers because they have not produced, according to the DEST criteria, justifiable research outcomes. To date, the only measurable outcomes of research are textual publications such as books, book chapters, refereed journal articles and conference papers although this is slowly changing due to both internal and external pressures. Even within the academy, it has only recently been acknowledged that what is produced for the outcomes of a PhD by creative project does indeed fulfill the definitions of research according to DEST, especially the point that states: Any activity classified as research, which is characterised by originality; it should have investigation as a primary objective and should have the potential to produce results that are sufficiently general for humanity's stock of knowledge (theoretical and/or practical) to be recognisably increased.†

Nearly ten years on, despite a decade of successful PhD projects completed in art practice in Australia, little has changed in the acceptance of art's capacity to contribute new knowledge in University culture. The related pressure of chasing Government funding for further research with an appropriate publishing track record is still to be resolved. My observation of the acceptance of art projects as original research in academia is that it is in a retrograde phase. As an early PhD candidate in art practice, I felt I had to produce two PhDs, the equivalent of a written thesis as well as produce an extensive visual project. Ever more ubiquitous is the pressure to publish in top tier journals or publish books in academia. The prioritizing of word over image persists in University culture, but in my awareness of this, I also made sure that my visual projects were substantial in both scale and substance.

I kept a PhD work diary with daily log on and off times for most of my PhD, as a way of checking that I wasn't deluding myself that I was working hard. This was for no-one else's reference but for myself. Having a scholarship contract that allowed two weeks holiday for the year and 40 hours minimum

---

† Duxbury & Grierson. (2007), p. 9.

research per week was a clear indication of how seriously I should use my time. As new personal relationships developed during my research, having already established a rigorous working schedule, my work routine tended not to be impacted. Social activities were worked around my research objectives or people were co-opted into my research.

I attended many advice sessions on how to manage doctoral research. I tried software that captures bibliographic material for ease of retrieval, but ultimately once an electronic draft is formed, the most useful process for me is to print a hard copy for reworking text by overwriting by hand. Cut and paste processes also become very tactile. Once I had commenced writing, I explored various ways of constructing a dissertation. For example, I attempted to avoid all footnotes as a method for filtering out unnecessary information.* A parallel experimental process occurred in the studio through casting plaster of architectural detail and then deliberately smashing it to discover new ways of putting elements together. As a response to the densely packed iconography of eighteenth-century art, I attempted to withdraw as much recognizable imagery as possible and all metaphor from my prints. By contrast, in other phases of drafting text, my supervisor alerted me to the colouring of language use from the eighteenth century. No surprise really, as I was immersed in historical literature, manuscripts, art and architecture and was undertaking that research in libraries and sites of the same historical era. My writing style had always been rather convoluted and dense, so the stripping back and rebuilding my approach to writing and studio methodology was a valuable experience.

Waiting for months for overdue examiners' reports was a confronting aspect in the final stage of my PhD, contrasting markedly with a fully active engagement in my research process. The most memorable resonance I felt while in the embrace of my work was the realization that I had a great detective task – that I could and must travel across the world to search out original sources. Reading manuscripts in the British Library of the real-life character from the nursery rhyme Sing a Song of Sixpence 'the king was in his counting house counting all his money' (Lady Conolly and her sisters regularly helped King George III count his coins), chancing on prints amongst the many thousands in the Bibliothèque nationale de France that identified the key images in

---

* Of course footnotes reappeared later.

Lady Conolly's print room, with all the identification inscriptions intact. She had cut off authorship details in order to shape and frame elegantly edited prints for her wall arrangements. By making miniature architectural models I was connecting with the contrast of scale that Jonathan Swift had applied in *Gulliver's Travels*. We had also both fingered through the dusty books at Marsh's Library (he as a resident clergyman and myself as a reader) and made the same familiar journey to Celbridge (he to visit a friend nearly three centuries earlier, me to Castletown House nearby). I relished being addressed as a scholar by the keepers of historical libraries and was astounded by the quiet but intense research competitiveness of those rewarded with readers tickets.

Through the artificial lens of retrospectivity I would have avoided the temptation to keep refining my exegetical text to the submission deadline. I would set aside a generous amount of time for a recommended professional editor to work through the document and then plan for a further period for my final adjustments. While I sought out proof reading by disinterested parties, a professional editor familiar with art theory and practice would have removed some of the corrections that examiners often feel obliged to point out as part of their duty. While corrections assist in perfecting the archive, it is a distraction that takes away from the real task of assessing the contribution to culture. I saved a great deal of backtracking in my written documentation by acquiring a style guide early on. Finding the appropriate style guide is not easy, but one with extensive detail and examples is worth its weight in gold. Of course there is always more that can be done on text and there is an increasing pressure on the design of documentation given the growing sophistication of, and access to, design software.

My advice to prospective doctoral candidates is to find a profoundly intriguing project that will drive you for the duration of your candidature, one that can allow you to manoeuvre across media and concepts as, or when, necessary. There should be a genuine enquiry to pursue, a set of questions that do not already have answers. Towards the end of candidacy I recommend to arrange a month after completion of writing to have a professional editor check your dissertation before you submit it for examination. Examiners love to make themselves useful in correcting your spelling (less so your grammar) so while it may be useful diversion for them to make corrections it also takes away from the major job at hand, to confirm that you are successfully contributing to cultural knowledge.

Following the completion of my PhD and now just over a decade later I still have an unfortunate relationship with reading. Speed-reading and targeting particular detail in text has reshaped my reading processes, perhaps permanently. The pleasure of reading for its own sake is still to re-emerge. Happily, exhaustion at examination, to the point of delirium, passes. Adrenaline depletion can have a more permanent impact and some care needs to be taken in this regard. Establishing a keen and regular research routine early on may have benefitted me. While the task of aligning with appropriate supervisors is not always easy, ultimately I think that you have to own the project first and foremost. If supervisors can act as a sounding board for your own voice, perhaps that is all you can expect. Lengthy waiting for overdue examiner reports caused me some consternation. Examiners' list of suggestions for minor amendments in the form of typographical corrections tended to recklessly expand in my imagination, so I recommend repeated reading of the reports to assist in rationally preparing the final amendments for submission. In the end I found as many typographical errors that I wanted to correct as they did, and it is certainly a reasonable expectation, even for the highly articulate, to have to amend their dissertation before final lodgement.

I harbour some regret that I did not have the advantage of luxuriating in the completion of my PhD. Life took over; a prospect of a new artist studio-residence complex seemed timely, but absorbed any available time for reflection on my previous six years of doctoral research. However reworking text for various post-doctoral publications and readjusting and adding to artwork for new exhibition sites serves to extend the life of my research project. Often the post-doctoral stop is unfortunately forced through illness, out of exhaustion. If a post-PhD forced stop can be possible for reflection and celebration, then indulge in it.

References

Duxbury, L. & Grierson, E. (eds.). (2007). *Thinking Through Practice*. Melbourne: RMIT Publishing.

Mayes, E. (ed.). (2011). *Castletown, Decorative Arts*. Trim: OPW.

MAKING IT MATTER

Robin Kingston

*Title of study: The limiting conditions:
An investigation into intuitive and rational thought in the
construction of contemporary abstract painting*

RMIT University, 2008

Abstract

In Surrealism the role of the unconscious and the psychoanalytic was a rich source of imagery, usually figurative. Today more than ever the role of the intuition is dismissed, as it is in scientific terms unable to be quantified. However some artists refer to their intuition or subconscious as a rich source of strategies and imagery they employ, while constructing abstract paintings. It is at once process and content.

To contribute to the examination of abstract painting incorporating an investigation of the roles intuitive and rational thought is relevant at this time. In our technological and economically dominated society, an examination of the manufacture of abstract painting in relationship to its 'non-logical self'[*] incorporating non-technological issues such as the body, psychology and the unconscious is to present a balance to the former view. 'The non-logical self' is a term used by Eva Hesse when referring to subject matter of another order that she thought lay under the formal visual logic in her sculptures. 'The formal principles', Hesse wrote, 'are understandable and understood. It is the unknown quantity from which and where I want to go. As a thing, an object, it accedes into its non-logical self. It is something, it is nothing.'[†]

---

[*] Briony Fer (1997). *On Abstract Art*. Yale University Press, p. 112.
[†] Ibid. Quoted in Eva Hesse (1976). New York University Press.

Through the rise of installation art in the Twentieth Century, aspects of viewing and reading meaning in an image has affected content in contemporary abstract painting. The experiential response of the viewer has become of primary consideration. The painting's relationship to its site affects meaning, as paintings are no longer viewed as separate to the conditions of display. The experience of looking at a painting not only includes the visual, but also the body in relation to the artwork. By using strategies and structures from my earlier works and reusing in paintings both on and off the stretcher, in actual spaces and sites, I will contribute to and examine this dialogue.

My research is pertinent at this time, when Formal abstraction is such a familiar language, common within our society, used in everything from advertising to architecture. The importance of investigating the role of intuitive and rational thought in the construction of abstract painting will add to the meaning attributed to this visual language and reinvest it with the embodiment of humanness and the handmade rather than the historical view of a formal pictorial language and banality.

--

The decision to commence a PhD, was motivated in part by just how fruitful my previous Master of Fine Art degree had been to my understanding of my practice, enabling the contextualisation of my reading and of my painting and their relationship to the broader art world. In the MA the writing component of twenty thousand words gave voice to my studio research and methods, which centred on what I termed 'not knowing' and the intuitive. I found the reverberations continued for many years after completing the Masters both in my practice and in teaching. The philosophical, psychological, theoretical and art references considerably enhanced my experience going forward as it had been an opportunity to take stock of my understanding of art practice and a place to gather those findings in an objective and contextual manner. It had been an opportunity to focus in a way that studio practice alone had not delivered, a chance to work within and to stand outside and analyse my painting practice.

I had lived overseas for ten years after completing my first degree in

Australia. An opportunity to travel at nineteen had opened my understanding of how viewing art work unmediated by photography, secondary sources or someone else's interpretation could enhance my understanding of the complex activity of viewing work for myself. In a seminal experience of standing where the artist stood before the work, as though before the motif, it dawned on me the movements mental and physical that had made the work became critical to my understanding of the work and a glimpse into the artist's practice. At the time it was hard to put into words as to why this was so important to me. It just was. Looking back now, I know why. At the time I was following an intuitive impulse that was to become so important to me. Much of the art that I am interested in cannot be understood without the direct experience of the work. A photograph pictorializes the experiential. It does not describe the same experience of actually being in the presence of artworks. Standing in front of them, walking through the site of display, experiencing the scale, presence and nuances of the work. This issue became an important as I progressed through the PhD. The experiential became critical.

It was with these issues in mind the decision to undertake a PhD was taken in around 2001 in the unspoken but increasingly obvious climate within the university (my place of employment) that it was becoming mandatory to have one to teach. I also was mindful that the masters allowed me to gather much information in one place, including a long bibliography and how beneficial that had been. There was a sense of focus, and a reason to put it all in one place and examine motivations and underlying issues in my practice.

The decision to undertake my study at my place of employment was being acquainted with colleagues, I believed, would be suitable supervisors. I knew their areas of expertise far better than those of academics from other institutions and had observed them in their supervisions and successful completions. It was still quite early in the history of PhD supervision of visual arts candidates in Australia, so not many lecturers had the qualifications to supervise one. Having supervised masters for many years prior to embarking on my PhD and having a long history of acting as an examiner for Higher Degrees for multiple universities I felt capable to benchmark the standard and quality of supervision within the School of Art, RMIT. I gauged it to be excellent with a good track record of completions and suitable and sympathetic engagement between supervisors and candidates. Supervision and candidature is a two-way negotiation and at its best is a close and sensitive relationship. It is motivational, guiding, supportive and analytical. There are both internal and external processes to be navigated. In one word—complicated.

I undertook the PhD in part-time mode due to a full-time workload in my employment, so the journey was a long one. Six years, and I took an extra year in the form of a period of leave from the formal study. This was used to pull the focus together and to concentrate on the writing in a manner that had been impossible during the previous years. It had been hard to hold the focus working full-time, so the leave of absence from study relieved the pressure somewhat and allowed me to take stock of my findings. The School of Art was very supportive allowing me three months replacement teaching to complete my PhD at a critical time in my final year. I could not have completed without this time away from teaching.

Working full-time as a painting lecturer at RMIT and completing a PhD, especially over a long period of time in part-time mode was difficult, but rewarding. The one research day a week and the weekends became critical and every evening, though tired I felt the pressure to create and analyse and to keep the threads of the study together.

I devised an unwritten, informal plan as the PhD progressed of how to use my time fruitfully. I had a very young son, a husband and two hounds to consider. After embarking on the period of study, cooking, gardening and walking the dogs, all activities I enjoyed came with a layer of guilt. I felt I should be spending all my time engaged with the PhD and what did that mean regarding my personal life and activities? It was something I learned to negotiate and to sort out just how important those activities were to my practice, so in many ways the PhD had profound findings not only for my practice, but also for my personal life and that of an artist. Early on there was the constant pressure (self-imposed) as study is a serious endeavour and I wanted it to be meaningful to me, and the time well spent. It was a privilege to have this opportunity and it was not to be squandered. I had colleagues who had withdrawn from their PhD candidature, as they could not properly address their study because of work commitments interfering with their focus. The constant pressure was not an issue I discussed even with my family or my supervisors. It seemed petty though on reflection it was important. I internalised it and there was the realisation I had to use my time judiciously.

As my research progressed, my focussed reading and investigation of artwork and artists enhanced my teaching conversations at work with students. This thread of investigation has always been a source of inspiration in my practice and life and every trip back to New York yielded interesting issues on which to elaborate that were directly influential to the PhD. For example, the exhibition of Richard Tuttle (2004) and a Tantric Drawing exhibition (2004), two of the important exhibitions the then director of The Drawing Center Catherine de Zegher curated. I came to find her writing and thinking critical to framing and voicing my research. She was able to put into words and to highlight intangible, tangential and ephemeral concepts directly related to arts practice that were definitely not concrete, but were there to be experienced. She spoke about the making and the reading of artwork and also championed an artist I had discovered in 1989 to my delight at PS1, when living in New York–Hilma af Klint, a little known Swedish artist who was making abstract paintings in 1908 based on ideas of Theology. De Zegher's writings encouraged me to believe one could write about difficult conceptual and experiential issues and elaborate authoritatively on the in between spaces of making and understanding. What happens in the studio, the making, is an introspective activity and it is hard to find the words to articulate this deep thinking in a way that can be understood and made manifest by the reader. De Zegher was able to do this in a poetic and articulate manner that allowed those processes to live. The PhD allowed for a bracketing or a focus for my investigations, which are far-reaching and tangential as my interests are broad. One never knows exactly what is going to be important. A sense of enquiry and finding out is crucial to the way I go about much in my life.

Working out the voice in the writing was important. I did not want the writing to be a dry academic document. It needed to be useful and meaningful to me, and reader friendly. It became vital that the exegesis mimicked what was happening in the studio, the methods and the content and that there was a flow and a coming together of the understandings that reflected the experiential nature of the studio. The studio in my practice is a place where one thing leads to another and the strategy of working in a not knowing way or doing it to find out way of working takes precedence. The relationship between the writing and the studio was that the artwork and findings were not an illustration of the exegesis. The writing was another form of understanding, that of contextualising the practice, which ran parallel to the studio practice and research. It gave voice in another form to the studio research and it was difficult as I was trying to give voice to very subtle intangibles, issues that were difficult to describe in words, attention to detail that came through discovery and the experiential. Philosophers and artists' thinking and writing became crucial as a way to elaborate on and to give validity to my findings so they could be understood as more than subjective. There was a broader context for my thinking and practice and I evidenced it.

I do not think like an academic (or the trope I suppose one is) or write like one. I am a painter and write as such. I make and I understand through the making. It is experiential in the first instance and this builds knowledge and understanding. The issues I discover through the making are then built upon as the work progresses. The issues I discussed in my PhD are relevant to the field and I can speak in a knowledgeable and erudite manner about them. The PhD made me think about how I wanted my voice to be perceived. I knew from past experience when I spoke on panels, or gave lectures about my practice to masters candidates, I received great feedback from the audience about what I had to say and to my approach. Many of the audience were my peers and they had invited me to speak. There had been a connection and a resonance and identification with issues I raised and interest in my experience. I had learned to trust that feedback as very valuable and an indication of my worth. It gave me confidence that I may be able to make my ideas coherent through writing.

Every artwork I examined within the PhD was experienced either whilst I lived in New York or on my annual visits back there when conducting the New York Study Tour. As mentioned previously this element to the research was vital – that the artwork was unmediated and I was able to bring to the writing an understanding of the experiential nature of the encounter. During the time of living in and visiting New York during the PhD it became increasingly obvious to me why I needed to be there. It was the vastness of the art world, both historical and contemporary and the breadth and depth to which one was able to study directly from the artworks unmediated.

Creativity is a difficult beast and doubt and attentiveness crucial elements. As I began to read and collect citations for the text I kept notes in a specific spiral bound journal and by the end of the study there were a number of them. It became a way I could keep the writing and studio findings and even the activities and the procedural notes regarding the PhD in one place. Each was numbered and dated and I wrote from the beginning of candidature–vague musings and notes on findings in the studio, things to do as well as judicious citations that had what I thought were accurate notations of sources. (I say this as at least one, and of course a vital one caused me much grief at the end as I could not find the original source and was in danger of having to leave it out. Thankfully it was found, but not without a great investment of time and angst. Note to oneself and to candidates: keep very accurate citation notes as over the period of candidature recollections become hazy. There is just too much information and time that passes.) I had attended workshops on how to use Endnote, but due to work commitments was unable to learn it sufficiently well to enable its use in my candidature. Others have and it is recommended.

In these spiral notebooks I made hand written notes from my reading. Writing by hand helps me to understand. I had no idea as to the validity of this fact in the broader sense (and much has now been written about the use of cursive writing) but I knew from past experience that for comprehension of difficult ideas that if I physically wrote out the information I somehow retained and understood it. Personally, even the use of the computer does not help in this activity. It has to be done the old way – with pen and paper.

I found that as I continued to research and nearing the end of the PhD that many of the footnotes and even in the body of the text that writings referred to other books I had read on the topic, or artists I was looking at. The texts either referred to a common source or were quoting each other. My research became cyclical. When I remarked about this finding to a colleague he suggested that if this was happening you were becoming a bit of an expert in the area as all the research seemed to be coming together and reflecting ideas in each other. The research/circle was becoming smaller as you start off your candidature with a wide pool that you are examining and it becomes more and more focussed as you frame your area of interest.

As the research developed I realised walking and play were vital issues within my practice and also in shifting ideas and my understanding. Play or what I call play has always been an important motivator in the studio. It gives me permission. Permission to go further than what I know. Walking the dogs daily was, and still is motivational. It cleared my head and allowed me to actively think. Movement shifts ideas and lets thoughts co-mingle and develop. As the candidature reached conclusion and in the period after I realised activities I had thought to be side issues and time takers away from study to be front and centre of my study and artwork. They enabled them. Life is not aside from art. It is part of it. These activities including walking grounded me and enabled understandings.

At the conclusion of candidature, the selection of examiners by supervisors is critical to the examination and successful conclusion. At the time of my completion it was an early time of visual artists having completed a PhD in Australia. This meant there was not large numbers of Australian artists who had the qualifications to examine one. Even how to do a PhD was in flux. There was the emergence at this time of a few collections of writings from academics about the topic of producing a PhD within arts practice with titles such as Practice as Research setting forth methodologies that were deemed adequate on how to identify or frame a research enquiry or how to engage in critical reflection at this level of research. Some used almost a scientific method to analyse and outline what was happening in the studio and the findings thereof. Some of these collections were about how meaning and matter relate in the context of art making and education. There are many ways of analysing findings from studio research and visual practice and in introducing the examiners to the project it behoves the candidate to set forth the conditions for framing the research and the findings. I had done this. My project and analysis was broader and more poetic examination, one that could be called an eisegesis which was more subjective and diaristic, and firmly contextualising my practice and findings in the studio within the broader art world, philosophy and ideas.

I did not have a smooth examination. One examiner had no problem with my project and the other wanted major revisions to the exegesis. The exegesis was referred to as a thesis and two lines of a six-page report addressed the studio project and the practice lead research. It seemed that I was examined not on what I had set out to research, but on what I should have researched.

As the third examiner needed to be engaged, the Higher Degree authority within the university thought it was satisfactory for me to submit photographs of the exhibition for the re-examination. As my artwork is and the project was experiential and photographs are simply pictures, the Head of Higher Degrees within the School of Art was able to put forward the case for me to resubmit by making another spatial artwork. My findings were in the form of painting directly on the walls of a site making an interactive artwork that was experiential and therefore needed to be experienced in person. I was asked if I could resubmit in two months. Impossible, as the work takes form and planning takes longer. I worked on the ideas over a period of time and know what the first move or strategy is to be and everything is relational to that first painting strategy.

The second examination was six months after the first and I was heartened by the reports when they came through at how perceptive the third examiner had been. I used examiner one's report and examiner three's report to refute examiner two's report. The rules of the university deemed I had to respond to all three. In my time previous to my examination as a supervisor I had only known of one other re-examination of a PhD and as there were careful processes to ensure a candidate is ready for examination and I had complied. On reflection it was a galling experience and I wondered if I had not had been as experienced an artist what an effect it would have had on my arts practice? Was what was said relevant? What if any reflection was applicable to the art school, or me or the examiner who seemed not to understand my project? The reactions of my colleagues and my supervisors gave me great support and when I bumped into the final examiner in New York the following year they asked what had transpired to have them invited to examine. After I had explained what I understood, they suggested that that was why it was important that artists such as myself had a PhD, so practitioners were examining practitioners.

On conclusion of this reflection on my period of candidature, I discovered a printed copy of an email from a student who was writing about her practice. I had tucked it away in the hard copy of my Durable Visual Record submitted for Research Repository. This student had been sitting at home reading my PhD regretting she had not had access to it earlier–nodding and muttering out aloud in agreement with what she was discovering within the pages. The student sent the correspondence to thank me as she realised my PhD illuminated how to engage in the translation of the complexity of visual practice into meaningful writing and acknowledged just how much it had helped her.*

When I began my candidature the requirement was three hard copies of the Durable Visual Record—one for the university, one for the school and one for me. By the end there was the requirement to submit it to the Research Repository so it could be viewed on the World Wide Web. This made me very uncomfortable as it was not written with this platform in mind and I am a painter, not a writer and the bulk of my candidature was studio based, and the work did not reproduce well in photographs as I have explained earlier. The work is experiential.

Eventually I was persuaded by a colleague to submit my PhD to the Research Repository at RMIT so it could be viewed on the web. They had been circulating with my permission a digital version to their Masters by Coursework candidates as an example of writing about visual art practice that made sense regarding tangible and intangible issues and enabled the candidates to believe they could write about theirs also. It gave them permission to find their voice and to trust it.

To date my PhD has been downloaded from the Research Repository 523 times since mid-2012. I hope it has been of use as it illuminated much for me, and despite the difficulties, was more than worthwhile.

---

* Gasteen (2013), pers. Comm., 20 June.

DOCTORAL RESEARCH AROUND SLAPSTICK TACTICS

Laresa Kosloff

Title of study: Slapstick tactics:
Staging a performance of video in contemporary video art

RMIT University, 2011

Abstract

This research project explores propositional similarities between early cinematic slapstick of the silent era, and examples of contemporary video art that feature the performing body. Films made by Charlie Chaplin and Buster Keaton are analysed and formulated into a 'slapstick methodology', which has been tested and applied in my own art video art practice. Contemporary video works by Bruce Nauman, Kate Gilmore, Robin Rhode, Bas Jan Ader, Francis Alÿs and others are used to support my claim that slapstick manifests as a method of approach in video art. It is argued that despite different time frames, contexts and intentions, early slapstick films and contemporary video art employ corresponding techniques involving comic humour, expressive physicality, ironic perspectives and the virtual properties of the moving image.

These methods are examined in relation to Laleen Jayamanne's (2001) claim that Chaplin and Keaton stage a 'performance of mimesis' in their films (p.181). This observation structures and informs the research premise; that slapstick methods are self-reflexive in approach, and that these techniques are employed to highlight and expose representational function in my own video artworks. Critics and theorists such as Thomas McEvilley, Michel de Certeau, Lisa Trahair, Gunter Gebauer and Christoph Wulf, Walter Benjamin, Griselda Pollock, Henri Bergson and Sigmund Freud inform this study, particularly in relation to concepts of mimesis and performativity. The exegesis outlines the practical and conceptual implementation of slapstick methods throughout my candidature, and provides a critical context for considering these ideas.

--

I have worked as a lecturer in various art schools for close to fourteen years and exhibited my work continuously since graduating from RMIT University School of Art in 1995. During that time I have developed a broad skill set as a practicing artist, from plastering walls to digital video editing. I have cultivated ways of working in the studio that enable instinctual and acquired knowledge to develop into new creative forms. Academic writing does not tend to feature in this process. I daydream, take notes, draw, play with materials, film myself doing things, research artists and theorists, talk to other artists and work very hard to try new and interesting things. I rarely write before making an artwork, with the exception of a broad pitch for a funding application. This chapter outlines my experience of undertaking a PhD at Monash University and RMIT University, and the impact (both positive and negative) that this has had on my art practice and teaching career.

I started my Master's degree at Monash University in 2008 and upgraded to a PhD in 2010 before transferring my candidature to RMIT University. I chose Monash University because I was working there at the time and a Professor indicated that I had a good chance of getting a Postgraduate scholarship. My incentive for doing a PhD was largely motivated by the lure of a scholarship to end the poverty trap that I was in as an artist and a sense that I might need a PhD to secure fixed employment as a lecturer later on. I did not choose to undertake postgraduate study for the sake of my art practice, as I was busy with projects at the time and not particularly interested in an academic context for my work.

It was unusual for artists to undertake PhDs around this time; in fact postgraduate study seemed to have a negative stigma as something that was too academic and stifling for artists. Consequently I rarely mentioned my PhD candidature to industry professionals, in case they presumed that I wasn't properly committed to my art practice. Thankfully that stigma no longer exists and some of Australia's better-known artists have completed doctorates in recent years. These PhDs provide fascinating insights into current methodologies in art, both locally and internationally.

Like many PhD programs in art schools around 2008, Monash University was relatively unstructured in their approach. I attended a vaguely relevant research methods class and gave a one-hour presentation as part of the PhD upgrade process. I had two supervisor meetings within a two-year period, one of which was ten minutes long. I never went through an ethics process despite the fact that people feature in my video works. I was largely left to my own devices with very little sense of what a PhD was or how to go about it.

I mention this experience reluctantly because it was symptomatic of the times and Monash now run an excellent PhD program. Monash had a rigorous undergraduate program but was still in the process of working out how to accommodate contemporary art as a doctorate degree. Most of the staff didn't have PhDs and therefore couldn't relate to the process, despite being terrific lecturers and practicing artists.

The PhD upgrade process was relatively straightforward and I submitted a 3,000 word essay about my research and gave a public presentation on my work. I was not required to submit a detailed proposal at the commencement of my PhD. This suited me, as I was able to build content over time and to uncover my findings through the artworks that I produced. Had I produced a detailed proposal at the beginning of my candidature I think that I would have ended up with a less creative topic. Intensive reading and studio time nourished my research during the first two years and it was only later on that I developed a framing argument for my PhD.

In terms of the development of my topic, I started by researching the things that I was interested in, mainly feminist perspectives on modernism and cinematic slapstick of the silent era. These topics seemed quite disparate, however I trusted that there must be a connection between them as they resonated with me and were evident in my own video works. I absorbed new concepts through reading and synthesised these insights into new artworks. The artworks that I produced steered the direction of my PhD, which became a study of slapstick methodologies in performative video art.

By gradually cultivating my topic I was able to develop a project that sustained and interested me. My artworks informed the research topic, as opposed to producing outcomes at the service of a written proposal. This allowed me to capitalise on the intuitive skills that I have developed as an artist including drawing, collecting imagery and enacting playful gestures in front of a video camera. These activities helped me to cultivate new forms and surprising content. My best thinking happens in the studio and so it was important to not privilege written analysis too early on in my candidature.

The large amount of reading that I did was positively enlightening and inspiring. The best moments of my PhD occurred when there was a synthesis between this reading and the artworks that I produced. Sometimes I was able to draw parallels between a pertinent text and one of my artworks, and sometimes I produced new artworks to explore particular concepts. It was fascinating to theorise my interests on a deeper level and to generate new methodologies within my art practice. I continue to creatively draw upon these findings to this day.

A creative synthesis also occurred through other influences, primarily video artworks and silent slapstick films. I had always revered early cinematic slapstick but did not understand the reasons why. It was a turning point within my PhD to find a book that analysed slapstick in relation to theories of mimesis. This book enabled me to explore slapstick as methodology (as opposed to a genre) and to understand the deeper significance of its influence within contemporary art.

These discoveries affected my art practice in terms of connecting me with philosophy and broader histories. I produced a lot of artwork during my PhD but the real benefits of postgraduate study manifested later on in my art practice. A few years after the completion of my PhD I noticed a development in terms of testing new mediums (sculpture and live performance) and having greater confidence in my underlying content. Postgraduate study refreshed my art practice and stopped me from becoming repetitive, as can happen to mid-career artists. Interestingly these developments occurred once my PhD was finished, as I felt free to experiment beyond an academic context and I also had more studio time to develop new projects. The legacy of postgraduate study has been a greater capacity to conceptualise my ideas and to try new things out.

Around two years into my candidature I realised that I would need more supervisor input to finish my exegesis. I had produced a large number of artworks and tested these through exhibitions. I received most of my critical feedback through external means including press reviews, catalogue essays and peer feedback. When it came to formulating my findings into a coherent exegesis I knew that I would need more academic support.

I had recently taken up a teaching position at RMIT University at the time and so I spoke to my line manager about needing more academic support. I was impressed by our conversation and asked him whether he would be prepared to supervise me. He agreed and I transferred my candidature across to RMIT in 2010.

Having my boss as my PhD supervisor was both convenient and inconvenient. It was convenient in the sense that we could have informal conversations on a regular basis. It was inconvenient in that I felt that I had to hide any difficulties for fear of seeming incompetent. Overall we had a very good rapport and he offered key insights along the way that had a positive impact. I had a second supervisor assigned to me however we never met up. This was not an issue as I felt that I had enough input from my first supervisor to complete my PhD.

During the final year of my PhD I wrote exclusively and did not produce any new artworks. This was difficult as I missed making art and had to say no to several opportunities. I found writing incredibly slow and wondered how I could spend a whole day at my computer and only produce a few sentences. Research leave was not available and I regularly woke up at 5am to work on my writing before a full day of teaching.

One of the most difficult aspects of producing an exegesis was the level of detail required in terms of contextualising my creative decisions. For example, I laboured over a chapter about the video medium despite the fact that this had been part of my art practice for over sixteen years. On the one hand this led to rigorous analysis as everything was questioned anew. On the other hand it was tedious to explain myself in written form when the results should have been evident in the artworks themselves.

In retrospect I can say that doing a PhD was a valuable and useful experience. It was also difficult in terms of compromising my studio time. This was largely to do with having to develop a written argument for my work, which I found painstakingly slow. Artworks provide a unique encounter that is primarily not language based. A PhD exegesis is separate to this and yet related. At times I felt like I was doing two PhDs, one in visual form and the other as text. These required different skill sets. I had to cultivate playful and intuitive thinking for the artworks whereas the exegesis required a more methodical approach. Both outcomes explore the same findings, however in different form.

The benefits of writing an exegesis became more evident over time. I found that I was able to write better artist statements and applications, which contributed to new opportunities. It also improved my lecturing skills, as I had more information at hand and could articulate concepts more efficiently. There were positive psychological benefits in terms of persisting with something that was difficult and experiencing a sense of achievement at the end.

The requirements of a PhD and how you might go about it are much clearer to me in retrospect. The timing of research activities is not just a pragmatic thing; it can directly affect the outcomes. Formulating a project too quickly can restrict creative scope, and conversely procrastinating with the exegesis can limit opportunities to refine the project.

As a PhD supervisor, I continually meet with candidates who misapprehend what a PhD is. They often neglect to write about their own work, thinking that the exegesis should be about other theorists or artists. They are sometimes very caught up in their defined topic, which can cause them to produce artwork in a prescriptive rather than responsive way. More often than not they find writing arduous and limiting in comparison with making art, which is their primary means of expression. Undertaking a PhD is an opportunity to develop new skills and critical insights. Conversely artists need to value the uniqueness of studio practice and to trust the rigour of their processes, even if these feel ad hoc compared with academic study.

It is impossible to start a PhD with the knowledge that you have at the end, and therefore it's difficult to say what I would do differently other than not worry quite so much. It's a good idea to keep track of pertinent references and quotes as you find them, including page numbers. Seek help in a timely manner – your supervisors should be working for you. It's also useful to think of a PhD as one large project rather than a life's work. There is life beyond it ...

References

Trahair, L. (2007). *The comedy of philosophy: Sense and nonsense in early cinematic slaptsick.* Albany, NY: State University of New York Press.

THE HEROINE OF THIS STORY IS ME

Keely Macarow

Title of study: Disturbance: Bodies. Disease. Art
The University of Melbourne, 2006

Abstract

Disturbance to the body through the onset of disease is for the most part, neither called for, nor welcomed. On the whole, people prefer to be in good health and to remain disease-free. The advent of disease disturbs the course and expectations of our lives and what we can achieve. For these reasons, disease is a vexing political, biomedical and personal experience.

This thesis explores the body and agency of people affected by HIV/AIDS and cancer in film, video and photographic works produced from 1961–2004, by artists' and activists based in the United States, the United Kingdom, Canada, France, South Africa and Australia. The research considers how artists responded to their experiences with HIV and cancer to make sense of what it is like to live with these conditions. For instance, whilst people affected by HIV and cancer share commonalities, their lived experience varies as a result of their cultural, racial, gendered, sexual and economic backgrounds. As such, the research probed territory generally presented as discreet and separate through examining work produced by artists living with HIV/AIDS and cancer, and by exploring the cultural analysis, activity and production that these immune disorders have inspired. As a result, the research reveals how the bodies of people living with HIV and cancer are as marked by the cultural conditions that they reside, as they are by the disease that affects their corporeality. Here, the representation and performance of the diseased body is central to many artworks examined in this thesis.

Embedded into the research is the notion of disturbance and dialogue – as a manifestation of disease and as conceptual and political strategies that artists affected by HIV and cancer used to make artworks about living with, or dying from these conditions. In turn, many of the artists who I discussed chose to use the disruption to the body and the legacy that illness has had on their life as the focus of their work. For instance, I examined bodies that dehydrate, bloat, become constipated, have sex, become weak and literally shit themselves away. Thus, the disturbance to the healthy functioning of the body provided an artistic and cultural framework to consider personal and political outcomes of disease. However, not all illness narratives lead to positive and empowered outcomes. While many of the disease narratives discussed in this PhD contain resilience and power, they also reveal emotional and physical ramifications of chronic illness. As such, this research bears witness to the stigmas, anxiety and functions of ill and diseased bodies, and their relation to the body politic.

--

There is no better hero of a story than the writer himself and there's no better authority on a disease than the diseased.
Bordowitz, 2000, p. 65

In 1994, I was diagnosed with malignant melanoma, my mother was diagnosed with bowel cancer and I lost two friends to HIV related illnesses. It was one of those life-changing years that shaped my life and marked my body for years to come.

As a filmmaker interested in art and political activism, I turned to the work of other artists and activists to make sense of my situation. I discovered a plethora of artworks, cultural debates, conversation and activism regarding HIV/AIDS but not as many cultural responses and activism around cancer. Through watching films and videos, viewing artworks, listening to music, attending forums and meetings, reading literature (novels, theory, memoirs, journalism and medical articles) I discovered that there were many commonalities but also many differences to the lived and political experience of HIV/AIDS and cancer.

However, I did not find anything that elucidated and aligned these illnesses together except for Susan Sontag's illuminating texts, *Illness as Metaphor* and *AIDS and Its Metaphors* (1991), which I found very inspiring.

> In *Illness as Metaphor* (1978) and *AIDS and Its Metaphors* (1992) the late Susan Sontag examined illness as a condition inscribed with religious, cultural, sexual, gendered and militaristic metaphors. Such use of metaphor has laden cancer with meanings that could be seen as counter productive to the healing process. (Macarow, 2007, p. 36)

Sontag's books literally changed my life as I decided to apply for a PhD to write my own text about HIV/AIDS and cancer. Whilst I was inspired by Sontag's work, I had not found the book I wanted to read. As a result, I decided to research the area through doctoral study so that I could source the material I needed to grapple with and make a contribution to the discourse I found useful during the years that followed my cancer diagnosis.

I applied for a PhD at The University of Melbourne in 2000 and was accepted as a doctoral candidate into the School of Art History, Cinema, Classics & Archaeology. I decided on The University of Melbourne for pragmatic reasons. I lived close by, which was important, as my son was two years old when I commenced as a mature age student and working mother. The university had an excellent international reputation, and I thought that this would be useful for securing employment and other opportunities once I had completed my PhD. I enquired about two other universities but decided to take up an offer from The University of Melbourne due to its resources, location and reputation. My supervisors' expertise was in Cinema Studies, Art History and Cultural Studies.

As I moved through my study, I became aware that I needed a supervisor who could provide guidance and support with the medical orientation of my research because I did not want to have any omissions and gaps in the thesis. I worked in media arts and film and video and was educated in these areas. I did not have a medical background and realised that a failing of my thesis would be my lack of knowledge of medical epidemiology and the issues and aetiology of HIV/AIDS and cancer. After a year and half into my candidature I changed to two new supervisors: a lecturer based in Cinema Studies, and a medical anthropologist who was the Director of the Key Centre for Women's Health. My PhD solidified as I progressed through the research, found my voice and changed supervisors.

Deciding on the topic was easy as it came from a deep yearning. I had a personal investment in the research because of my need to read a text which explored the lived experiences of people affected by HIV/AIDS and cancer through an interrogation of art, medicine and politics. My investigation crossed a number of mediums and disciplines: fiction, film, video, photography, painting, installation, cultural and medical theory, economics, epidemiology and medical anthropology. It covered the narratives, artefacts and political agency of people residing in the United States, the United Kingdom, Canada, France, South Africa and Australia.

I am not sure that my topic changed much as my study progressed. However, I framed the scope of my investigation in a tighter, robust and clearer framework as I worked through the research. For instance, it was important that I understood and engaged with cultural and medical discourse to be effective with my investigation. This was no small feat. Through my research study, I learnt the language of medicine and how to read and discuss statistics. I used medical anthropology to understand the lived experience and corporeal signs of people living with HIV and cancer. I still turn to statistics to present evidence and to provide substance for my research. My PhD training in medical anthropology gave me experience in ethnographic research and an understanding of the signs and culture of disease.

Understanding medical literature and discourse has continued to be useful to projects that I have worked on since completing my PhD. I have moved from examining the representation and etiology of disease to working on collaborative interdisciplinary projects which seek artistic and design applications and solutions for healthcare environments. These projects are inspired and informed by my PhD research, which was in turn influenced by my personal experiences with cancer and the death of friends due to AIDS related conditions. It is no surprise that my PhD is in fact my autobiography, although it is only briefly autobiographical:

> At the start of 1994 I was diagnosed with malignant melanoma, which is a particularly virulent skin cancer unless surgically removed

in its early stages. In the same year, two friends died from Human Immunodeficiency Virus (HIV) related illnesses and my mother was diagnosed with bowel cancer. I spent the following year searching for texts that examined the cultural construction and representation of HIV/AIDS (Acquired Immune Disorder Syndrome) and cancer to provide an insight into my family's experience with cancer, and my friend's experiences with HIV and AIDS. I wondered whether activists working around issues connected with HIV/AIDS and cancer shared common objectives and whether people living with HIV and cancer had similar narratives. (Macarow, 2006, p. 2)

The methodology for my research was determined fairly early into my candidature as my PhD was by thesis. My methodology was very much based around my literature review, which was broad as I examined a diverse range of artefacts from feature films, short independent films, experimental film, video documentary, video art, photography, installation, novels, paintings, music, brochures and PowerPoint presentations for my research. My methods were very much led by my research, as I did not have to submit a methodology prior to commencing my candidature. Instead my research enquiries led me from one clue to another similar to a forensic scientist.

The first year of doctoral research was wonderful. I read texts, examined artworks, watched films and videos, listened to music, went to seminars, visited libraries, consulted my supervisors, wrote notes and a first chapter (which was later ditched). My investigation was iterative, with my exploration leading to materials and people that would reveal new ideas and challenges for my examination. Not surprisingly, I always encourage my doctoral students to relish the early stages of their PhDs. In the beginning of my PhD, the territory that I scanned was quite broad but became focused as I framed the research. However, I was always very clear on what I wanted to research for the PhD, and determined that my voice would be central. I was not interested in using what I considered fashionable theorists (quite often dead white male philosophers) to base my argument. Instead it was the artists and activists who were my guides and heroes, including the American artist, Gregg Bordowitz who I cited at the start of this chapter.

I note the contradiction of challenging the use of often cited philosophers who are male, European and long passed, given that my thesis explored the work of many artists and writers who were male and had died due to AIDS related conditions or cancer. The point I am making is that many doctoral students and researchers use the work of continental philosophers to give leverage to their scholarship because they believe it is the correct thing to do as a scholar. I am of the view that the author's own voice is crucial to their writing and that it does not need to be constantly interrupted by the inclusion of a small coterie of what I deem dead white male philosophers. I realize some may take offence at this and acknowledge the value of the likes of Foucault, Deleuze and Heidegger. However, it is important to locate and amplify one's own voice in our writing and to converse with the people that are relevant and inform and inspire your research. It is important to be bold and find our own community of practice in order to make distinct and original contributions to knowledge.

Some time into my research, I received ethics clearance to interview artists and AIDS and cancer activists for my PhD. In the end I only interviewed three people for my PhD. One was a high-profile artist/writer who was well known for his AIDS activism. I also interviewed two women about their experiences with breast cancer, including a Canadian artist and the Melbourne-based National Coordinator of the Breast Cancer Network Australia. My initiation into ethics proved to be very difficult as the University ethics committee's response to my ethics application and request to interview AIDS and cancer activists and artists was initially misunderstood and dismissed. However, this experience gave me insight into the little understanding that many University ethics committees have of artistic and creative practice research, which I have since championed for many years with my own research students and through my research leadership roles. In the end I received ethics clearance, but it was a lot of work and very stressful.

In 2003 I undertook fieldwork in the USA where I conducted research about artists' video in the distribution organisations, Electronic Arts Intermix (NYC) and Video Data Bank (Chicago) and of photographic, visual and installation works located in the archive at Visual AIDS (NYC) and in the collection at Ronald Feldman Gallery (NYC). It is very important for researchers to consult primary resources as much as they can and especially when they are studying PhDs.

My research in New York and Chicago proved very useful for my PhD and a great initiation into these two wonderful cities. I made two field research trips to South Africa in 2007 and 2008 to follow up the research that I conducted for my PhD about South African artists and activists response to the enormous challenge of HIV/AIDS in the African continent and in South Africa. Whilst it may seem odd to interview people and organisations that you discuss in your PhD in the years after completion, it turned out to be exhilarating. I met people I admired from my PhD research and spoke with them with more confidence and understanding than I would have done whilst I was studying. I also adapted text from my PhD into book chapters which were published after my completion.

The writing of a thesis is regarded as a traditional research activity but it should also be considered as an exercise in improving a candidate's writing. I am very grateful for the difference the PhD has made to my writing, which improved over the course of my study due to the sustained feedback from my supervisors and my own practice and interest in the art of writing. My expertise in editing my text extended through the writing of my PhD. Through much hard work I developed skills in recognizing over long sentences – the curse of the PhD candidate. I am at pains to share this skill with my doctoral students as they write their dissertations to provide context to the artworks that they have created for their PhDs. It was important for the prose to be fluid and graceful in my thesis because I wrote about the challenge people have to find the words to express their thoughts and responses to those living with and affected by illnesses such as HIV and cancer:

> … we do not always have the power of speech to communicate how we feel when we hear of someone's diagnosis, decline in health or passing. Sometimes our use of language is awkward, when we try to discuss the lives and deaths of others. Words in this instance may fail us and we may be at a loss to offer our empathy or condolences. We may stumble as we try to convey our sorrow or our confusion at the plight of others. In the end we may offer little, because we cannot find the right words to

> express our feelings about illness and death. We may try to articulate our feelings about disease and dying, but unless we are clear and confident with our speech, we may try to avoid such discussions, preferring to cut conversations about these matters short, to move onto the next topic. If it is difficult to talk about disease, imagine living with it. (Macarow, 2006, pp. 200–1)

I lectured for half a day a week in the Visual Arts/New Media TAFE Department at Swinburne University and was the artistic director of Experimenta when I commenced my PhD in 2000. My Experimenta position was a three days per week intensive high profile role. This ostensibly meant that I was remunerated for part-time work, but contributed much more time to the role, which is not unusual for small arts organisations. My task was to set the artistic direction and to curate the program of exhibitions, screenings, performances and talks, and edit publications for the Melbourne-based media arts organisation. I also had to co-write funding applications, work with the Board of Management, external partners and coordinate our artists.

The first major project I curated for Experimenta was *Viruses and Mutations* (Macarow, 1998), which included an exhibition located at Melbourne's St Vincent's Hospital and a conference program at the Cinemedia @ Treasury Theatre (now the Australian Centre for the Moving Image). The project explored the intersection between art, technology and biotechnology and was presented in the 1998 Melbourne International Arts Festival Visual Arts program. This project included artworks and a conference program, which explored issues concerned with HIV, cancer, the human genome project and the ethics of genetic engineering amongst many other topical concerns related to biomedicine. The project was also inspired by my interest in cancer and HIV/AIDS, and was presented prior to my realization that I could research this area in a more intensive fashion through undertaking a PhD.

I had a very young son who was two years old when I commenced my PhD. I resigned from Experimenta in 2000 during the first few months of my study, because I soon realized that would not be able to juggle my two jobs with fulltime study and motherhood. I continued with my sessional teaching and was fortunate to be offered another two days a week casual teaching in the

Media Arts undergraduate program at RMIT University. Through the course of my studies, my employment conditions and teaching changed somewhat. In the beginning, I worked as a sessional lecturer before being appointed to a 0.4 and then 0.7 fraction post.

By the end of my PhD I had a full-time position at RMIT University and had long resigned from my casual work at Swinburne University. While I was studying and teaching, I also continued to work as a curator on media art projects collaborating with the Centre for Contemporary Photography (Melbourne), Chunky Move dance company (Melbourne) and the Video Data Bank and the School of the Art Institute of Chicago (US) on screening, web and installation projects. Prior to completing my PhD I developed an audio vision performance project with Media Art colleagues, Philip Samartzis and Philip Brophy. *Northern Void* was premiered at the Australian Centre for the Moving Image (Melbourne, 2007) after I completed my PhD but I remember the stress of completing my final draft of my PhD while I submitted funding applications for this project.

My PhD and curatorial projects were quite different as my thesis was based on artistic responses to disease and my curatorial projects focused on experimental film, video and sound projects which explored digital materiality, and the relationship between audio and vision. If I was more alert to this, I may have run things differently and combined the subject matter of my thesis with my curatorial projects. However, I have always believed opportunity leads to opportunity and took on curatorial invitations and challenges as they arose. I also investigated professional opportunities in teaching and curation while I studied for my PhD as I have always worked on a number of projects at the one time. In all, I was the producer and curator of five projects while I worked on my PhD. This is not unusual for those that work as artists and academic, but becomes difficult at times when you are also the single parent of a young child and undertaking a PhD!

If you have a young child and paid employment, you learn to work fast, smart and well on your PhD. There is no time for waste. You become pragmatic and fearless in what you have to do and how you do it. I was given one day's teaching relief for a semester near the end of my PhD so that I could complete my final draft. This was helpful, but would have been more supportive if I had a full semester to work on my thesis. For this reason, I am proud that we are now supporting staff in the School of Art (RMIT University) to receive PhD completion leave for a semester so that colleagues can have uninterrupted time to complete their PhDs.

My advice to those considering doctoral study is that you have to love your PhD. If you do not love doing your research you should question why you are doing a PhD that you do not care for. Doctoral study is an intense time, with great demands on the student, their supervisors, family and friends. I maintain that a PhD is not hard but completing a PhD is. This is when fatigue sets in and the struggle to complete final footnotes and finalise printing of artworks, and the spatial installation of a speaker system for exhibition can be complicated by the doctoral student's overwhelming tiredness. Enjoy your PhD. It will come to an end, and there will always be a new project to be challenged by and to accomplish.

References

Bordowitz, G. (2000). Which is More Powerful: The Word or the Idea? In J. Bryan-Wilson & B. Hunt, *Bodies of Resistance*. New York: Visual AIDS, 65–9.

Macarow, K. (2010). 'You Have Cancer.' In V. Kalitzkus & P. L. Twohig, (eds.), *The Fallible Body. Narratives of Health, Illness & Disease*. Inter-Disciplinary Press: Oxford, 29–39.

Macarow, K. (2008). Transmission Routes: The Global AIDS Epidemic in South Africa and France. *The Global South*, 2(2), 92–111. Bloomington: Indiana University Press.

Macarow, K. (2007). Producer of *Northern Void* (video, live performance, 1 hr) directed by Philip Brophy and composed by Philip Brophy and Philip Samartzis. Funded by City of Melbourne and Film Victoria. Supported by RMIT University and the Australian Centre for the Moving Image. Premiered at ACMI, February 2007 and screened at Performance Space, Sydney, 12 May 2011.

Macarow, K. (2006). *Disturbance: Bodies. Disease. Art*, University of Melbourne: Melbourne (unpublished PhD manuscript).

Macarow, K. (2003). 'I am a heterodemon.' *Refractory*, Vol. 3, 27 August. Retrieved from http://www.refractory.unimelb.edu.au/journalissues/vol4/macarow.htm

Macarow, K. (1998). *Viruses and Mutations,* exhibition and cultural symposium, the Melbourne International Arts Festival Visual Arts Program, Experimenta Media Arts, St Vincent's Hospital – Melbourne, and the Cinemedia @ Treasury Theatre, Melbourne.

Sontag, S. (1991). *Illness as Metaphor and AIDS and Its Metaphors.* London: Penguin Books.

ECO REVISITED: HOW TO 'WRITE' AN ART THESIS
Maggie McCormick

Title of study: The transient city: Mapping urban consciousness through contemporary art practice

The University of Melbourne, 2009

Abstract

The research undertaken through *The transient city: Mapping urban consciousness through contemporary art practice* is about the impact of the collective experience of The Transient City on urban consciousness. It brings together urban theory and art practice to address some of the fascinating cultural phenomena of today. In a time when the world's population is increasingly urban, our understanding of what it means to be urban is in flux and current perceptions of the nature of culture and belonging are under review. This research is based on a position that argues we are born transient, the impact of transience on perceptions of belonging has not been fully investigated and indicators of shifts in consciousness are more likely to be found in visual vocabulary than in the linguistic lexicon. Through a focus on two urban phenomena, namely Biennialisation and the China Phenomenon, this inquiry is into the extent to which contemporary art practice maps changes in urban consciousness.

The multi-layered research process combines artistic practice with analysis of the practice of contemporary curators, artists and audiences, combined with a study of interdisciplinary theoretical positions. The creative components are two transient exhibitions comprising photography, montage and drawing, utilizing visual metaphors of the body, tattoos, subway maps and windows. The hypothesis was initially formed through art practice in Beijing and consolidated through converging theoretical positions within urban and art inquiry, and exhibited in

Beijing, Vienna and Melbourne over 2006 and 2007. A composite picture of today's urban consciousness emerges from the juxtaposition of an analysis of viewers' responses, the outcomes of a study of the changing practices of Chinese born curators and artists represented in biennales in Asia, Europe and Australia during 2006 and 2007, as well as the findings resulting from a study of cultural change in China that has shaped that practice. The second exhibition was part of the final synthesis and takes the form of nine original art maps that travel to the viewer. Both exhibition formats invite the viewer to assume an active role.

The research outcomes indicate a growing awareness of cultural blind spots brought about through a changing sense of cultural scale and a growing understanding of fakeness in the formation of existing cultural concepts. Both indicate shifts in consciousness and perceptions of cultural belonging. A blind spot that remains, namely gender asymmetry cannot be ignored because of its prevalence and possible impact on further inquiry into urban consciousness. It is argued that shifts in consciousness challenge existing cultural paradigms through the perplexing questions that arise at points of cultural convergence, not so much out of difference, as out of collective experience of transience as an everyday urban aesthetic, within which one feels at home. I refer to this state of mind as urbaness and transphilia.

The thesis integrates text and visual material in two boxes, including *A Transient City Atlas for the Urban Century*. It is argued that both research rigour and artistic sensibility are needed to decipher signposts within contemporary art mapping that point to the nature of conceptual cultural territories beyond today's paradigms. New perspectives within urban and art studies are presented by focusing on transience within art practice to address the themes of the transient city and urban consciousness in the first Urban Century.

--

Eco revisited: How to 'write' an art thesis

'As I stand at my Beijing window,* in one of the world's fastest growing cities

---

* In August 2006 I undertook a research residency in Beijing, China, awarded by Red Gate gallery, a member of Res Artis, the International Association of Residential Art Centres. While there I staged a research exhibition at the 798 Art District.

surrounded by some sixteen million people,† my thoughts turn to what it might mean to be urban in the first Urban Century'.‡ (McCormick, 2009, p. 17)

These are the opening sentences to my PhD thesis, *The transient city: Mapping urban consciousness through contemporary art practice* (2009), undertaken at the Faculty of Architecture, Building and Planning at The University of Melbourne. On reflection, my choice of this first sentence encompasses what doctoral research means to me. It is essentially about burning questions that need to be asked. In the process of finding answers it is about the need to cross boundaries. Doctoral research provides space within which essential questions can be identified, asked and debated, to better understand the world you are experiencing. While there are ongoing public and academic debates about what role universities play in today's society, who they are for and what constitutes research, doctoral research remains a key element in a society's understanding of itself and its capacity to reflect on and renew itself.

My first studies were in the 1970s; my doctoral research did not start until 2006. Why did I wait so long? There are many reasons, but essentially it is because the capacity to create new and original knowledge requires life experience, depth of understanding of the complexity of issues and a recognition of, and desire to, understand what you do not know. On completion of a PhD it is hard to remember what you did not know in those first few days of excitement at being accepted and receiving a scholarship. The reality is that your personal 'new knowledge' has expanded excrementally through the process of the research. Most importantly you know yourself better, your ideas and capacities and what you can bring to a whole new world of ideas, philosophical thought, critique and debate has been opened up to you. My journey back to academic research had started with a Master of Fine Art at RMIT University 2004/2005 so why did I choose to do my doctoral research at another university and in another field? Having worked and practiced in the arts for many years, moving to a new 'box' emerging out of architecture, design and urban studies was the transdisciplinary challenge I was looking for – new ideas, new people, new

---

† At the time of writing the thesis, the population of Beijing was 16 million. It is now over 21 million.

‡ One of the earliest uses of the term Urban Century is by Peter Hall and Ulrich Pfeiffer in *Urban Future 21: A global agenda for twenty-first century cities*, 3, associated with the Global Conference on the Urban Future 21, Berlin, July 2000.

approaches, new questions. It proved to be a challenge worth taking up.

The questions that still intrigue me are related to the collective experience of the first urban century. In a time when the world is increasingly urban, our understanding of what it means to be urban is in flux and perceptions of the nature of culture and belonging are under review. The research began from the premise that in the contemporary world we are 'born transient' (McCormick, 2009, p. 17) in body and mind and as such transience* was used as a critical tool of inquiry. Within this context of transience, the question asked was – What form does contemporary urban consciousness take and how is it redefining perceptions of being urban and belonging? I argued that while a new urban lexicon was emerging in response to the changes in urban consciousness including terms like 'space of flows' (Castells, 2000), 'cityness' (Sassen, 2005), 'Liquid Times' (Bauman, 2007), and 'urbophilia' (Radovic & Dukanoic, 2007), critical clues to shifts in consciousness were more likely to be identified in visual vocabulary and visual metaphor. Building on the existing lexicon, I contributed to our capacity to express such new ideas through introducing new definitions such as 'urbaness'† (McCormick, 2009, p. 7) and 'transphilia' (McCormick, 2009, p. 6) and conceptual frameworks for artwork such as *MelBeiVien*.‡ The first gave clear voice to the perception of being urban as central to cultural identity, the second embraced a growing love of transience embedded in our capacity to move rapidly both physically and digitally across space and time, and the last added to our visual vocabulary through the title and the nature of the artwork itself. Through a focus in my doctoral research on two urban art phenomena, namely Biennialisation[§]

---

* In this context transience is defined as multiple 'impermanent' convergences. Soanes, C. and Stevenson, A. (eds.) (2005). *The Oxford dictionary of English* (revised edition). Oxford: Oxford University Press.

† Note urbaness can also be spelt as urbanness. The former is used here as a new addition to the linguistic lexicon.

‡ *MelBeiVien* was exhibited at Two Lines Gallery, 798 Art District, Beijing August 2006, Palais Porcia, Vienna September 2006 and at Fortyfivedownstairs, Melbourne, July 2007.

§ While the first biennale was held in Venice, Italy in 1895 it took until 1951 for the second significant biennale to appear on the scene in Sao Paulo, Brazil with others gradually appearing through to the 1980s. The term biennialisation has emerged as a commonly used expression in response to the now proliferation of biennales, biennials and triennials since 1990. The biennales in this doctoral study were Biennale of Sydney 2006, Asia Pacific Triennial 2006, Singapore Biennale 2006, Shanghai Biennale 2006, Venice Biennale 2007 and Documenta 12, 2007.

and the China Phenomenon¶, the study inquired into the extent to which contemporary art practice maps contemporary changes in urban consciousness. Biennales made an interesting field of inquiry because of their proliferation and changing practices that increasingly create moments of cultural convergence. An explosion of interest in contemporary artist and curators emerging out of China's rapid urbanisation and cultural re-evaluation provided the basis for a pertinent study from which broader conclusions could be drawn. Through an inquiry that mapped practice and employed practice I identified significant aspects of perceptions of scale and cultural fakeness emerging out of urban transience.

When I was first studying art in a university context in the late 1970s, Umberto Eco (1932–2016) was writing a book in Italy titled *Come si fa una testi di laurea: le materie unmanistiche* (1977). *How to Write a Thesis* was not translated into English until 2015 so I was not aware of it until quite recently. During my doctoral research I had been influenced by another of Eco's translated books *The Open Work* (1989) in relation to my doctoral methodology, so I wondered if his thoughts might relate to my experience first as a PhD candidate and now as a PhD supervisor. There are many books advising on how to undertake doctoral research but this one caught my attention because of the author himself whose interests ranged from semiotics to medieval history and who while a university professor also wrote novels. In his recent obituary he was described as 'a polymath of towering cleverness' and 'impishly humorous and robustly intellectual' (Thomson, 2016). *How to Write a Thesis* reflects these qualities in that while practical it reads more like a novel which at times is humorous. For example, he titles one section 'Must You Read Books?' (Eco, 2015, p. 103) and even tongue in check suggests plagiarism as a possible research methodology (2015, p. 4).

The first chapter heading, The Definition and Purpose of the Thesis, caught my attention with the question: What is a Thesis and Why is it Required? Eco's opening line addresses the first question – 'A thesis is a typewritten manuscript, usually 100 to 400 pages in length, in which the student addresses a particular problem in his chosen field' (Eco, 2015, p. 1). It is meant as a straight-forward

¶ The term China Phenomenon is taken from the title of the art journal *Artlink*, Vol. 23, No. 4, 2003 co-edited by Stephanie Britton and Binghui Huangfu that investigated why contemporary Chinese art had become so prolific on the world scene.

definition, but of course some forty years later it is more likely to be her typing on her laptop. Chaper 6 in his book is even typewritten rather than word-processed! His question Why is it required? has a number of practical answers but in essence some things do not change. PhD research is understanding and reflection on existing thought in pursuit of new knowledge, new ways of thinking and acting. While furthering the discipline, research also has a responsibility to further society. Eco argues for the relevance of political and social inquiry back in the 1970s. Doctoral research today within universities accepts and promotes this challenge. One example can be seen on the current RMIT University Research Degree Information web page headed Why a research degree? It talks of candidates who can 'conduct research that aims to solve critical global problems affecting communities and the environment'.

The questions What is a Thesis and Why is it Required? are particularly pertinent to doctoral research in art. Universities in various formats have been part of societies across the world for a long time. Universities from Cairo to Cambridge lay claim to be the oldest university. Because it has never been out of operation it is the University of Bologna in Italy founded in 1088 that holds the title. Coincidentally Umberto Eco became the first professor of semiotics at Bologna University in 1971. Within the historical framework of universities doctoral research in art is a new concept. Although it now exists in some universities, questions about its legitimacy and role remain a part of academic discourse. In part this is due to a misunderstanding of the difference between the art practitioner as artist and the practitioner as art researcher who is 'a conscious practitioner who sets out to realizes an objective that has been defined in accordance with the question, for as with all research, the research question is central to the creative project' (Duxbury & Grierson, 2008, p. 11). How does contemporary doctoral research in art differ from Eco's 1977 more conventional concept of a thesis? Interestingly Eco was engaged in a debate about the scientific nature of research and how research in the humanities might fit into this perspective that is relevant to today's discussion about doctoral research in art. Arguing within the premise that research should be scientific, he notes that research is scientific when it fulfills several conditions – it deals with a specific object, it is defined so others can identify it; it says or revises things that have not been said about that object from a different perspective;

it is useful to others; verifies or disproves the hypothesis it presents to provide the foundation for future research. He argues the case for the humanities, in particular for political and social enquiry, but it seems to me doctoral research in art, while employing different methodologies, also fits the general criteria.

Doctoral research in art can take multiple approaches. The investigation can be for art, into art or through art (Frayling, 1993). While the first two of these criteria sit easily in a more conventional approach to research, the latter is more problematic within academia. Australia and in particular RMIT University, have taken the lead in relation to doctoral research through art amongst only a handful of universities that validate the making of artworks as the research itself. Lesley Duxbury, Elizabeth Grierson and Dianne Waite (editors) note in their book, *Thinking through Practice: Art as research in the academy*, this style of research 'has not been readily recognized as research according to the Australian Department of Education, Science and Training (DEST) criteria, nor is it well understood within the academy itself' (2008). Currently the Department of Education, Employment and Workplace Relations, Higher Education Research Data Collection (HERDC) data collection criteria acknowledges that 'Research and experimental development comprises creative work undertaken on a systematic basis in order to increase the stock of knowledge, including knowledge of mankind, culture and society, and the use of this stock of knowledge to devise new applications'. So while some advances have been made over the last few years, in essence the validity of art practice as research is still often questioned within academia and its accrediting bodies.

My doctoral research took a different approach to Frayling's definition of art inquiry. While agreeing with Leon Van Schaik's premise that theory should be derived from practice rather than the creation of practice obedient to theory (2003), I took an interwoven conventional and unconventional approach. Mine was not exclusively research for, into or through art but rather the style of the research methodology and the structure and format of the thesis presentation reflects the focus of the study itself. Words and images, theory and creativity, objectivity and subjectivity, the individual and the collective, all create dialectical patterns and arrhythms that converge and collide throughout the research and dissertation. A visual hypothesis took the form of an interactive exhibition in the *798 Art District* in Beijing, China and at *fortyfivedownstairs* in Melbourne, Australia. The visual synthesis took form through written text and art images. While conventional in its substantial text, images played a vital role in the argument with one chapter entirely visual. The hypothesis and the synthesis reflect a body of research in which visual practice and observation combined with theoretical readings and analysis. The visual components do not illustrate the text and the written thesis is not designed to describe the artwork. Rather the making of images and the writing of texts by myself and others are positioned as equal research practices from which new knowledge emerges.

Some reflections

Be *passionate* about your topic and enjoy the research journey. Eco gives four practical rules for *selecting your research topic* that will enhance that passion. He advises that the topic should reflect your experience, be materially accessible, be manageable in relation to your ability, experience and background and employ a methodology appropriate to the subject matter (2015, p. 9). While not being aware of his rules at the time of undertaking my doctoral research, I did unknowingly follow them.

Make the *doctoral research central* to your life during the time you are undertaking the PhD. It's a unique time and space. It's a privilege so treat it as such. Choose your *supervisors* carefully. They will need to challenge you as well as foster you and at times defend you. You will need to respect their views but also be able to argue your case. An important thing I learnt as a candidate and now carry into my role as a PhD supervisor is to never lose the researcher's voice. In many ways doctoral research is an individual pursuit and we each bring our own way of understanding, writing and visualizing.

Changing questions and titles are part of the process. If they don't change then you have not changed in your thinking. My topic started as *The Architecture and Cartography of the Imagined City* and ended up *The transient city: Mapping urban consciousness through contemporary art practice* focusing on the practice of artists and curators emerging out of contemporary China in global biennales over a specific timeframe. The latter reflects the process of clarification and discovery during the research. It also reflects the process that all candidates need to go through of moving from a broad field of inquiry to a more focused one.

Have several *backup systems* kept in a logical and clear way with dates to distinguish different versions. You will very quickly accumulate multiple versions of your texts and images. Don't delete anything as sometimes elements of an earlier version end up being what you come back to. You will definitely come back to your notes, preliminary art works and outcomes after your completion. These together with your reference list will be an invaluable resource for further work.

Never underestimate the *accidental encounter* or what Eco calls 'Academic Humility' (2015/1977, p. 142). What he meant was that sometimes the best ideas do not come from the major authors or artists but rather stimulated by chance encounters that are not necessarily academic. Libraries and bookshops still offer this through the book sitting next to the one you came to borrow or buy that catches your eye through its colour, typeface or sheer boldness of its title. In the digital 'library' of the Internet you search and soon find yourself in a labyrinth of links, a rhizomatic wonderland. Eco's experience of this was his discovery of a book by the abbot Vallet. He says, 'I found at a stand in Paris a little book that attracted me at first for its beautiful binding' (2015, p. 143). Years later Eco realized that the abbot had not formulated the idea he remembered being so inspired by. Rather the encounter had clarified Eco's thoughts and helped him complete his own thesis. He notes that had he found it earlier 'I may not have caught the hint' (2015, p. 144). For me many key accidents lay in footnotes and citations that opened a door into a whole area of study of the city and the nature of urban space and how that might be mapped. By discovering a text or image through footnotes and citations you then find others and 'so on, potentially infinitely' (Eco, 2015, p. 92). Along this line of thought, things will always emerge out of the research that are not central to the study but in themselves warrant attention – *side tracks for later investigation*. In the process of research and writing which involved the tracking of curators and artists participating in biennales, I became aware of a striking gender imbalance across biennale artists and curators.[*] Gender asymmetry was included as a noted blind spot in urban studies. Later this was the starting

---

[*] In my biennale study 2006/2007 none of the artistic directors were women and of the eighty-one artists in my study only fourteen were women. While there have been some improvements in the last ten years, it is still worth counting.

point for further writing on the subject outside of the doctoral thesis.*

Keep to a *timeframe*. In years gone by people would stretch out their doctoral research across many years. This is not so common now. A concentrated period of time focuses your mind and will deliver the most productive outcomes. Remember there will always be *more to be said*. At the end of all doctoral research there is always another book, another art work or artist, another thought, something you have not yet considered, but it is important to remember you are at the start, not the finish line. The knowledge gained in the doctoral research informs an ongoing artistic, curatorial and publication practice. Eco sums it up well when he talks of his own experience – 'with time, a writer becomes more astute and knowledgeable, but how he uses his knowledge will always depend on how he originally researched the many things he did not know' (2015, p. 6). While my dissertation was not published at the time of completion, sections have since informed numerous chapters, papers, presentations and artworks. The titles of some writing bear witness to this – *Carto-City Revisited: unmapping urbaness* (2017); *SkypeLab: The Invisible City* (2016); *The Transient City: the city as urbaness* (2013). Equally the research has deepened my artistic and curatorial practice with *SkypeLab*† (2012 ongoing) as a key example. This interdisciplinary lab connects universities, cities and artists across the contiguous space of continents and the digital world as an ongoing mapping of urban consciousness, in this case mediated by the transience of Skype screens. Several publications and art works, including *MelLingen* and *MelShangLingen*, are integral to the investigation and outcomes of this ongoing research.‡

All are part of my ongoing research in art that began with my doctoral research in art – *The transient city: Mapping urban consciousness through contemporary art practice*.

In conclusion, just a reminder that as Umberto Eco said in his 1977 introduction to *How to Write a Thesis*, 'research is after all an adventure' (2015, p. xxv).

---

* *Suitcases, Maps, Wolves and Glass Walls: mapping urban consciousness and reflecting on gender asymmetry in contemporary art.* (2007). UNESCO Observatory e-journal, Vol. 1, No. 1, http://education.unimelb.edu.au/__data/assets/pdf_file/0004/1105735/suitcases.pdf.
† www.skypelab.org.
‡ *MelLingen* and *MelShangLingen* were exhibited at Staedtische Galerie, Reutlingen, Germany, 2017. The works can be viewed in the SkypeLab publication pdf at http://www.skypelab.org/publication/.

References

Bauman, Z. (2007). *Liquid times: Living in an age of uncertainty*. Cambridge, UK: Polity.

Castells, M. (2000). *The rise of the network society* (2nd edn., 1st edn. 1996). Malden, Massachusetts: Blackwell.

Duxbury, L., Grierson, E. & Waite, D. (eds.). (2008). *Thinking through practice: Art as research in the academy*. Melbourne: The School of Art, RMIT University.

Eco, U. (1989). *The open work*. Translated from the original *Opera Aperta (1962)*. Cambridge, Massachusetts: Harvard University Press.

Eco, U. (2015). *How to write a thesis*. Translated from the original *Come si fa una testi di laurea: le materie unmanistiche* (1977). USA: MIT Press.

Frayling, C. (1993). *Research in art and design*. UK: Royal College of the Arts Research Papers, Vol. 1, No. 1. Retrieved from http://www.transart.org/wp-content/uploads/group-documents/79/1372332724-Frayling_Research-in-Art-and-Design.pdf.

McCormick, M. (2009). *The Transient City: mapping urban consciousness through contemporary art practice* (unpublished doctoral dissertation). The University of Melbourne, Melbourne.

McCormick, M. (2013). The transient city: The city as urbaness. In E. Grierson & K. Sharp (eds.). *Re-imagining the City: Art, globalization and urban spaces*. Chicago: Intellect, The University of Chicago Press.

McCormick, M. (2016). *SkypeLab: The invisible city*. In H. Eichinger & M. McCormick (eds.) *SkypeLab: Transcontinental faces and spaces*. Bielefeld, Germany: Kerber Publications.

McCormick, M. (2017). *Carto-City revisited: Unmapping urbaness*. In E. Grierson (ed.) *Transformations: Art and the city*. Chicago: Intellect, The University of Chicago Press.

Radovic, D., & Dukanoic, Z. (2007). *Urbophilia*. Belgrade: Faculty of Architecture, University of Belgrade.

Sassen, S. (2005). *Cityness in the urban age*. Urban Age Bulletin 2. Retrieved from www.urban-age.net, February 2007.

Thomson, I. (2016). 'Umberto Eco Obituary'. *Guardian* (UK), 20 February. Retrieved from https://www.theguardian.com/books/2016/feb/20/umberto-eco-obituary.

Van Schaik, L. (2003). *The practice of practice: Research in the medium of design*. Melbourne: School of Architecture and Design, RMIT University.

THE ROAD TAKEN

Grace McQuilten

Title of study: Mis-design: Art in a consumer landscape

The University of Melbourne, 2008

Abstract

This thesis examined the collusion of 'art' and 'design' in contemporary artistic practices as a means to investigate the possibilities of critique in a commercially driven cultural landscape. It proceeded through an analysis of the work of Takashi Murakami, Andrea Zittel, Adam Kalkin and Vito Acconci, four contemporary artists who claim to be working in the field of commercial design rather than the traditional sphere of artistic practice. As I argued, this turn away from the institutions of art signals an attempt to address the increasingly commercial directive of contemporary art. The work of Murakami was presented as a counterpoint to illustrate the ways that contemporary art reinforces the systems of capitalist exchange. By contrast, the work of Zittel, Kalkin and Acconci was explored for its capacity to reactivate the critical practice of art in a more direct engagement with commerce through what I termed 'mis-design'. The work of all four artists reveal a fracture in contemporary society—the displacement of human desire in consumer culture. Engaging with design in a consciously provocative manner, I argued, opens up the potential to produce active objects that exploit the internal irrationality of late capitalism and insert difference into the homogenised sphere of consumer production. In this way, artists have the ability to make consumers aware of the alienating effects of capitalist exchange, the design of human life in our post-industrial landscape and the potential for becoming-human in a designed world. In this thesis I traced a move away from 'oppositional' practices toward work that emerged from within commercial systems. Contemporary art, in this context, was considered as a critical engagement with capitalist systems of production, misdirecting the product-based methodology of commercial design. This examination of design responded to commercial design's cannibalisation of art. Moving critical and conceptual practices into overt fields of architectural, landscape, interior and fashion design, art becomes a critical practice within the commercial sphere. By acknowledging the inherent complicity of art with design, this thesis began to conceive of and affirm a future for art within the complex socio-economic and cultural predicament of late capitalism. Can misdesign provide the means for artistic critique within the designed spaces of contemporary cultural production?

--

> *Two roads diverged in a yellow wood,*
> *And sorry I could not travel both*
> *And be one traveler, long I stood*
> *And looked down one as far as I could*
> *To where it bent in the undergrowth*
>
> Robert Frost, *The Road Not Taken* (1995)

This chapter follows a winding path that starts with a poem and returns to a poem and hopefully by the end of it we understand the road that was taken.

I started with a Masters, which turned into a PhD, and then somewhat unexpectedly I found myself running a social enterprise, The Social Studio, and now I am back working as a researcher. There is a connection between my research and professional experiences, however at times it is not obvious, even to myself. I will start with an outline of how my study turned into PHD research, and how this shaped my direction in terms of my career and other community based work.

My interest in art history evolved alongside my own artistic practice during my undergraduate studies. I was studying a Bachelor of Creative Arts which enabled me to combine interests from a range of disciplines; media, photography, visual art, creative writing and critical theory. I had always been a writer and relished the opportunity to study poetry alongside visual art. I had a very passionate art history teacher, Ken Wach, who introduced me to the poetic side of art history. His lectures were mesmerizing and his words brought every detail of the artworks to life. His passion was the study of Surrealism and so Surrealism crept into every part of the curriculum. As I pursued my studies in art history it became apparent to me that the interlinking of art with words not only had a long history, but also a rich and dynamic relationship that was part tango, part war, part love. So perhaps it was not surprising that my Honours thesis combined a study of contemporary art with my own practice in poetry.

After my undergraduate degree, I decided to take a year off to travel, think and gain some work experience in the art world. My research into contemporary art had awakened a real interest in curatorship and I wanted to see what this industry was like in practice. I spent six months living in New York and during this time I completed two internships. The first was a marketing/education internship with the New Museum of Contemporary Art in New York City. I was exposed to the true mechanizations of the art world – money, wealthy people, trends, and the business of art. I found this to be both compelling and horrifying. The second internship was with the Dia Art Foundation, where I was placed as a research assistant in American minimalist artist Dan Flavin's archive. Here, alongside inspiring curator and researcher Tiffany Bell, I assisted the team in preparing Flavin's full *catalogue raisonné*, a catalogue of his life's work, in preparation for a major touring retrospective. This was a truly amazing experience – I sat in an office adjacent to the store-room where Flavin's lights were stored, restored and installed. I also experienced painstakingly detailed research work, checking facts, chasing up page numbers from articles published in obscure magazines many decades before. And I think it was here that I fell under the spell of research.

My New York experience also sparked a deep frustration with the art world. So much commercialization was evident everywhere I turned – art was a commodity that helped to sell brands across a variety of industries and commercial spheres, artists were brands themselves, and the art world was full of pomp and superficiality. I started searching for the aspects of art that had always inspired and motivated me – critical thought, creative freedom, braveness, rebellion. What I found was several artists that were addressing the increasingly commodified face of art, not by rejecting it, but by declaring themselves to be designers while making products that were either dysfunctional, absurd, or useless. I found this to be a fascinating approach to dealing with our own embedded relationship to consumer culture and capitalism. Un-doing the machine from the inside-out, so to speak. And this inspired me to start my Masters in Art History in 2004, which then evolved into a PhD that I completed in 2008.

The distinction between art and design has been a contentious issue throughout the twentieth century, from early attempts to unify the disciplines, found in movements such as De Stijl and the Bauhaus, to Minimalism and Conceptualism's questioning of the art object itself. Recently, it is the lack of distinction between art and commercial design that is of concern to many artists and theorists. At the same time as design practice and discourse is infiltrating the art world, a number of contemporary artists have abandoned the traditional institutions of the art-world by explicitly taking up design as an experimental practice.

Vito Acconci, for example, was a notorious performance artist in the 1960s who rejected commercialism and the power structures of the art world, and an unlikely suspect to transform into a designer.

His artwork evolved from poetry, where he was interested in testing the limits of the page, to performance, testing the limits of the human body. This was a means to question power structures in modern art and society – and to draw attention to a loss of human agency in the systems of contemporary culture. His various works questioned perception, language and communication. This led to an interest in design and architecture. He was less interested in the aesthetics or function of architecture, however, and more in how architecture and design control us, how we might become activated in public space, to become critical agents rather than passive subjects.

Many critics and commentators describe Acconci's design as 'bad' because he does not prioritise aesthetics – his work is quite bizarre and doesn't look like slick design. Herein lies the effectiveness of his practice – he is not trying to create 'good design,' he is using design to stop us in our tracks, to think twice, and to consider the influence of design on our environment and lives. A good example is the public artwork *Face of the Earth* (1985), installed in City Hall Park in New York City. It is a seating space, a play space, and a park space carved in the shape of a human face. The face is not particularly well formed, however, and looks more like a bad masquerade mask than a portrait of a human head. The result is absurd and elicits laughter and confusion from visitors. It is also a functional space that can be used to sit, to play, to congregate. Audiences encounter the work, are surprised by it, consider how such a strange thing has been created as public infrastructure, and then also use the space. It is 'bad' design that draws our attention to its own construction, to its *design*. This lies in contrast to the underpinnings of much public design, which often disguises the processes of its construction. In this way, Acconci makes viewers aware of the systems and structures that underpin our public spaces.

Art theorists and historians have tended to respond sceptically to the engagement of art with design, utility and commerce, for many valid reasons including the risk of losing the critical qualities that have defined art since the advent of modernity. In his strident critique *Design and Crime*, Hal Foster revisits Adolf Loos' influential modernist essay of 1908, 'Ornament and Crime,' looking at the dangers posed to art and criticism with the increasing interconnection of art, architecture and design in contemporary consumer culture. He likens this recent interdisciplinarity to Loos' criticism of excessive ornamentation in Art Nouveau, suggesting:

> This old debate takes on a new resonance today, when the aesthetic and the utilitarian are not only conflated but all but subsumed in the commercial, and everything – not only architectural projects and art exhibitions but everything from jeans to genes – seems to be regarded as so much *design*. (Foster, 2002, p. 17)

It is this idea that was central to my research – how everything in contemporary life is informed by design, and how design has become the language of capitalism. Design is constantly shaping things, relationships and experiences in the form of commodities. I started my research journey with questions rather than answers. Was there hope for art beyond the market? What does freedom look like today? Is there any form of resistance – creative, social, philosophical – that can be effective in the machine of global capital?

My PhD therefore focused on two main ideas: firstly, an acknowledgement that the collusion of 'art' and 'design' is a symptom of the total commodification of art and creativity in contemporary capitalism; and secondly, I argued that the way through this complex territory is in critical practices that occur on the *inside* of commercial culture, rather than claiming a position *external* to consumerism.

I looked at the work of four artists; along with Acconci, I looked at Takashi Murakami, Andrea Zittel, and Adam Kalkin, all who claim to be working in the field of commercial design rather than the traditional sphere of artistic practice (to greater and lesser degrees). The claim to 'design' by these contemporary artists constitutes an acknowledgement of the relationship between cultural production and capitalist production. The distinction of art and design was not as significant, in my argument, as the issue of artistic freedom and critical space, which is at stake in both the commercial realms of the art world and in the commercial realms of design.

What I discovered early on in my research was that working at the intersection of two disciplines can be divisive – and I often received polarised feedback to my work. Looking at design from the context of art could be seen as a kind of betrayal of art's presumed autonomy, its irrational, dysfunctional and critical aspects – design being utilitarian, commercial and unapologetically complicit with dominant social systems. At the same time, looking at design from a critical point of view, considering ways that artists were challenging, upsetting, rebelling against the design of their practice – didn't fit seamlessly within a design discourse either. And so began a wonderful journey into problematic, complex territory.

The research journey

I chose to study at The University of Melbourne because of their well-recognized art history department and my familiarity with the research culture there. My methodology involved a mix of primary and secondary research. I made site visits to exhibitions and artists' studios, looked at artworks, interviewed two of the artists and gathered as much historical and archival material as I could find. This involved travel to Europe and the USA, scouring through archives and libraries and visiting key sites for selected artworks. While I had originally intended to interview all four of the artists in my study, only two agreed to participate – Adam Kalkin and Vito Acconci. Adam's response to my first written questionnaire came in the form of children's drawings scrawled over the questions. As soon as I received it I realized that it was a perfect response to questions of artistic freedom in an institutionalized and over-designed world. The interview with Vito Acconci was somewhat more productive, if terrifying. Acconci was in his 70s at the time I met him in his studio in Brooklyn, New York. I was met with a deep, crackling voice and an intense set of dark eyes. All my questions were met with succinct, rehearsed answers. On reflection, it occurred to me that I could have sourced all of the same responses by trawling through his previously published interviews. But I provoked him at one point, when I asked a question about the relationship between his art and architecture. It became clear that he did not want his architecture to be reduced to the terms of contemporary art, that he wanted to be taken seriously as an architect.

Without conducting a formal interview I also undertook a site visit to Adam Kalkin's house and artwork, *Bunny Lane* in New Jersey, USA. This was a truly Alice in Wonderland experience, with surprises around every corner. The house contains a perfectly preserved 1800s cottage at the heart of a large airport hangar, creating a fusion of inside and outside, old and new, industrial and handmade. Adam was incredibly generous with his time and we discussed in great depth aspects of his practice and his thoughts on art, social politics and contemporary culture. This provided great insights that ended up informing and transforming some of my research questions and assumptions.

The most difficult stage of my research came in clarifying my key argument. This took a lot of time, challenges and provocations from my wonderful supervisor Anthony White, and a willingness to shift from vague and general statements to a much more specific, detailed and nuanced articulation of ideas. Once I could clearly explain – to myself as well as others – why and how art can change our perspective on the design of contemporary life, the rest of the thesis followed. But getting to this point was the real crux of the project, and it probably happened about halfway through my PhD journey.

Around the same time, I took a six month break from my research due to personal and family responsibilities. Up until this point, I had been lucky enough to focus on the PhD close to full-time, thanks to an Australian

Postgraduate Award scholarship. Alongside this, I had been working across a range of *ad hoc* jobs, from tutoring work in art history to community development with a focus on migrant settlement. The six-month break was a challenge, both financially and personally, however it also gave me a priceless opportunity to take time to reflect on my research, and to wrestle with some of the key questions and problems it posed. This made a huge difference in resolving the key argument I wanted to make, and focusing my research in a way that was coherent and translatable. My six months break also became a time of compulsive art-making. This was not planned, but with the space away from writing and research, my creative practice took over effortlessly. It also deepened my understanding of the relationship between practice and theory. When I returned to study I was very grateful for the opportunity to research, and understood the responsibility I had to do justice to this incredible opportunity. Studying at a postgraduate level is a privilege that many people cannot access, whether for financial or personal reasons.

From research into the world

A few of the central ideas in my research help to explain why I ended up taking an unexpected path into social enterprise after finishing my PhD, or how I found myself taking 'the road not taken.' While thinking about the impact of consumerism on our daily lives, I was struck by the question of what true freedom looks like in contemporary society. We find ourselves conforming to so many social rules and norms, from the bureaucracy of Centrelink to how we move through city streets, observing arbitrary delineations between public and private spaces, passing security cameras or security guards at every corner. We are almost entirely dependent on these same systems of society to survive, and yet we sacrifice so much personal choice in the process. When we shop, we are presented with the appearance of choice–a dazzling array of colours, sizes, shapes and products to choose from. And yet none of these are really free choices – they are predesigned sets, manufactured and distributed. And then there is social media, a system for maintaining professional and personal relationships that is almost impossible to avoid, and almost completely privatized. We freely hand over our most personal details to global companies that use our data to market more effectively and to understand our consumer behavior so they can target us with products and services we don't really want or need. So, the question arose, how can we inhabit these systems in a way that allows for creative difference, for multiplicity, for social change?

What I found fascinating about all of the artists I was studying in my PhD was their interest in process and production, rather than the end point of consumption. This is fundamental to transforming the conventional power structure of much design, which tends to rely up on a hierarchical relationship between the designer, who determines an outcome, and the end user, who passively receives this outcome. It is through process, rather than plans, that the potential for difference emerges. And art has a powerful role to play in generating change. Philosopher Gilles Deleuze articulates this beautifully in *Difference and Repetition*:

> The more our daily life appears standardised, stereotyped and subject to an accelerated reproduction of objects of consumption, the more art must be injected into it in order to extract from it that little difference which plays simultaneously between other levels of repetition ... Art thereby connects the tableau of cruelty with that of stupidity, and discovers underneath consumption a schizophrenic clattering of the jaws. (Deleuze, 2007, p. 293)

These ideas led to my interest in the idea of social enterprise – enterprising activity that sets out to change social systems and structures, rather than simply generating financial or material outcomes. Another key point in my research that informed my subsequent ventures was the idea of embracing failure. By shifting focus away from an end-point and instead engaging with process, we are much more vulnerable to failure. However it is in this uncertain field that new possibilities emerge.

And so it was that on completing my PhD I turned away from both academia and the art world and collaborated with a group of people working across community development and design to start a social enterprise called The Social Studio. I was building on my previous work in community development, while also being informed by my artistic practice and research. The Social Studio set out to provide training and employment opportunities to young people from refugee and migrant communities through the vehicle of a design studio. The

Studio has multiple dimensions to it, including a fashion label, digital textiles studio, café/gallery, fashion school and community drop-in space. It runs as a not-for-profit that prioritises education and community development over financial gain. Precarity, the possibility of failure, and uncertain outcomes are all part and parcel of the daily life of many social enterprises.

It was five years after embarking on the journey into social enterprise that I finally returned to research in a considered way. During this time, I curated a number of exhibitions, wrote occasional articles and engaged with academic research from the sidelines. While none of this was intended to support my academic career, in fact these various experiences have deeply impacted on my research trajectory and approach. At heart I am an artist, although I wear many guises. And what my PhD journey taught me over and above all else, is that art does have the power to change us, and to impact the world around us.

For those considering embarking on a journey into doctoral research, my main advice would be to think less of what you will achieve by completing a PhD, and more on what you can learn in the process of your research. Academic study is a wonderful privilege, an exciting journey, and an opportunity to cherish. But it can also be precarious, competitive and goal-driven. I hope you can enjoy the process as much as you can, and be surprised by the way that your questioning of the world unfolds into practice, and be prepared to take risks and venture to places you didn't expect. And at this point it's time to return to Robert Frost's poem *The Road Not Taken:*

> *Two roads diverged in a yellow wood,*
> *And sorry I could not travel both*
> *And be one traveler, long I stood*
> *And looked down one as far as I could*
> *To where it bent in the undergrowth;*
>
> *Then took the other, as just as fair,*
> *And having perhaps the better claim,*
> *Because it was grassy and wanted wear;*
> *Though as for that the passing there*
> *Had worn them really about the same,*

And both that morning equally lay
In leaves no step had trodden black.
Oh, I kept the first for another day!
Yet knowing how way leads on to way,
I doubted if I should ever come back.

References

Deleuze, G. (2007). *Difference and Repetition*. Trans. Paul Patton. London, UK: Continuum.

Foster, H. (2002). *Design and Crime: And Other Diatribes*. London, UK: Verso.

Frost, R. (1995). *The Road Not Taken and Other Early Poems*. New York, USA: Penguin Press.

ONE DAY AT A TIME

Sally Mannall

Title of study: The use and abuse of the garden as a cultural artefact

Monash University, 2017

Abstract

The use and abuse of the garden as a cultural artefact considers the garden as a highly complex cultural artefact and explores correspondences between this idea and practice-based creative projects that employ intervention in garden contexts. I pose the question: if gardens are polysemic, combining cultural ideas about nature with site, natural force, human power and control, how can artistic interventions expose, disrupt and extend understandings of this complexity? I propose that in utilising the unique combination of site, interventions, actions, play and mimesis in distinct vernacular gardens in Austria and Australia this complexity is revealed. This exegesis frames a conceptual understanding of the garden as a microcosm of a cultural moment through a series of case studies of the historical and contemporary contexts of the gardens in Austria and Australia that I have worked in. These case studies have been deliberately chosen for the opportunity they offer to engage the histories (ownership, landscape design, labour) of the food garden. These specific sites enable me to develop the landscape culture in the periods of these gardens' emergence and the cultural attitudes towards the landscape. Correspondences to these ideas in the creative works synthesise the theoretical and creative outcomes of this research. The materials and formal vocabularies I have employed include site-responsive works, artistic interventions, kinetic sculptures, uniforms, and photography, moving image, time, duration and anamorphic illusion.

What was the motivation to study? Were you encouraged/supported by your institution?

The decision I made to enrol in a PhD was twofold. Firstly, I had arrived at a point in my practice where I was looking forward to a focused period of study on a topic I had been researching for many years. As an academic I was also aware having PhD was becoming a necessary qualification in my field.

Why did you decide on the university?

The choice I made to undertake my PhD outside the university I was teaching in was informed by a postgraduate research training session at RMIT. This session took as its subject the merits and problems arising from undertaking a PhD as an academic staff member in one's current institution. I benefited from the honest and open discussion that took place in that forum. The overriding conclusions were that studying externally had the benefit for academics of extending their professional networks. In addition the forum identified complex and at times incompatible expectations and roles where PhD supervisors were also working colleagues and line managers. Studying at another institution gave me the freedom to be a student in a manner that was not complicated or enfolded into my concurrent role as an academic. Additionally my studies fostered strong networks with academics I would not otherwise have developed such good relationships with. I based my choice of institution on two criteria: first I wanted regular access to my supervisor so I investigated universities based in Melbourne, and secondly I researched available supervisors against the expertise in my discipline and field of research. I selected the most appropriate supervisor over and above any perceived status of the University in which I was to enrol.

Comment on the process you underwent to decide on the topic/thesis/project and how it changed/emerged.

The topic for my thesis *The use and abuse of the garden is a cultural artefact* was arrived at circuitously and in mid-candidature. The PhD research project had commenced examining the psychological state of anticipation relative to the perception and imagining of the future framed by ideas of fear, disquiet and the banality of the everyday. This initial research topic was identified as an ongoing theme and interest in my practice from as early as 1996. I had developed an interest in how threat and fear conveyed via politicians and the media (particularly post September 11), could be internalized within the populace as an anticipatory circuiting displaced from any actual event or outcome.

Numerous works produced early in the candidature sort to engage with this topic. The body of work titled *The Good Life* exposed for me the schism between my research topic and ideas the work was generating. What was apparent was that my topic was not demonstrably retrievable from the artworks. A second project *Hope, Eddies and Microclimates* also enacted in a garden context opened space for a necessary reappraisal of my initial topic. The feedback I received when presenting these works at a mid-candidature research symposium suggested a shift in the thesis topic. The art historian and garden theorist Luke Morgan who attended this presentation suggested key ways I could bring the projects together through addressing the way my garden interventions activated the cultural, social and historical contexts of the gardens I was working in. The questions of fear and hope for me remained meta-narrative within the project. I examined the role of gardens and food production in relation to self and heteronomous determination, order and control, agency and power.

Comment on the process of determining the methodology for the research and how it changed/emerged.

The approach I take to creative practice is informed by a concept of directed play. I work intuitively and responsively with set propositions and materials. The process involves trial and error, experimentation, ingenuity, evaluation and reworking. With a long and established history in creative practice I am experienced and comfortable working in this domain. Reading and research have always informed and enfolded into studio processes and outcomes.

Writing the thesis on the other hand was far more challenging. The initial supervisor I had recommended I did not commence writing until I had finished all of the creative works. He had suggested the thesis, no less than 30,000 words would take three months full-time or six months part-time to complete. In hindsight, I can see the value in formulating the thesis through critically reviewing the outcomes of all the creative works. But commencing the thesis late in the candidature where little prior research and writing could be used, the task ahead in length, scope, and depth of critical inquiry was daunting. As someone that was not in the habit of a critical writing practice it took months to find and reestablish my writing skills and voice. There is a single paragraph late in my first chapter where this comes alive with confidence and attitude that the prior writing missed. The initial writing was slow and laboured. It took three months to complete my first chapter that ran to 15,000 words in it first fully edited draft. I approached the writing by breaking it down into small tasks, a section at the time. When things got sticky I used voice recognition and free writing to invigorate the flow. The learning curve through the thesis writing was steep but rewarding. It was not until I had completed the introduction and all of the chapters in fully edited drafts that I could see I would actually be able to complete the thesis. Prior to that, negotiating looming deadlines against actual daily word accounts had kept the completion horizon as something of a mirage

How did you organise your work/employment to allow you to study?

I commenced my PhD as a 0.8 employee with an ongoing role in postgraduate education onshore and offshore teaching. At 0.8 I had sufficient time between my teaching role, my research allocation, my non-employed day and my weekends to commence the PhD part-time. Early in my candidature I was asked to temporarily act in the role of MFA Program Manager, a full-time position. Initially this was for six months but extended to five years. In spite of having one day a week allocated for research in my workload, the reality of work demands as a program manager resulted in little time to concentrate on study and undertake creative practice. To address this I applied for a three month international residency and used long service leave and accrued annual leave to take a full semester off work. That residency gave me the opportunity to develop a large project with multiple exhibition outcomes resulting in one of the main bodies of works in my PhD. Subsequent to the residency and time off my return to full-time work brought about the realisation that I would need to renegotiate my role and responsibilities if I was to finish my PhD. In response to this I took 12 months leave from my PhD while I continued to work full-time. The following year I negotiated to step down from my position and work 0.5 with a view to completing my PhD that year. Midyear the appointment of a new Head of School opened the opportunity for staff to apply for PhD completion leave. I was awarded 12 weeks pro rata which I supplemented with annual and long service leave to extend to five months off work. The majority of exegetical writing was completed in this time.

How did you organise your life (and family) to allow you to study?

The study program I set up to write the thesis rotated around a very organised daily routine and the almost complete withdrawal from my social life. Murakami's description of his daily writing routine in his book *What I talk about when I talk about running* was the inspiration for this. My weekdays were organised around a schedule of reading, researching and writing. Aside from Murakami, one of the other most useful tips on effective writing came from a workshop at Monash University. Put simply – pay attention to when your mind / body is most alert. This was rather generally presented as 'Were you are morning or evening person?' I was to discover I was most alert at 5.00am and would arise, have a cup of tea while my head was running full steam ahead formulating clear thoughts and arguments. Initially I resented this early waking but got accustomed to embracing it. In the last three months of my exegesis and facing what looked like an impossible deadline I would write from 5.00am to 9.30am on non work days, break for breakfast, a shower and a short mindfulness meditation and return to writing until lunch time. My levels of productivity during this time were very high and the quality of my writing was good. Afternoons were sluggish for me. I found I could reinvigorate myself by using the early afternoon to exercise. A short stint shooting hoops at the basketball court in the local park served to relax my shoulder and make me laugh (I was terribly inaccurate at this). Alternatively I would take 1.5 hours to do a 6km walk around Lake Wendouree or a 1km swim (far more effective than walking), before retuning to my desk to research or edit until 5.00pm. I would break for dinner, attend to any necessary domestic tasks before retiring to read for an hour or so before sleep. That reading would set me up for the following morning. In the last three months of my thesis I worked on a 10–12 hour a day program. The down side of this was that I was so mentally consumed that I found it hard to transition from my thinking/writing brain to being companionable. After working with such intensity and concentration for so many months I equated finishing and submitting the thesis to a high-speed crash – when you come to a sudden stop but your body and adrenaline keeps going. It took a considerable amount of time for me to reset my 5.00am 'ready to go' body clock and generally unwind from working that intensely.

What were the main issues you confronted throughout your period of study?

On enrolling at Monash University I was allocated only one supervisor who was an art historian. At mid-candidature I changed supervisors because I became aware that Luke Morgan, lecturer in Art History was also a garden historian. His expertise in my field of research was extraordinary. The insight, knowledge and direction he was able to provide for the writing of the thesis opened for me a whole new area of research that provided pertinent theoretical frameworks to examine how my creative works were activating the garden landscapes they were located in.

The writing process gave rise at times to considerable frustrations for me about constraints on what could and could not be included in the thesis. This arose from differences of value placed on 'knowledge' between my art historian supervisors and myself as an artist. I was to observe that both my supervisors' knowledge and articulation of artworks was predominately framed and authorised via written publications. As an artist the knowledge that I make and read through artworks includes the tacit, the felt and the experiential. Observations and conversations with my audience are part of my knowledge gathering in understanding what ideas and content are generated by my work. I missed not having an artist as a co-supervisor to advocate and advise on how to approach and articulate this knowledge in the thesis. At the end of my first chapter I wrote a two-page evaluation of audience responses to my suite of photographs *The Good Life* reflecting on this relative to the cultural and theoretical frameworks I had set up throughout the chapter. The response to this by my primary supervisor was that none of this knowledge could be 'substantiated' and needed to be removed from the chapter. Similar responses were made to my inclusion of feedback on my work *Hope Eddies and Microclimates* by the gardeners who hosted the project in Austria. However quoting from the short catalogue essay on this work by the Viennese curator Alexandra Hennig was acceptable. Interestingly one of my examiners notes in his report that I did not 'engage in discussion concerning viewer responses to the work.' This was a bittersweet criticism given I had, but it had ended on the editor's floor. What the assessor's comment did was to endorse my position in the debate I had with my supervisor about the inclusion of these observations in my thesis. It also highlighted for me an embedded power dynamic between supervisor and student that operate relative to authority and trust. It also exposed a potential pedagogical divide between art historians and fine art practitioners in what is authorised as knowledge in creative practice.

What was the most memorable time during your research?

The most memorable situation of my PhD was to find myself at a summer garden party for the Viennese cultural elite in the small country town of Zwettl. I have been invited to install my work *Hopes eddies and microclimates* in the garden at the country home of a senior and well-regarded Viennese painter. Every year she hosted a garden party for around 200 people. The installation of my work in her garden was to coincide with this event. It rained that day and most of the guests retreated indoors spread across the large multi-storey house. Seated around a huge dining room table in an upper room of her home were the most famous of her guests. I was introduced to this inner sanctum and left seated between two people who were not very interested in talking to me. The man to my right rather disparagingly asked if Australia had an art scene and how famous I was. What followed was an extraordinary introduction into Euro centric snobbery. He appraised the town of Krems that were hosting my residency as having a beautiful landscape but populated by people with small minds. He then proceeded to ask me if I knew who the people were around the table. I knew no one. Without introducing me to anybody he began identifying person by person their role and status in the culture of Vienna: Vienna's most famous composer, Vienna's most famous conductor, most accomplished soprano singer, most famous contemporary composer, appraised film maker and so on. My host was good humoured by my encounter with her long-term friend. While I was clearly out of my depth culturally, socially and linguistically in this context I did establish a wonderful creative dialogue with her and made through her some other valuable contacts that opened opportunities for my work in lower Austria.

What was the most difficult memory of the time as a candidate?
The examination experience

The University I studied at required the submission of the thesis two months in advance of the examination exhibition so it could be sent to the examiners. As a pedagogical structure having the writing preceding the exhibition to my mind is problematic. It prioritised the explanation and framing of the examination exhibition through the philosophical, contextual, and methodological frameworks explored in the exegetical text. This process inadvertently weights the writing as precursory to the creative works. There were no options within the established structures of the examination timelines to request that the thesis be made available at the time of the exhibition.

To describe the examination process I would choose the words, tough and confusing.

The delay between the examination exhibition and receiving the assessor's reports was in excess of the 8-week timeline I had been given. By the time I got the examiners' reports four and a half months had elapsed since the submission of the exegetical text. The two examination reports contained significant disparities between the assessors' appraisal of the examination exhibition and thesis. One of the assessors had graded the PhD as strongly competitive at an international level, praising the originality of the research, the methodology, and the exceptionally high quality of the writing. In spite of having employed a senior publishing editor to correct the thesis on the minutiae of grammar and punctuation this assessor had found an additional 30 minor typographical errors. These were listed in the examination report for correction and were the only amendments required by this assessor for the final submission of the thesis.

In contrast to this, the second assessors report evaluated the examination outcome two grade levels lower than the first assessor, in the 'good' category and returned 13 pages of major amendments. It appears in reading the assessors report that umbrage was taken with the introduction that may have got this particular assessor off to a bad start. There was some repetition in the introduction that I had found hard to avoid. This is criticised. Conventions on chapter outlines also came to focus. The fact that I hadn't provided a précis of every single key reference, conceptual idea and artist I examined relative to my work in the chapter outlines was listed for amendment. At the core of the criticism was that I had not provided enough of a road map for the exegesis. Reading through the report was confounding. There were some absolutely excellent observations and recommendation for amendments that would improve the thesis. There were numerous clearly articulated compliments about the critical frameworks, the insight it provided to reading the work and to the various successes of the creative projects. These critically astute comments and observations were balanced out by the most bizarre list of artists and other cultural and critical frameworks that apparently I should have also written about. This read as a quick-fire brainstorming list without any due reflection. So on one hand I had great comments but on the other I doubted whether the assessor had actually understood the nuancing of the project or if indeed had spent any time duly reflecting on the appropriateness of references suggested or listed as required amendments. My supervisor appraisal of this examination report was that what was being returned for major amendments were the equivalent of a completely different exegesis. Through my supervisor's guidance and weighting the disparity between the two assessors, we arrived at an agreed list of amendments.

The significant disparity between the two assesses reports suggested to me that current processes employed by the academic institution I studied at are open to a reasonably subjective interpretation of the grading criteria and overall expectations of PhD in the fine art discipline. As a student going through this process at no point in time was a grading matrix or specific grading descriptors made available. So making sense of the significant disparity between two assessors' reports had no substantiating references that could be drawn on. The use of three assessors may have provided a more balanced examination and reporting process.

In retrospect what would you do differently?

Undertaking the PhD part-time extended the study over eight years and during this period there were some major shifts to my art practice and the focus on the research. The constraints of my employment and available time necessitated this study mode. In hindsight, full-time study with a dedicated time to focus on a research project looks to me like the preferred option for a PhD

What advice would you give to prospective doctoral candidates?

As an academic teaching masters degree students there has been an increase in the number of graduates that want to continue their studies by enrolling in PhDs. There appear to be several motivators to this. One is that the PhD scholarship provides a means to continue with creative practice in an economic environment where financially sustaining art practice is difficult. Secondly prospective PhD students are frequently looking for a critically engaged community of practice in a supported study environment. Third, any possibility of moving into an academic role at university requires a PhD that is motivating for some prospective students. There is also a noted increase in the number of PhD candidates that have been in continuous study since the commencement of their undergraduate degrees. Undertaking a PhD is tough, it requires focus, discipline and a sustained time of writing that takes the artist away from the studio. It also requires the examination of one's art practice, though a depth of theoretical enquiry that can at times feel antithetical to creative practice and it can impose a very tight focus on that practice. It's also quite a solo journey. So if considering a PhD my advise is as follows: know why you want to do one; don't expect a close knit community of practice in postgraduate research; if you have come straight through from undergraduate do a couple of years of self-directed practice before entering into a PhD because sustaining an art practice outside a formal institution will provide invaluable skills in working independently, and finding your voice and practice as an artist. While having a PhD can open opportunities for teaching in tertiary institutions, this is not always the case, nor does it provided any assurances for stable and secure employment in the tertiary sector. Finally understand that the PhD journey requires openness, excellent communication skills and courage.

READING, WRITING, MAKING FOUNDATIONS TO IMAGE A CONTESTED SPACE

Nikos Pantazopoulos

Title of study: How to make a monument
Monash University, 2013

Abstract

For this practice led PhD I have produced three new works: *A Spartan Monument, Ongoing Monument to Indecent Activities 399BC,* and *A Monument to Toilets: An exhibition and procession.* In this exegesis, which supports three artworks and their problems, I have devised a structure that places at the centre of my writing the work of Felix Gonzalez-Torress (FGT). On the one hand, this reflects the enormous importance of his work to my own. More importantly, however, it is an attempt to deploy his work – and to ask questions of his work – as a means to ask, and answer, questions regarding my own work.

This PhD project responds to my own experiences growing up as the son of Greek immigrants, and, specifically, to what this means for the way that I 'came out' as a gay man, and how I encountered the city as a space. For me, there was no pedagogical model or any identifiable histories that paved the way for a homosexual's rite of passage. It was in this context of the heteronormative city that I became the author of my own education. I explored the metropolis to find and realize my desires and turned to invisible spaces to piece together my own path. In these explorations I discovered a tradition of homosexuals continually resisting the patriarchal state, struggling to be recognized as different and sovereign.

This PhD project has evolved as an articulation of this experience. That experience is, above all, the experience of the city, framed by the complexities of being gay, the constant process of coming out this entails, and being the son of Greek immigrants for whom the city was something to be negotiated through their children.

This exegesis has sought to support, contextualize and unpack the three works I present in my examination exhibition. I have sought to answer: *How might a monument articulate a gay experience of the city?* I have relied heavily upon the process of researching and producing an archive of information on the history of homosexuality. This, along with a strong emphasis on participatory process, has become the material that has yielded a set of works that might be understood as anti-monuments. I have identified that the position of homosexuality in the patriarchal city means that the process of coming out is ongoing, and I have attempted to understand what this means for art making. In the model of FGT's work, and in my own work, this ongoing process finds its expression in the structure of the work itself, which then resists both the classical tropes of a monument, but also the closure that these tropes imply. These anti-monuments become a means to avoid both assimilation and the stereotypical image of homosexuality. Above all, they are a way to honour a set of experiences and a tradition of resistance, and to build, through art making, the knowledge and resources for that resistance to be ongoing.

--

In the following section I will attempt to describe my doctoral journey. I will reflect and touch on the academic, personal and professional issues that are related to my study and my employment. I will conclude with how I emerged at the end of this process that has marred and currently remains a keystone to my continual learning.

Academic PhD student

As an early career researcher I had expectations projected on me through the academy where I studied that was not particularly clear to me. My experience and understanding of what a PhD might be, was limited, I did not know what feedback or assessment form for the process of the exegetical writing and exhibition would look like. This is because I had not been presented or shown one. I had entered into a process of learning without any incremental feedback. As I had very little experience, if next to none, and the doctoral process was foreign to me, my expectations were to just get through this alienating process quickly and to complete my milestones as they had been presented to me through the academic board.

Unlike the current climate in postgraduate study where candidates are given two supervisors, I only had one allocated to me, Dr Tom Nicholson. He was a very good supervisor who helped me through my milestones with abundant pedagogic generosity through our interactions. Dr Nicholson had a flourishing art practice, which I had the opportunity to experience by volunteering on his projects. He had a busy schedule this was in one sense difficult because he was travelling internationally, making it difficult to have conversations with him in the present so I had to rely on developing the scholarly relationship through the written form and through deadlines.

I look back on my aspiration to complete and I see it as not enough to just complete but to reach a level of academic rigor in which the project has very solid foundations to grow from in the future. However and in spite of very lean resources and support, I was expected to work through my trajectory of the postdoctoral in solitary, this challenged my constructive space of learning and it was also the paradoxical successful component to the project; which is not visible in the document. I touched on what it means to self-reflect on the situation of making and writing and carved out a pedagogical structure that continues to assist my academic development.

Preparing for a submission and receiving a report

I completed my PhD in April 2013 so there is a significant amount of time passed; however the experience of producing the practice led project and the written document has left me with plenty of problems to consider in my work as an academic and as an artist.

When I received the report it came to me unexpectedly, as I did not discuss once with my supervisor how I would receive the examination feedback and what this feedback might look like. When it did it was a very poorly written rubric with a very short paragraph of critique.

I was not asked to resubmit my exegesis, I was asked to fix up and extend certain details in the writing such as: I need to explore the concept of hegemony further in my writing. It was also noted that I repeated the word homosexual many times in my exegesis it would have been stronger to have edited out the over use of this word or if I am to repeat it I should think about how I can play with this word more poetically through the text and use it as punctuation. I was also asked to explain my own work in the postscript in more slow and objective detail in the way that I described other artist's work in the chapters. Some of the positive comments were that I have an engaging written style and that it clearly articulated the problems I was addressing and I was commended on the confident understanding and exploration of materials.

Having started my PhD with very little command of the written form I was writing timorously – with more time I would have been more autonomous and considered these structural and grammatical issues more intently. The structure of the exegesis was introduced to me by my supervisor (the script embodied the main argument here I talked about artists and artworks that have informed and contributes to my research. The postscript is the text that unpacks my own work. This framework is very useful and I recommend it as a written form.

Receiving the report made the exegesis that I submitted to a deadline, the underdeveloped concepts and threads in my writing and the exhibition was revealed to me in my underdeveloped report, which itself needed work. However with distance and time I do see that I did not having enough time to reflect on the document. There was an expectation and an urgency to complete put on me from both the University I was employed by and the University I was a candidate at.

On the completion of my PhD I was then asked to complete a tertiary teaching training course and this experience took up a lot of time in which my research time was being used up in this area and was an encumbrance to working through the unresolved aspects of the PhD which I see now as the 'problems' in the work, things that need attention and to be resolved. If I had more support and encouragement to complete my PhD in the time frame in which I was given with teaching time off I would have produced a much stronger document that articulated and threaded the projects I researched more coherently.

I had begun my doctoral journey in 2009 as a Masters candidate and I upgraded to a PhD at my confirmation six months into my project. My PhD supervisor worked with me through my milestones and my exegesis with a firm and a pedagogical approach that was at times extremely challenging and rewarding. The relationship to my supervisor was important and at times on the verge of needy. I was vulnerable and I relied on thinking through the work and the opening up of research both in the studio and in the writing. Tom Nicholson not only had a grasp of my practice he was also aware of the community that I was relating too and I volunteered on his social practice project for The Melbourne Urban Sculpture Prize that was an important factor in extending my understanding of reflecting and making at that time beyond a material and theory driven process. We entered a psychoanalytic conversation that informed the basic argument in my practice in which I argue through my writing and through other artist's works that I am interested in about the personal as politics and material. I placed a lot of trust and asked for a lot of guidance because I felt that I needed to complete my PhD at a speedy time for my employment at RMIT. Whilst working at RMIT I was under the impression that if I completed my academic studies on time and if I also completed my Essentials in Teacher Training course that my academic career would open up for me and more work would be available as I would be more useful across the school. This has not happened. I have had to teach a lot during and after the process that has impacted on my workload and into my own studio time. These boundaries have become blurred.

What was the motivation to study?

I completed my MFA in London in 2007 and returned to Australia in 2008 for personal reasons. My father had passed away and my mother in her early 80s was living alone. I wanted to contribute to my family as a youngest son of three children. My oldest brother has three children and one has passed away from cancer/leukemia and lives in Melbourne with his wife and is an owner operator of a fresh fish shop at the Camberwell market and is busy with those aspects of his life. Although he is also very close to my mother she lived alone in Brunswick and would have to find independent ways to grief and mourn her husband of 50 years. My sister lives in Athens with four children and her husband and was also busy rearing her family. As the youngest son I had recently come out of a short term gay relationship in London and had recently completed my Masters. It felt like the right time to return to Melbourne and be close by my mother and support each other through the mourning process of her husband and my father. I moved to East Melbourne in a bed sit and applied for an Australian Postgraduate Award scholarship at Monash University which I was successful with.

Were you encouraged/supported by your institution?

From the perspective of being a student

At Monash University I felt supported by the fact that I had received a scholarship and had developed a strong relationship to the other lecturers on the course in the lead up to doing my PhD through external research projects. I initially turned to them for advice and research strategies, however as my individual project developed external influences seemed impossible to access. In my first year I tutored Art Theory to the first-year students under the supervision of Robert Nelson at Monash University. As the research got more involved and I needed more time I worked purely on my project trying to find a discipline on my research days reading appropriate texts that related to my writing and interests. The PhD felt like a very difficult terrain to mine when nobody was offering any help or advice. When the writing eventually began to find a form my supervisor was very good at critiquing my every single expression making me self-reflect on the position I was taking. This at that time was not clear to me where and what kind of field I was projecting, the writing was shaping my position through the questions that he would pose to me and I was relying on my defense as a strategy of moving through the writing.

From the perspective of being of being a lecturer in the school of Art

When I returned to Melbourne in 2008 I was offered a sessional teaching role in the Fine Art Photography studio through Lyndal Walker who had been working in the studio for several years. She in the first two semesters would introduce me to the teaching structure of this particular studio area. I taught first years 'Photographic Ideas' and we worked in semester reviews together. I was encouraged and supported to develop my teaching role in the following three years and I would move from a sessional lecturer to a fixed term 0.5 lecturer with an increasing sense of roles and responsibilities. When the merger begun with Printmaking and Photography, my PhD became pressing, the deadline was consciously looming that I had to complete. It was mentioned several times during my performance appraisals that I needed to finish my PhD in due time to confirm my position and to make my contract from a fixed term to ongoing. This added a lot of pressure to the situation and I lost sight of the goal of the PhD. My work went from being a research driven project that was to be crafted and made with quality to an intensive in which I had to complete my PhD so that my job would become secure. In this process I was not given any time off except when I was presenting my exhibition in which I took one week of PhD leave to install my research project.

Why did you decide on the university?

I chose to go to Monash University because I was interested in the profile of their staff with whom I was at that point collaborating with on social engaged projects. Monash University had been promoting a new rigorous and experimental postgraduate program and it has a vast array of national and international artists, curators and academics speak at their lunchtime forums and their symposiums. They are interested in engaging with a global art discourse from within the institution, which is made evident through the public profile of the staff. The postgraduate course is also located next to their gallery MUMA in which they research and present high profile exhibitions. Through my professional relationship with staff and engaging with the program of their public galleries I was enthused to apply for an Australian Postgraduate Award in which I was successful.

Comment on the process you underwent to decide on the topic/thesis/project and how it changed/emerged.

My project was practice led and I worked in the studio and on sites until I allegedly found a thread in my work that I could reflect on beyond the aesthetics and its physical material. My initial project was about exploring my practice through studio related experiments and it evolved into a site-specific set of projects. I applied for a travel scholarship in my second year of research and it was through this travelling scholarship that I began to reflect on site-specific practice in a deep and meaningful way. With my travelling scholarship I went to London and had an exhibition in the Whitecubicle – a curated space in East London in which I developed a research project based on the Queer working class homosexual community of this particular area. I invited the public in to participate in a socially engaged project in which they helped me to realize a monument to a gay bashing and the closing down of gay bars and the beginnings of gentrification in this area. When I returned back to Melbourne after having worked through a site-specific research project as a way of making, I worked with a local Spartan/Greek community to make a monument to an historical leader that stood as a role model to the first wave of Greek immigration. The folklore that this leader exemplified was that of a person who defended his countries to his death. These relational activities then led me to think through my final project, which was about a public space in which illegal homosexual activities took place. This building was a very famous architectural site designed by Roy Grounds for the Melbourne City Council, despite the building impressive architectural vision and the architectural communities rallying to preserve this site as a heritage building; the homosexual activities that took place on this site outweighed the necessity of preserving the Australian architectural landmark. The conflicting politics around this site became a catalyst for my research and became the foundations to re-imagine a contested homosexual political space.

I found that my interests were at that time about using cultural history about underrepresented spaces in which I was a part of as material to make-work. I was researching other artists that were interested in anti-monuments and monuments and it was then they decided to write my question. How to make a monument as an overall arching title to my practice led PhD.

Comment on the process of determining the methodology for the research and how it changed/emerged?

I determined the methodology of the research as I gained momentum in my research, which was expanding outwards with artists and writers. I began to find a thread, which was useful to me developing a position that framed a self-reflective approach to making. The way I reflected on my personal experiences were mirrored by a more communal experience made possible through the way that homosexuality operated around and in architecture and public space.

How did your practice develop over your candidature?

My practice developed during candidature through engaging in my research in the studio and in the reading and writing process. These disparate activities were weaved together through finding a point of connectivity in making, reading and writing. The very activity of following an inquiry and allowing the process to unfold became a very significant and important method of working. Instead of becoming fixated on an outcome I focused on developing a process as a method of working that I could reflect upon. For instance I was interested in particular sites. I used these sites as a way to collect information that I could generate knowledge on. I would then use this knowledge to build a narrative around the space and to also construct architectural/sculptural forms. The content that I collected about the sites that I was researching operated as references and an index to the making and the writing. All these activities would weave in and out of each other till a particular shape took place based on rules that I imposed on each project. Rules where made because of the limitations that where imposed by the project and the sites that I chose to work with. For instance does the site still exist? If not, what could I gather about the site? What could I do with the information that I gathered about the site that reflects upon my experiences of using the site? These types of self-reflective and process driven questions formed and framed my research.

How did you organize your work/employment to allow you to study?

I worked as a sessional at RMIT in the first two years; I was then offered a 0.5 position in the last two years of my PhD. The School of Art was undergoing structural changes, Fine Art Photography amalgamated with Printmaking and my line manager changed. The PhD was and seemed critical to my employment and it felt critical that I completed on time. My line manager in my new situation did not have a PhD and it was an uncomfortable position to be in to be discussing the progress and to discuss the project with someone who had not yet begun there own journey in this process. I felt as though it was imperative to turn to someone who had completed a PhD so that I could obtain applied knowledge on the process of completing a practice – led PhD under the circumstances of working and study under such tight deadlines and pressures of the Universities.

How did you organize your life (and family) to allow you to study?

I lived by myself in a bed-sit in East Melbourne I would visit my elderly mother in Brunswick twice a week so that I maintained a healthy relationship to my family. I had a personal life on the weekends and I tried very hard to maintain a scholarly practice during the week. I worked from my kitchen table and at the State Library of Victoria.

What were the main issues you confronted throughout your period of study?

I had problems with writing and reading and focusing on a project. My ideas networked and spiraled outwards away from a center having to bring them back in was difficult at first. What was more of a problem for me was trying to unpack the process of my work, staying focused on the actual work that was just made and looking back in reflection. It was as though I was looking for content beyond the surface and the process of my practice. This could be or was interesting for an introduction or a conclusion however reading by unpacking its process materiality and its spatial intent would have given the project a deeper reading. I would have been able to articulate in the writing the way that my materiality moves from the sculptural into the photographic and from the photographic back into a spatial practice. My biggest problem was that the work repeated the grand old theme of homosexuality and this became a barrier to looking deeper at other was that I its materiality was a repetitive part of the writing. There should have been more moments in which I did more objective analysis and a thorough analytical unpacking of my own works. Not just of the other artists that I analysed.

Therefore I had several threads running through my work. I needed to start with the basics with my writing. It was all very stream of consciousness. I struggled to understand how to write a structure for an essay and how to write a paragraph. I had a lot of readings that I wanted to read and I also was reading from a lot of different sources. I was finding it difficult to focus my reading in one area as I was concerned and interested in so much different content.

What was the most difficult memory of the time as a candidate?

There where so many difficult memories of the PhD that it is difficult to recount only one; from trying to make a decision about what my work would be about for the purpose of a pedagogical project to having to learn to write concise sentences. At the beginning of my candidature I had two supervisors. Dr Daniel Palmer as my primary and Dr Tom Nicholson as my secondary supervisor. In the first six months Dr Palmer went on sabbatical and I only had Dr Nicholson for the following three years. Whilst now reflecting on the supervision only having one supervisor meant that I was encouraged to go in one particular direction with my work, I was not censored from going in other directions however there was also no conversation about taking another course with my work. I did explore several methods of making and writing before committing to my final project but these where all my own insular decisions. The narrative arc in my making was broad and with a big wide lens I framed an autobiographical exploration to do with my relationship to City of London and the City of Melbourne as sites of making. (It is only now after the PhD that I am slowing down and working more directly with the materials to understand the craft, materiality and the direct relationship I have to studio in my practice.)

Probably the most difficult thing that I found however was that I had no one at all to discuss my readings with or to develop my writing, except when I would submit chunks of writing to my supervisor. There were no readings groups or writing groups that where appropriate to my particular focus. These are the nuances of a practice – led PhD that as the researcher and the maker you enter uncharted territories alone.

Learning how to write and address the things that are important for me was the key to forming my PhD project. The research was about ways of framing and highlighting places in which I discovered and explored my homosexual coming out; that to me under the illegal circumstances were safe place.

The silence I experienced by my supervisor as we met was very alienating and strange. He would arrive and not speak waiting for me to say something that was about my research. At times I was very lost and could not find a way into a discussion. I didn't really understand what the purpose of a meeting in which he didn't speak would amount to. I now reflect on those times as being when he was really trying to tell me something the meeting was not drowned out in other meaningless conversation and he left a lot of space between what he said. This gave gravitas and impact to his comments.

What was the most memorable time during your research?

Completing my documentation studies and presenting the conclusion to my research was my most memorable moment. The conclusion was presented in the form of a presentation in the last six months of my candidature. At this presentation I unpacked all the site-specific projects that I had made during the time of my candidature. It was in producing the writing and delivering the presentation that the research had finally come together and I had a frame to hang my writing on and around.

In retrospect what would you do differently?

In retrospect, I would slow down, I would use my intuition more and I would engage the process of art making and the various relationships to writing more rigorously. Slowing down to write can be a very difficult task when you are wrapped up in ideas and wanting to produce. I would take the time to think about what it is that I just made, how did I make it what was the catalyst to the object that I made, is the object or photograph in response to something else I have seen? I now try and do in my work those these particular qualities as a studio practice. If I slow down and clearly write and articulate what it is that I am trying to produce using short sentences I now write as I make continually and I read and scout for writing that I find informs my own studio methodologies.

ON THE CONSIDERATION OF VALUABLE TIMES

David Thomas

Title of study: Extending duration: Time and timing in contemporary painting and painting/installation practice

RMIT University, 2004

Abstract

The research project produced paintings and painting/installations that examined how time and timing can affect delivery and content in a work of art, and how, through the application of the principles of duration, and the structures of the composite and multiplicities, readings of a work could be extended in both time and space. Painting is defined to include Painting / Installation as a hybrid category of practice where the component elements of painting are articulated in and pictorialize actual space and time.

The works aim to focus the viewers' attention on being and perceiving in time and space. The works addressed key the following research questions:

How can the principles of duration be applied to enable various meanings to unfold in time and in turn affect the perception of content in a painting and/or painting installation?

Can the use of duration reconcile heterogeneous experiences and codes within a work of art?

Content in this context becomes understood as both a cultural operation, external to the viewer, resulting from the manipulation of the artist's language, and as an internal operation embodied in the viewer, as sensation, affecting and affected by the viewer's experience, perception and memory.

The exegesis supported the practice, addressing relevant philosophical and historical links, in particular, two key aspects Henri Bergson's model of duration: the idea of the composite, a model/idea that is composed of components, different in kind; and, the model of multiplicity, which aims to reconcile the heterogeneous nature of experience (moments) within the unity of the continuum of time.

Other important references discussed included: Merleau-Ponty's work on the phenomenology of perception, the embodied experience and his idea of the chiasmic, an intertwining of inner and outer experience; Deleuze and Guattari's ideas of hybridity and pluralism, as manifest in the idea of the 'rhizome', and Paul Crowther's Principle of Reciprocity, which discusses the iterable in relationship to language and perception in creating meaning. These theoretical and philosophical models were complemented with a discussion of the painting of Pierre Bonnard, who I term an Impressionist with a memory. I analyse his work with regard to memory, experience and the issues of time, timing and humour in pictorial space. European movements of Constructivism, Suprematism, de Stijl and Unism and French art of the 1960s and 1970s including the work of François Morellet, Supports/Surfaces and BMPT and their relevance to my practice were discussed.

Although the roots of my practice lie in the Australian, British and European traditions of Concrete and monochrome art, these were contextualised by a review of selected contemporary practitioners in the field from other cultural sources including the USA and Asia. Global and local approaches to reductive painting were acknowledged. The exegesis concluded by discussing the passage of my practice and how it enabled questions of content, authentic experience and its relationship to the conditions of Contemporary Painting to be engaged with.

--

What was the motivation to study?

Primarily I returned to formal study as I wanted to clarify my practice and its context. I wished to be more articulate about those things that one can be conscious of in a practice. I also recognized that in order to keep teaching at a tertiary level in the future, I would need this degree and it would give me more opportunities. However I also realized that it was not a guarantee for these things to occur.

Were you encouraged/supported by your institution?

Yes, although I was hampered by not receiving an Australian Postgraduate Award (APA) as my previous results were ungraded, as was the practice during my undergraduate art study. Again this throws up questions regarding of how practice led research in Fine Art in Australia is valued and its relationship to traditional academic attitudes of what constitutes a PhD research within universities. Funding for practice led research (pure/primary) is still very rare whilst funding for Fine Art historical research (secondary) or design research (applied) is more prevalent. That being said RMIT does recognize the value of practice led research and it has supported many artist/academics through the PhD process.

Why did you decide on the university?

I decided to study at RMIT University. On one level that might appear as mere convenience as RMIT was the institution in which I worked. However I knew its strengths and weakness. I had done enough research and I did not wish to waste my time so I chose the university because of its supervisors.

My supervisors importantly were not from my direct department but were experts in relevant fields to my research. I had been invited by other universities to undertake a PhD but I felt the supervision was more appropriate at RMIT and their understanding of practice led research was well established and regarded. The formal supervision was complemented by colleagues and peers from elsewhere through discussion. This is also important for candidates to understand as the issues being researched go beyond individual supervisors and individual universities.

Deciding on a topic

It was a long process to find an appropriate language by which to articulate my questions and to reflect the complexity and multiplicity of fine art practice. During my MA I was often using an accepted given terminology. This seemed inappropriate for my PhD. Eventually I found after 20 or so attempts, a satisfactory set of questions and appropriately personal terminology began to emerge. This continued to be defined and clarified as the PhD progressed. My practice led research was both logical and intuitive. My thinking theoretical and contextual research slowly became personal and related to my practice as the project progressed. Research is organic, it has different rhythms. It became important to understand these and that at times it was important to be reflective and do nothing. It was important to give myself time to understand and accept as normal the uneasy spaces that research sometimes led one. I learnt to understand that failure can be good – success is not just summing something up neatly according to the popular conventions of the day. Failure is an important and necessary part of the process. My writing slowly began to clarify methods, processes and facture and importantly context.

Comment on the process of determining the methodology for the research and how it changed/emerged.

An artwork is a unique set of relationships, which operate in the reality of the world, both culturally and experientially as a multiplicity of ideas sensations. These occur in a non-linear fashion. The experience of the work is not simply transferable to another idiom, particularly one like writing, which is linear. The actual experience of an artwork differs from what is written about it. An artwork's actuality brings the material, conceptual and sensory together into a holistic construct that unfolds in time and space not necessarily in a logical manner. It is important to understand that the PhD is not simply a written text.

Heuristic models were used. Experimental studio practice was developed into exhibitions. This enabled me to reflect upon and evaluate the diverse public responses to the work and were eventually written up. This however, was not done employing a scientific quantitative method of analysis. The very nature of art, of poetics is qualitative and deals with the reality of the subjective. Therefore my evaluations reflected this.

How did your practice develop over your candidature?

I was determined that my practice lead the PhD and that theory be integrated into it. Theory is an important part of an informed practice, as is history, but practice is not simply an illustration of theory. The practice needed to respond to the actuality of experience as well as idea. I wanted a holistic approach knowing and feeling were important, irresolution, failure, questioning, fuzziness were important to accept, as these are part of life … my work had to reflect this. In fact it was these very conditions that would often enable to work to have life/energy. Learning how to accommodate, the incomplete, the sense of continuing, of becoming was critical in order that I could sustain my research. I continued to exhibit, seeing these moments as key mechanisms for testing my outcomes. This is a normal practice for an artist. I tested aspects of my research through my personal responses and criterion in the studio. Was my content clear and presented in a way that actualized the complexity of experience in a succinct manner. The works were then presented in solo, group exhibitions, collaborations and studio experiments for comment by others.

How did you organize your work/employment to allow you to study?
How did you organize your life (and family) to allow you to study?

I took leave, paid and unpaid when I could. I was working part-time in an Art school and I muddled through. Family and friends were critical to my stability and support. I needed to balance time with them. My professional practice as an artist working within Australia and abroad was important to maintain. It was also important to recognize the limits of my PhD project and not get this confused with my general ongoing practice – they were obviously connected – but the PhD project was specific. It was not everything, not the total sum of my knowledge and practice. It was a project of research.

What were the main issues you confronted throughout your period of study?

Time and energy – the discipline to balance these was critical. Time to laugh and vent outside the world of the PhD was important. Life was bigger than the PhD. Trying to understand that the PhD did not have to be academic and justified by theoretical writing alone but should be research in my field – which is painting – a practice of Art. At the early stage of my candidature (all those years ago) people implied that the written form was the PhD bit as there was not a lot of experience around Fine Art Practice. Many assessors and supervisors were art historian or theoreticians not practitioners. This was due to the history of how higher degrees and university art schools developed. Thankfully things are changing.

What was the most memorable time during your research?

A recognition that my research was valid and useful to others as well as myself. That I could be articulate in arrange of ways in diverse forums.

In retrospect what would you do differently?

I would write less. I would not try to write an encyclopaedia of everything but would limit the scope of my writing more. I would understand how to waste time profitably. I would recognize that time is a gift it does not have to be filled with frenetic activity but with USEFUL ACTIVITY.

What advice would you give to prospective doctoral candidates?

Panic slowly, take your time, talk, discuss. Do not fear making mistakes. For Fine art candidates understand that your practice is the primary form of research and that theory and practice are intertwined.

Laugh a lot support each other.

Use humour.

This is an underlying present in some of my work, most of my teaching and hopefully for your sakes in some of this writing. In your PhD it can be employed as a tactic for destabilizing tropes of practice, enabling you to be surprised and challenging content to be addressed in non-threatening ways.

Read widely at times beyond your discipline. My ideas have been informed by numerous thinkers as diverse as Michel de Montaigne and Henri Bergson, artists and movements including; Pierre Bonnard, William Turner; Supports Surfaces, BMPT, Gerhard Richter, Blinky Palermo and Lee Ufan, as well as contemporary iterations of Non – Objective practice and importantly my artistic peers. INSIGHT NOT ONLY SIGHT was my aim, to paraphrase the Danish painter Per Kirkeby.

Understand your context in which you are making working – the real politik and conditions of the world. Our contemporary society is materially orientated, its agenda is driven by a particular brand of economic rationalism forgive my gross over simplification here which tells us things; like time is money. Time is not money, as we all know. Time is a gift, time is valuable, not only in what it enables us to produce and consume materially…but in what it enables us produce and consume intellectually, emotionally, spiritually. For time enables us through its passing to consider value. For me art is my chosen means of reflecting on these issues and valuing time.

Regarding the written component: Be succinct (excuse my hypocrisy here!), use the titles/subheadings to help in the exegesis/dissertation, don't underestimate the value of the Post-it note, use post-it notes to materialize the structure and content of your PhD on a wall, table, floor. For artists this is often a useful strategy for seeing how ideas become concrete and how they connect.

Other issues or comments

Stress less, take a big picture view. Have fun and realize what a privileged position we are in. That unlike most of the world we have the potential to make, to think, to feel, to act to question whilst contributing to a field we love. And finally it is how you say something/ make as much as what you say/ make your research with passion. This time does not come around again. Value every moment!

WHAT JUST HAPPENED?

Darrin Verhagen

Title of study: Noise, music & perception:
Towards a functional understanding of noise composition

RMIT University, 2015

Abstract

This research explores the compositional mechanics of Noise Music. It seeks to understand both the grammars of Noise when compared with traditional musical styles, as well as the types of experiences it elicits from its audiences. It acknowledges the academic work undertaken to date in relation to the genre but identifies that extant academic analysis has been strongly informed by sociopolitical readings, cultural context or philosophical claims (whether for or against the genre). With that in mind, this research bypasses such approaches and instead uses systematic musicology to gain a better understanding of the genre's compositional mechanics. Acknowledging the fact that Noise hit a brick wall of maximum intensity almost at inception, it then asks the question how arousal levels in response to contemporary Noise practice might be heightened. Experiments in attempting to maximize the experience has pushed sound into light, vibration and physical movement. In so doing, a number of the deeper questions that usually lie latent in musical experience have assumed greater presence and demanded answers.

--

Motivations to study

The starting point was certainly institutional encouragement. I had never really thought strategically about the value of a PhD before. Even when it was first raised for consideration, the frame presented was more around the PhD as a finish line, rather than a starting point for enabling/supporting further research. Whilst I achieved greater clarity about the doctorate as the equivalent of a driver's licence as I progressed through the PhD, my initial thinking didn't really extend beyond 'OK. I'm doing a PhD – what should it be?' I chose Noise (the most extreme genre) simply for the poetry in counterweighting with my Masters which had explored delicate instability in very minimal 'lowercase' musical forms. Both provided the means of using the extremities of experimental genres to interrogate an expanded perspective on what music is and how it works at a psychophysiological level. Whilst recent systematic musicology – the exploration of the neurobiological basis for music consumption – has brought musical discourse into the 20th century, the nature/position of most academics writing about the subject results in a focus that can still be very conservative. I was interested in interrogating existing theories about what music is and how it works by exploring the edges.

There was another layer of motivation. Ultimately, I was annoyed that the primary forms of academic engagement with the Noise genre were always from socio-political and philosophical standpoints. The idea that my work practice would neatly divide so that anything noisy was some kind of inherent statement – an antagonism to the musical hegemony – when writing for an orchestra wasn't, seemed both myopic and puerile. My initial intention was to argue with these positions – ones which that felt like they were making claims for a genre which were far removed from my experience as a practitioner. A great piece of early advice from an Associate Professor of Psychology at Melbourne University however, was simply 'Don't engage'. As he suggested, rather than spending a PhD grounded in negativity, arguing against positions for which I lacked any respect, I should simply sideline the establishment from the outset and instead concentrate on a new way of thinking about the form – an alternative position to the established order rather than an unrelenting series of corrections to their misguidance. So whilst the anger was an initial motivation, the choice to focus on a positive alternative instead of spending three years sniping at theorists who annoyed me, paved the way for a far more fulfilling experience. Simply saying 'that's one way of looking at it; here's another' allowed for greater time to explore what I wanted to do, rather than undertaking an exercise in trench warfare.

Choice of university

RMIT has a strong pedigree in experimental musical forms. It was also an opportunity to source co-supervision across schools – as a means of covering not merely extreme music, but also media psychology. I had explored the idea of a similar interschool approach elsewhere, and whilst one supervisor was perfect, the school of music in that institution wasn't. I would argue that the choice of supervisors is always the most important consideration, rather than the institution. Whilst I can understand that questions of prestige and reputation may strategically influence some candidate's choices – that a doctorate in a particular discipline at a particular university may carry more weight for future post-doctoral positions – I went into the PhD without any kind of long-term thinking. I just wanted the right people's guidance for the sort of research I was interested in. A sound artist who understood noise and a media psychologist were the perfect blend.

Process

At the point of my initial application, the topic began as an exercise in the challenge of fusing creative practice experiments – taking a high art form – *musique concrete* – to be mashed with a 'low' art form – Noise. Whilst creatively exciting, this starting point didn't have a series of genuinely interesting research questions at its core. The far more fruitful drive for my research was the aforementioned dissatisfaction with academic literature's engagement with noise – where it is viewed only as a socio-political or philosophical statement rather than a creative exploration no different from any other genre. As a practitioner who worked with a range of styles, I was keen to find a frame that could shift that paradigm. In that regard, the process of working on the confirmation document was a useful opportunity to focus and refine my interests. Early on I was curious to see what happens to the arguments if I framed the experience of Noise as the equivalent of a bungy jump or roller coaster ride. This became an important mechanism for shutting down politics and philosophy.

This whole process helped clarify that creative interests aren't necessarily always aligned with academic interests. In much the same way that a Noise academic had never influenced anything to do with my music practice, an interesting creative idea isn't necessarily the best stimulus to generate research questions. I'm not suggesting the two are mutually exclusive. In my case, however – initially at least – they were.

In hindsight, the research methodology was as dynamically responsible for the changes in my topic as any conscious decision. I was exploring in a sandpit, raising questions rather than using the practice to answer them. Rather than the research being a means by which I could further develop a pre-existing expertise, the truly experimental nature of the multimodal experiences I was designing was leading me to more and more interesting research questions in an effort to understand what was happening in audience experiences. These in turn, were helping identify the limits of Fine Art philosophy and critical theory as useful tools in the generation of new knowledge. As a result, I was finding new disciplines (anatomy, psychology, ethology, neurotheology) were offering more effective mechanisms to interrogate the mechanics of what I was developing creatively. Furthermore, the more distant Kansas was becoming, the more important it was that I start surveying and interviewing others in order to ensure the psychophysiological claims I was making for the installations I was crafting weren't just limited to my own experience.

Methodology

At its most basic, my three questions of the Noise genre were What is it? How does it work? Why does it work? I considered a PhD by thesis, but discounted this early on. Firstly, I reminded myself that, despite curiosity, I had no skills in neurology, psychology or any of the other fields I would need to draw in to the study. My field of expertise is my creative practice: music, so that should be at the forefront of the research. Secondly, I assumed that within a six-year (part-time) framework, many of the questions I'd be asking about music and the brain would probably have been answered, given the ongoing developments in systematic musicology. Embarking on a practice-based research project, however, would allow me to feed this knowledge in to the project, rather than potentially feeling trumped by any published discoveries. Having decided on a PhD by project, I felt strongly against the traditional framing of the research in a Fine Art context. Having heard the phrase 'the practice is the research' repeatedly, I found it necessary to continually explain why – for me – the work was merely a means to an end, not an end in itself. The music being generated was the mechanism by which hypotheses could be interrogated, and new research questions generated.

An early curiosity – how Noise might be made more extreme – decisively shaped the nature of the work. And the most exciting aspect of the research was that the hypothesis which drove the methodology was completely wrong. Taking the starting premise that noise as a musical stimulus can't get any more sonically intense, I had erroneously considered that adding additional senses into the experience of power electronics would amplify arousal further. Instead of making Noise more intense however, adding vibration, movement and light actually made it more enjoyable. Understanding the psychophysiological differences between multisensory and monosensory noise became a key seam of research which I had never considered when starting the doctorate. The means by which this was being explored moved my practice into installation – which was a completely new area for me.

Developing practice over candidature

The exploration of multimodality shifted my practice from monosensory to multisensory. As such, it moved from simply musical explorations to more of a fine art installation practice. It is important to note that this wasn't an aesthetic development in my practice, however. It was simply the practical means by which I could explore and interrogate the principles I was studying. The other element which accompanied this development was the shift towards greater collaboration on my own projects. Whilst my sound design and soundtrack work is inevitably collaborative, to date it had always involved working on other people's projects. The PhD saw me developing ideas to which I would then bring in other practitioners. I began working with system designers, industrial designers, coders, motion programmers, and lighting designers. It is this key group of collaborators who now form the (((20hz))) collective and are active across a range of fine art outcomes.

The issues at the core of this research – essentially the psychophysiology of aesthetic experience – as well as the methodology (systematic musicology) have been fundamental interests of mine for the last decade of teaching. The doctorate never felt like it was separate from my interests or pedagogy, so there was never really a struggle. My previous research and teaching informed the PhD; the PhD informed conversations in the classroom …

Organisation

I worked through holidays to pursue my obsession, and took long service leave to work on the PhD rather than spend time with the family, or pursue any downtime. Far from being saviours of the planet, artists are just selfish. Learn (or at least come to terms with) what drives you. If you have a sad, psychological need to put your practice before everything else, understand and own your problem rather than hide behind any worthiness delusion. Ultimately, I loved what I was researching – so it never really felt like a burden to be endured. My partner is amazing – and was far more tolerant of how much fun I was having than she needed to be. My kids also saw through this idea of me 'going to work'. 'You make shit music and you ride in a chair' was actually a pretty astute summary.

Issues

The most difficult memory of the time as a candidate was being told by the Head of the Art School (at the time) that my research was a complete waste of time. Seeing how incensed other academics around me were getting when a traditional Fine Art research template wasn't being followed. Tiring of having to justify the idea that the work was a disposable means to an end in the interrogation of arousal/valence in multisensory experience rather than the hero of the PhD. Getting weary of the staff antagonism towards contemporary media psychology research methodologies. Fortunately, whilst all of this negativity was coming from the School I was in, there was serious enthusiasm for my research from other schools and universities – so it helped to clarify not that I was on the wrong track, but simply in the wrong school.

The most memorable time during your research was the excitement of running the audiokinetic jukebox at the NGV for *White Night* and that proving how completely wrong my assumptions (about 'more = more') had been. Suddenly, a far more interesting and complex series of questions opened up.

Changes

All of the negative experiences I previously outlined were fantastic tools to sharpen my perspective on which research paradigms were a fit for my interests. I was in a culture which had very restrictive ideas about what art was, what it was for, and what it might do. There were tensions in understanding sound. There were suspicions about setting aside philosophy and cultural theory in favour of the disciplines of psychology, neurology, nerotheology and evolutionary biology. By contrast, academics in other schools (and in the end, the examiners) were excited by the breadth of what I was doing. So whilst there were certainly frustrations when battling conservative notions of what an 'appropriate' approach might be, in hindsight it encouraged me to rethink whether I was in the right research environment. The PhD brought these matters to a head. The range of disciplines I was excited to draw from was chaotic, not singular. My interests extended across a number of fields rather than being nested in one 'home' discipline. I was enthusiastic to use my research findings to fuel collaborative opportunities – whether for 'pure' art ends or in the application of artistic approaches for practical outcomes. This was at odds with advice I was receiving that the PhD should be more insular and personal. Whilst I didn't know exactly where I fitted, it became very clear the research environment in which I didn't. With this gaining clarity from the mid-candidature review onwards, I was able to make plans to move Schools. Were it not for the PhD, the surprising directions in which it took me, and identifying enthusiastic research allies, I suspect I would have just muddled along with my soundtrack practice, rather than looking at the PhD as a starting point for further research and new directions.

CONTRIBUTORS

Colleen Boyle is an artist and writer working out of Melbourne, Australia. Her current research interests include: theories of perception and representation; history and theory of photography; space exploration and space imaging; philosophical interpretations of imagination; scientific imaging and theories of scientific observation. In 1977 her grandfather took her to see a matinee screening of the film *Star Wars* where the windows of the Yea Town Hall had been darkened with previously used black plastic that was ridden with tiny holes. The result was a galaxy of shining stars and thus began Colleen's life-long fascination with all things to do with outer space. Initially trained as a printmaker at Monash University, Colleen's art practice has now diversified into working with photography, sculptural elements, light, shadow, projections and mirrors.

Jazmina Cininas is a Melbourne-based artist best known for her technically demanding reduction linocuts, as well as an arts writer, curator and lecturer in printmaking at RMIT School of Art. For two decades now, Cininas has been charting the various incarnations of the female werewolf as a vehicle for her printmaking practice. Since completing her MA in 2002, Cininas has exhibited her ongoing Girlie Werewolf Project throughout Australia and in Lithuania, and has presented papers on female werewolves at international conferences in Philadelphia, Budapest, Oxford and Manchester. Her PhD research project, completed in 2014, saw her create a Girlie Werewolf Hall of Fame by identifying women from throughout history who may qualify as female werewolves for the purpose of creating reduction linocut portraits. Cininas' work has been shortlisted for numerous printmaking awards, and has been acquired for many public collections, including the National Gallery of Victoria, the Victorian Arts Centre, Broken Hill Regional Gallery and the Alice Springs Art Foundation. Her curatorial projects include Enchanted Forest: New Gothic Storytellers, which toured to significant regional galleries throughout Victoria and NSW between 2008–2009. Cininas also initiated the RMIT Summer Printmaking Residency programme with the exhibition Pelt in 2004.

Rhett D'Costa has more than 27 years of experience working as a professional artist and exhibiting regularly in solo and group exhibitions in Australia and overseas. He has taught and supervised in a range of capacities in tertiary institutions in Australia and overseas for more than 26 years. His doctorate is from RMIT University and currently works in the School of Art. His research includes the idea of the *'right to belong'* and the role of resilience and optimism in the intersecting areas of migration, identity, nationalism and belonging, in the context of a multidisciplinary art practice. His PhD project looks at how culturally composite ethnicities and mixed-race communities, negotiate the porosity of place, belonging and identity in the context of practice based research, which takes into account the shifting social and political circumstances, tensions and consequences of mobility and migration in transnational environments, examining the agency and role an artist as researcher can have within these often precarious and unstable spaces.

Lesley Duxbury is a Professor and artist whose research concerns include the natural environment, climate change and sustainability. Phenomenological experiences of extended walks in remote landscapes, such as Baffin Island, Nunavut, Canada, Tierra del Fuego and Iceland are the impetus for her investigations. She has exhibited for over 25 years in solo and more than 50 selected group shows in Australia, Korea, Austria and Hong Kong. She has undertaken artist residencies in Iceland (2015 and 2012) and in Paris at the Australia Council VACB studio (1996). She was awarded the Australia Council for the Arts New Work (established artist) Grant (2011). Exhibitions include: 2016: *Breathing Hemispheres* Blindside, Melbourne. *Out of the Matrix* RMIT Gallery, Melbourne. 2015: *Sky Lab: lines of sight and forces of attraction* Counihan Gallery, Melbourne. *27° South to 19° North: Contemporary Australian Photography* Museum of the City of Cuernavaca, Mexico. 2014: *Kyoto Hanga* Kyoto Municipal Museum & Fukuyama Art Museum, Japan. 2013: *Bogong ELECTRIC* site-specific artwork at Bogong Village, Victoria; *Local Weather*

Gippsland Art Gallery, Sale. 2012: *Luminous World* Art Gallery of Western Australia. 2011: *Out of the West* National Gallery of Australia, Canberra. Her work is held in all major public collections in Australia.

Phil Edwards has been a practicing and exhibiting artist for 34 years and a lecturer in the School of Art at RMIT for 12 years. He has much experience in both formal and experimental art spaces. He is a multi-disciplined artist whose current practice revolves essentially around the role of painting in the contemporary world. He is currently working on some music and sound projects. His research interests are only partly circumscribed by his formal studies. During his Masters he researched the possibility of an innate aesthetic that manifested itself in the casual assemblage of everyday objects. His PhD studies concerned themselves with an examination of the positioning of audio CDs in a Fine Art culture. Both these formal studies overlapped in the sense that within each was an examination of hybridity as it is expressed in the overlap between *art informale* and Fine Art. Phil's research focus and interests are in six themes: Children's art/ outsider art and its relationship to formal painting; Fake poetry and Fine Art; Alchemy in Art; Music brut; Temporality and Compression in Hybrid art forms.

David Forrest is Professor of Music Education in the School of Art at RMIT University. He has contributed to the fields of music, arts education, policy in music and arts, education and cultural development and doctoral education. He is a member of the National Executive of the Australian Society for Music Education and editor of the *Australian Journal of Music Education* and the *Victorian Journal of Music Education*. He has published *The Doctoral Journey in Music Education: Reflections on Doctoral Studies by Australian Music Educators* (2003) *Journeying: Doctoral Journeys in Music Education* (2009), *The Doctoral Journey in Art Education: Reflections on Doctoral Studies by Australian and New Zealand Art Educators* (2010) as well as three books on the Russian composer and educator D.B. Kabalevsky.

Ian Haig's practice refuses to accept that the low and the base level are devoid of value and cultural meaning. His body obsessed themes can be seen throughout a large body of work over the last twenty years. Previous works have looked to the contemporary media sphere and its relationship to the visceral body, the degenerative aspects of pervasive new technologies, to cultural forms of fanaticism and cults, to ideas of attraction and repulsion, body horror and the defamiliarisation of the human body. His work has been exhibited in galleries and video/media festivals around the world. Including exhibitions at: The Australian Centre for Contemporary Art, Melbourne; The Ian Potter Museum of Art, Melbourne; The Experimental Art Foundation, Adelaide; The Australian Centre for the Moving Image, Melbourne; Gallery of Modern Art, Brisbane; The Museum of Modern Art, New York; Artec Biennale – Nagoya, Japan; Centre Georges Pompidou, Paris; Art Museum of China, Beijing; Museum Villa Rot, Burgrieden-Rot, Germany. In addition, his video work has screened in over 120 festivals internationally. In 2003 he received a fellowship from the New Media Arts Board of the Australia Council and in 2013 he curated the video art show *Unco* at The Torrance Art Museum in Los Angeles.

Julian Goddard is Professor and Head of the School of Art at RMIT University, Melbourne. He has been an academic, writer and curator for over 30 years specializing in the aesthetics of the everyday. As well as an academic Julian is the founder and chairperson of the *Australian Centre for Concrete Art* – an international group that makes large public minimalist wall paintings. He is also chairperson of *The Bureau of Ideas* an international think-tank that promotes public discussion of art, design, architecture and philosophy through forums in non-academic environments. As a curator Julian has made over 100 exhibitions and published widely on Australian, Aboriginal and Concrete art, including three books, book chapters, articles, papers and catalogue essays. He is also an artist.

Professor Paul Gough is Pro Vice-Chancellor and Vice-President at RMIT University, Melbourne. A painter, broadcaster and author he has exhibited globally and is represented in the Imperial War Museum, London; Canadian War Museum, Ottawa; and the National War Memorial, New Zealand. In addition to two books on the British painter Stanley Spencer, his books include *'A Terrible Beauty': British Artists and the First World War* (2010) and *'Brothers* in Arms', John and Paul Nash (2014). He curated 'Back from the Front': Art, Memory and the Aftermath of War (2015) and has written extensively about the street artist, Banksy.

Michael Graeve is a visual and sound artist based in Melbourne Australia. He works across painting and sound disciplines through easel painting, site-specific installation, painting and sound installation, sound performance and composition. By engaging painting and sound art practices in dialogue, he seeks to extend frameworks for their creation and reading into oscillations between conjunctive and disjunctive relations. Installation space provides a playground for the juxtaposition of painting and sound, resulting in a suspenseful dialectic between causal relations and awkward un-relations. He has held over 25 solo exhibitions, and his work has been included in curated exhibitions surveying practices of sound art and non-objective and abstract painting in Australia and internationally. He is a Samstag scholar. Michael has been a board member of Liquid Architecture Sound Inc since 2007, and president and chair from 2011 to 2017. He was a board member and program manager at West Space Inc (2000–2004) and founding committee member of Grey Area Art Space Inc. (1996–1999). Michael lectures at RMIT University in Sound, Sculpture and Spatial Practice, Expanded Studio Practice, Honours and in the MFA Coursework program.

Richard Harding has participated in multiple solo and group exhibitions as an artist, coordinator and curator in Australia and internationally; the latest being Imagined Place presented at Burris Hall Gallery Highlands University, Las Vegas USA. His work is held in public and private collections in Australia and overseas including Australian National Gallery, Proyecto'ace Print Collection, Argentina and OCAD University Ontario Canada. He exhibits in various modes, from public and commercial galleries, to artist run spaces and community-based environments. He has worked in industry based print workshops, like the Australian Print Workshop Inc. as a studio supervisor, a custom printer and access artist. He has been involved with the Australian national print organization; the Print Council of Australia as a committee member, Vice President and currently holds the role of Secretary. Richard

Harding is part of The News Network Project, a Trans-Tasman network of artists that contributes to contemporary debate around current events and conflicts by exploring their representation through contemporary fine art practices. He is current project titled Break in Transmission seeks to address how we attempt to empathise the tragedies that befall others through news articles via image and text.

Shane Hulbert is a Melbourne-based artist and academic. His work celebrates the diversity inherent in Australian culture, with particular emphasis on understanding the effects of multiple narratives of immigration, settlement and tourism (including the ubiquitous 'Aussie backpacker') on Australian cultural identity. Borrowing from the traditions of landscape, documentary and political photography, and composed with a larrikin sense of humour, Shane's imagery features a combination of local and international places, personalities, icons and myths. Some photographs explore the importation of cultural icons into Australia, such as Bengali sculptures in the Grampians or Egyptian icons lining a suburban street in Coburg. Other images explore international representations of Australia, such as a miniature version of the Sydney Opera House in Shenzhen, China, or the startling presence of a Ned Kelly-themed bar in Hong Kong. Shane's work has recently been exhibited in *Melbourne Now* (National Gallery of Victoria, 2013–14) and as a finalist for the 2014 Monash Gallery of Art's *Bowness Photography Prize* (2014). In 2009 he was awarded the Excellence in Photomedia prize in the national *Contemporary Landscapes in Photography* (CLIP) exhibition at the Perth Centre for Photography (PCP). He has curated exhibitions in Australia and China, most recently an exhibition at RMIT Gallery acknowledging the 130-year history of photography at RMIT, and the contribution this has made to photography in Melbourne and Australia. His work is held in various private collections in Australia, as well as international collections including the Suzhou Art and Design Institute in China, the Department of Foreign Affairs in Xianyan, China, and Sangmyung University in South Korea. He is Associate Professor of Photography and Deputy Head of School (Higher Education) at RMIT University in the School of Art.

Ruth Johnstone is a Senior Lecturer in the School of Art, RMIT University. She commenced art school training in 1974 at Warrnambool Institute of Advanced Education, completed advanced undergraduate studies in Printmaking at RMIT in 1982, and prior to commencement of doctoral research in 1998, completed a Master of Arts in 1993 at the National College of Art and Design, Dublin. She was awarded an RMIT Research Award for her PhD in 2005 and an Emerging Researcher Grant in 2008. While employed in art schools continuously since 1981, an equally active art practice extends to 35 years. A recipient of Australia Council awards and residencies as well as national art awards in her field, her work is in collections of the National Gallery of Australia and Parliament House in Canberra, British Museum, London, National Gallery of Victoria and the State Library of Victoria, Melbourne, Queensland Art Gallery, Brisbane, Art Gallery of New South Wales, Sydney and Tasmanian Museum and Art Gallery, Hobart and many regional and university collections in Australia. Alongside a visual practice, written publications include *The Artist Curates* (ed.), 2015, a chapter on the print room for *Castletown, Decorative Arts*, 2011 and a chapter describing her PhD project in *Thinking Through Practice*, 2007.

Robin Kingston is a Senior Lecturer at RMIT University and a practicing visual artist. Her recent work investigates possibilities in contemporary abstract painting using traditional means as well as an investigation of painting, abstraction and site. Robin completed her PhD (2008) and the project examined the role of intuitive and rational through in the construction of contemporary abstract painting. She seeks to extend the understanding of the complexity of material processes and through that contribute to the content in the construction of abstract painting and how context placement can affect meaning. Robin teaches a variety of studio based courses in the School of Art, RMIT University including a course she developed in Abstraction. She also coordinates and leads the annual New York Study Tour for the RMIT School of Art and has done so for the past thirteen years – to a city she lived in a ten-year period, 1980–1990. Her research interests include abstraction, contemporary painting and drawing, installation practice, materiality, process and play, attentiveness and phenomenology, intuition, seriality and repetition, ornamentation and the performative in relation to painting.

Laresa Kosloff works as a visual artist and lectures at RMIT University, Melbourne. Her research interests include the performing body in art, new-situationalism, humour and participatory art practice. Dr Kosloff makes performative videos, Super 8 films, sculpture, installations and live performance works. Her artwork examines various representational strategies, each one linked by an interest in the body and its agency within the everyday. Dr Kosloff has been involved in several Artist Run initiatives and is currently a member of the City of Melbourne Public Art Advisory Panel. Selected solo exhibitions include *Lets do something*, Monash Prato Centre (Italy, 2015); *The Russian Project*, Margaret Lawrence Gallery (Melbourne, 2012); *CAST*, Anna Schwartz Gallery, (Melbourne, 2011); Sensible *world*, Artspace (Sydney, 2009) and *Solidarity for a Metaphysic*, ACCA @ Mirka (Melbourne, 2008). Selected group exhibitions include *Art as a Verb*, MUMA (Melbourne, 2014); *The space between* us, Art Gallery of NSW (2013); *Glasgow International Festival of Visual Art* (Glasgow, UK 2012); *ACCA Pop-Up* Project, 54th Venice Biennale (Italy, 2011). Dr Kosloff was awarded the Monash University Prato Residency in 2015 and the Jane Scally Art Award in 2011. She has received Australia Council for the Arts funding on four occasions and an Australian Postgraduate Award in 2004.

Keely Macarow is an Associate Professor and Deputy Head, Research & Innovation, School of Art, RMIT University, Melbourne. Keely has worked as a creative producer, artist and curator for film, video, performance and exhibition projects which have been presented in Australia, the UK, US and Europe. She has lectured at universities in Australia and England, and worked as an artistic director and arts administrator in arts organisations and in local government. Keely's creative practice has spanned media, sound and visual arts, performance, experimental film, curation and design. Her research is collaborative and focuses on socially engaged art, co-design, social justice, health and wellbeing. She is currently working on interdisciplinary projects with art, design, housing and medical researchers based at RMIT University

(Australia), Lund University, Malmo University and the Karolinska Institutet (Sweden).

Sally Mannall is a Senior lecturer on the MFA Programs in Melbourne and Hong Kong. She has over 25 years of professional art practice and 20 years teaching in tertiary education. Sally completed a Bachelor of Fine Art, Canberra School of Art in 1987, Master of Arts in Fine Art, Goldsmiths' College, University of London in 1994, and Doctor of Philosophy, Monash University in 2017.

Her recent work considers the garden as a highly complex cultural artefact. The focus of her PhD research was on domestic and productive food gardens as sites that engage personal, historical, cultural, ideological and environmental contexts. Her humorous and poignant artistic gestures in gardens respond to the sites, their histories and their use. She uses post studio strategies of working directly on site and often with materials at hand. In addition she has employed kinetic sculptures, photography, moving image, time, duration and anamorphic illusion. Her research investigates how artistic interventions in specific sites can reveal and comment on the garden as a manifestation of a cultural moment.

Recent solo exhibitions include: *The Polysemic Garden,* MADA, Monash University; *States of Play,* Conical Gallery; *Flight and Perchings,* The Engine Room, Massey University, Wellington, NZ. Group exhibitions include: *Concrete Post 3,* Bonn, Germany; *Forest garden breakfast tea,* Galerie IG Bildende Kunst, Vienna; *O Nude / On Boredom* TABAČKA Kulturfabrik, KOŠICE, SLOVAKIA; *The Weight of History* Switchback Gallery, Monash University and*Screenings: International and Australian New Media works,* NGV, Melbourne. She was a founding member of Ocular Lab Inc. an artists-run gallery in West Brunswick.

Maggie McCormick is a practicing artist, curator, writer and researcher who has exhibited, curated and undertaken research projects, exhibitions, presentations and publications in Australia, Europe and Asia and forthcoming in South America. McCormick is Head of the Master of Arts (Art in Public Space) program at the School of Art at RMIT University, Australia and

Professor at Reutlingen University, Germany. McCormick's research focus is on urbanisation, urban consciousness and contemporary cultural concepts. Her doctoral thesis at The University of Melbourne 2009 titled *The Transient City: mapping urban consciousness through contemporary art practice* examined the changing nature of urban consciousness and conceptualisation of belonging in an urban century and how this phenomenon is mapped through the visual vocabulary or art practice of artists and curators. Her current research focus extends these ideas into the digital space of Skype through *SkypeLab* (2012 ongoing) that investigates the relationship between urbanization, digitalization and perceptions of identity. The research is in collaboration with Professor Henning Eichinger, Reutlingen University, Germany, engaging to date with universities in China, Colombia and Brazil. www.skypelab.org Her most recent artworks were exhibited at Staedtische Galerie, Germany and her most recent publication is *Carto-City Revisited: unmapping urbaness* in Grierson, E. (ed.) *Transformations: art and the city*. Chicago: Intellect, The University of Chicago Press, both 2017.

Grace McQuilten was appointed Vice-Chancellor's Research Fellow in 2014 in the School of Art at RMIT University. Prior to her current appointment, she was an Honorary Fellow and Lecturer in Art History in the School of Culture & Communication at The University of Melbourne from 2009 to 2014. She has held numerous professional and industry roles in arts and cultural management since 2004. She has published two books, including *Art as Enterprise: Social and Economic Engagement in Contemporary Art*, co-authored with Anthony White (IB Tauris, UK, 2016) and *Art in Consumer Culture* (Routledge, USA, 2011). Previous positions have brought together industry, community and scholarly outcomes, and include roles such as: Founder and CEO, The Social Studio (2009–14); Conference Coordinator, Arts Project Australia (2014); Project Officer, Melbourne School of Government (2013); Guest Curator at the Ian Potter Museum of Art, University of Melbourne (2006; 2010–11); Co-editor of Al Muhajir / The Migrant Newspaper (2007–8); Research Intern at the Dan Flavin Archive, Dia Centre for the Arts, New York (2004) and Intern at the New Museum of Contemporary Art, New York (2004). In addition, she has worked extensively in the arts developing, curating, coordinating and presenting major exhibitions, public art projects, festivals, events and conferences across venues such as the Ian Potter Museum of Art, the NGV International, the Immigration Museum, RMIT Project Space Gallery, Federation Square, Viva Victoria Festival, Melbourne Spring Fashion Week, Emerge Festival, the State of Design Festival and the Melbourne Fringe Festival.

Nikos Pantazopoulos is a current Gertrude Contemporary studio artist and a studio artist representative on the Gertrude Contemporary Board. He has a Bachelor of Fine Arts from the Victorian College of the Arts, Melbourne; a Masters of Fine Art from Goldsmiths College, London and a PhD from Monash University, Melbourne in 2013. He is a lecturer in photography at RMIT. Pantazopoulos's recent projects include: Gertrude Contemporary studio artists exhibition, Melbourne, 2016; The Nude show LON gallery, Melbourne, 2016; Writing & Concepts Series, The problem is … The Design Hub, Melbourne, 2016; The Problem is I want to be more … VCA Artforum, Melbourne, 2016; These Economies, Sydney Contemporary, 2015; Australian Tapestry Workshop residency, Melbourne, 2014; Fucking in Solidarity, National Gallery of Victoria, Catalogue Essay for When This you See Remember Me, David McDiarmid Retrospective, NGV Melbourne, 2014; The Spirit & Spark of David McDiarmid Symposium, National Gallery of Victoria, Melbourne, 2014; The Purple Onion, TCB art inc, Melbourne, 2014; Re-building, The Substation, Melbourne, 2014; Private View & Occasional Performance, Dudspace, Melbourne, 2014; Decisions, RMIT Project Space, Melbourne, 2013; Dark Rooms, RMIT Project Space Melbourne, 2013; Octopus 10, Gertrude Contemporary, Melbourne, 2010; A Monument to toilets; An Exhibition and Procession, White Cubicle Toilet Gallery, London, 2010.

David Thomas was born in Belfast Northern Ireland in 1951. He arrived in Australia in 1958. He studied art and education at The University of Melbourne graduating in the 1970s. After travelling in Asia and living in Europe, he returned to Australia and had his first solo exhibition in 1981. He holds an MA by Research in Fine Arts and a PhD from RMIT University. He has taught in the School of Art RMIT since1992 where he is Professor of Fine

Art. He has received: Australia Council, AGNSW, Arts Victoria International Development grants and undertaken residencies at the Cité International des Arts, Paris, France, Two Rooms Gallery Auckland, New Zealand, the Centre for Drawing Research, Wimbledon College of Art, University of the Arts, London and in 2013 the Porthmeor Studios, St Ives, UK. He has exhibited in Australia, New Zealand, Korea, Taiwan, China, Singapore, the USA and Europe, including: National Gallery of Victoria, Australian Centre of Contemporary Art, Melbourne; Museum of Modern Art at Heide, Melbourne; Centre for Contemporary Photography Melbourne; ACP Sydney; Kunsthalle Dominikanerkirche, Osnabruck, Germany; Australian Embassy Paris; Talbot Rice Gallery, Scotland; Auckland Art Gallery, New Zealand. His work is represented in public collections including: The National Gallery of Victoria, The Australian National Gallery, Canberra; Art Bank, Trinity College, The University of Melbourne, RMIT University, Museum of Modern Art at Heide, Cripp's Collection (Australia and UK), Chartwell Collection, Auckland Art Gallery, New Zealnd, Canterbury University, Christchurch, New Zealand, Lim Lip Museum, Gong Ju, South Korea, Kunstmuseum Bonn, Germany, Kunstmuseum Ahlen, Germany and in private collections in Australia, USA, France, Germany, New Zealand, Singapore, and the UK. He has curated numerous exhibitions and has written on eastern and western art in relation to time and the monochrome.

Darrin Verhagen is an award-winning sound designer and composer, working across a range of media. In theatre, he has worked with the Melbourne Theatre Company, Malthouse, Daniel Schlusser Ensemble, Chamber Made Opera, Bell Shakespeare, Sydney Theatre Company, Griffin and Finucane & Smith; in dance, with Chunky Move, Australian Dance Theatre, Expressions Dance Theatre, Lucy Guerin, Sue Healey and Antony Hamilton. As a founding member of the (((20hz))) collective, his recent installations have fused sound with light, felt vibration and motion simulators, and have been exhibited at White Night, the NGV, Experimenta, Globelight and RMIT Gallery. His audiokinetic opera, a reworking Tarkovsky's *Stalker* will premiere in 2017. Darrin's most recent book chapter 'What's wrong: the sound of danger versus hearing dangerously' was released in *Endangering Science Fiction* (2016). His most recent remix was the Shinjuku Thief rewrite of Snog's *Clockworkman*. And his latest film score for *Boys in the Trees* was nominated for a 2016 AACTA award. He is a Senior Lecturer in Sound Design in the RMIT Digital Media program in the School of Media & Communication. He is also the director of the AkE (Audiokinetic Experiments) Lab where, with creative practice as a starting point, he researches the psychophysiology of multisensory experience. His applied research includes work with the Bio-Inspired Digital Sensing (BIDS) Lab, and the School of Aerospace, Mechanical and Manufacturing Engineering. Previously, he ran the Dorobo record label and was in the RMIT School of Art for 11 years.

www.ingramcontent.com/pod-product-compliance
Lightning Source LLC
Chambersburg PA
CBHW030853170426
43193CB00009BA/593